RUMSFELD'S WAR

RUMSFELD'S
WAR

The Untold Story of America's
Anti-Terrorist Commander

ROWAN SCARBOROUGH

Since 1947
REGNERY
PUBLISHING, INC.
An Eagle Publishing Company • Washington, DC

Cataloging-in-Publication Data on file with the Library of Congress.

ISBN 0-89526-069-7

Published in the United States by
Regnery Publishing, Inc.
An Eagle Publishing Company
One Massachusetts Avenue, NW
Washington, DC 20001

Visit us at www.regnery.com

Distributed to the trade by
National Book Network
4720-A Boston Way
Lanham, MD 20706

Printed on acid-free paper
Manufactured in the United States of America

10 9 8 7 6 5 4 3 2 1

Books are available in quantity for promotional or premium use. Write to Director of Special Sales, Regnery Publishing, Inc., One Massachusetts Avenue, NW, Washington, DC 20001, for information on discounts and terms, or call (202) 216-0600.

To my late parents, Rowan and Katherine

CONTENTS

[INTRODUCTION]

IN LATE SUMMER 1992, I TRAVELED TO TWENTYNINE PALMS, CALIFORNIA, HOME TO the Marine Corps' sprawling desert training venue. I was research-ing a story for the *Washington Times* on future military missions in the post–Cold War world. The 170,000-member Corps serves as the nation's expeditionary force. Marines onboard helicopter-carrying assault carriers are America's on-call force to put boots on the ground. These rapid deployment capabilities were increasingly important after the Soviet collapse and America's involvement in "peacekeeping" hot spots like Somalia, Bosnia, and Haiti.

My tour of Twentynine Palms took me to several mock opera-tions centers where war gaming was underway. In one room, Marines had painted dark blobs where a new enemy was emerging: Muslim fundamentalists. "We need to know, frankly, what the pil-lars of Islam are, which aren't bad when you read them," then–Major General Harry Jenkins, director of Marine Corps intelligence, told me. "But certain groups that carry those kinds of things to the extreme, and like to throw bombs, assassinate people and get into those kinds of activities or take on embassies. We have to be kind of concerned and be prepared to deal with it." The Marines knew first-hand. They suffered America's first mass casualties at the hands of

Muslim fanatics in 1983, when a truck bomb killed 242 personnel in Lebanon.

The military clearly had the right future threat in mind—long before many others did. But over the next eight years, as Osama bin Laden's al Qaeda terror network expanded and became more deadly, the American armed forces were largely kept on the sidelines by a Clinton administration more interested in "peacekeeping" than in terrorist-fighting.

When al Qaeda bombed two American embassies in Kenya and Tanzania, killing twelve Americans among 257 dead, President Clinton responded by ordering cruise missile attacks. Sixty Tomahawks hit bin Laden training camps in Afghanistan in a safe, arm's-length attempt to kill the terror master. Simultaneously, Navy missiles destroyed a suspected chemical weapons plant in Khartoum, Sudan. Neither assault succeeded. The terror master was not at home when the missiles hit, and at best the target was a civilian-military dual-use facility that did produce legitimate pharmaceutical products.

Two years later, when al Qaeda suicide terrorists bombed the destroyer USS *Cole* in Yemen harbor, killing seventeen sailors, the Clinton administration handled the attack as a Justice Department matter. The *Cole*—its hull torn open, its sailors killed and wounded— was a crime scene, not a battle zone.

Bin Laden had made his intentions clear in 1998, before the *Cole* and embassy attacks. He issued a *fatwa* (traditionally a religious order from a prominent Islamic figure) brazenly declaring war on America and urging his followers to kill us everywhere.

"By God's leave," he said in a declaration published February 23, 1998, in the Arabic newspaper *al Quds al Arabi*, "we call on every Muslim who believes in God and hopes for reward to obey God's command to kill the Americans and plunder their possessions wherever he finds them and whenever he can. Likewise, we call on the Muslim *ulema* [authorities on Islamic law] and leaders and youth and soldiers to launch attacks against the armies of the American devils and against those who are allied with them from among the helpers of Satan."

Not until September 11, 2001, did the nation wake up. President Bush declared a war on terrorism that goes on today and will likely last into the next decade. A senior Pentagon official conceded to me, "I hate to say this and would never say this in public, but 9-11 had its benefits. We never would have gone into Afghanistan and started this war without it. There just was not the national will."

In this global war against Islamist terror, the Pentagon is not fighting a foreign country with fixed leaders and infrastructure per se (though the Taliban regime in Afghanistan and the regime of Saddam Hussein in Iraq have been struck down as accomplices to terrorism). The enemy in this war is mobile, well funded, and exists in terrorist cells spread around the world. In some cases, our enemies can be defeated with advanced jet fighters, ships, and tanks—as was shown in Iraq and Afghanistan. But in most theaters, the Pentagon must find ways to penetrate the shadows, to find terror operators one by one. In this new war, our targets are individual people, their communications network, and their money.

ENTER RUMSFELD

Defense Secretary Donald Rumsfeld, a longtime national security figure in Republican circles, returned to government with the election of President George W. Bush. He was then sixty-eight years old and had enjoyed a twenty-five-year corporate career. He arrived in Washington not to wage a global war, but to lead a bureaucratic reformation that would shift the armed forces from a Cold War military to a lighter, suppler organization. It was not a terribly high-profile mission.

But Islamic terror turned Rumsfeld into an accidental war secretary, and he quickly emerged as a powerful leader—colorful, demanding, and dismissive of critics in the press as well as in the administration. His intellect and energy are legendary. He can conduct a three-day, eight-nation tour and get off the plane at Andrews Air Force Base looking as fresh as when he left. "I work long hours," he once said. "I like to work long hours."

This book tells the story of how the Rumsfeld-led Pentagon made crucial decisions in repositioning the 1.4 million-member active duty force to fight the new war on terror. I write of important, and often previously unreported, debates within the administration over the role of special operations forces, whether to pay ransom for hostages, what to do with captured al Qaeda terrorists, and who should run the war—the White House or the Pentagon. I also, to establish a point of comparison, look at how President Clinton used—or more often didn't use—the military to fight al Qaeda during its astonishing rise in the 1990s.

Rumsfeld's drive to succeed, his intellectual power, his insatiable appetite for work, and his willingness to fight bureaucratic wars all make him a unique figure in the modern history of American government. He has led the country in two major wars—Afghanistan and Iraq—while positioning the armed forces to fight a terrorist threat, the global dimensions of which are still unknown. History will surely judge him one of America's most important defense leaders.

Rumsfeld burst out of the Eisenhower 1950s. He grew up solidly middle-class in Illinois, graduated from Princeton, flew Navy planes, got elected to Congress, ran the Pentagon, rescued a failing corporation and, at an age when most men are ready to retire, came back to take over the Pentagon one more time. He has run with the bulls in Pamplona and run with bulls on Wall Street. He is a championship wrestler, fierce squash player, and master of the one-handed pushup. He married his high school sweetheart and raised three children. His net worth is in the tens of millions. His friends and his wife call him "Rummy." He has made friends on the political left and right. A longtime friend is CBS anchor Dan Rather, a consistent critic of Republicans and the Bush family. Rumsfeld confirmed to me in November 2003 through a spokesman that he co-owns a ranch with Rather. He later told *Time* magazine of the joint investment for its December 29, 2003, issue.

A Pentagon corridor displays two portraits of Rumsfeld, one as the youngest secretary of defense, the other as the oldest—artistic testaments to his ambition and his longevity.

For this book, I interviewed scores of Rumsfeld's friends as well as corporate and government colleagues. The portrait they paint is of a human dynamo. Arthur Laffer, the father of supply-side economics and a thirty-year economic adviser to Rumsfeld, says, "I've never seen a person who enjoys life more than Rumsfeld. I don't mean leisure activities. I mean he loves all of life. He loves his family. He loves his friends. He loves his jobs. He puts everything into it and relishes it."

Henry Kissinger, a rival in the Ford White House, wrote this in his memoir, *Years of Renewal*: "Rumsfeld afforded me a close-up look at a special Washington phenomenon: the skilled full-time politician-bureaucrat in whom ambition, ability and substance fuse seamlessly."

Judge Laurence Silberman, who sits on the U.S. Court of Appeals for the District of Columbia and has been a Rumsfeld friend for more than thirty years, says Kissinger shortchanges him. "Don has integrity and a first-class character. I've known him for years as the man you see go through all those press conferences all those times. He is decent and polite and very frank. I was talking with someone else about Kissinger's remarks that Don was a cunning bureaucrat and infighter. We both agreed this was a projection on the part of Kissinger because Don was very straight. Kissinger was so convoluted that he always thought Don's straightness was cunning."

I asked former president Gerald Ford about Rumsfeld's management style. "Don isn't the most flexible person in the world," he said from his Aspen, Colorado, office. "He had strong convictions. He would express them well in Cabinet meetings or at the NSC [National Security Council] and if his views did not prevail, he still was a team player and then would go out and defend what I said was the best policy. Don had great loyalty."

David Frum, conservative thinker and former Bush speechwriter who penned the first insider's book on the administration, had this assessment: "If you looked around the Bush Cabinet table . . . [y]ou saw a number of very able, solid and reliable people—but only one, Donald Rumsfeld, whose mind could truly be said to sparkle."

"Don is a tremendous student of history," says Rumsfeld friend and Princeton classmate James M. Denny. "And I think Don has attempted to model his life after characters in history who he thinks exemplify the best qualities. If you had to try to figure out where Don was going to go and what he was trying to be—he was trying to emulate those persons in history he most admired. Churchill was one."

Another was Theodore Roosevelt. "He especially admired TR's fighting spirit and strong desire to pursue what he believed in, even if it clashed with prevailing Republican views," says Princeton classmate H. Allen Holmes, a career diplomat and Pentagon policymaker. Holmes's grandfather, Henry J. Allen, had put Roosevelt's name into the nomination process at the 1912 Republican convention, and then led a large number of delegates out into the street to start the Bull Moose insurgency for TR. Recalled Holmes, "Rummy once said to me with undisguised admiration, 'Your grandfather was a rebel.'"

Newt Gingrich, a close confidant of the defense secretary, said that to understand Rumsfeld you have to analyze his early passion for high school, collegiate, and Navy wrestling. "Wrestling is a very lonely business," Gingrich says. "You're by yourself in the arena. It's also a business of great precision. If you snatch wrong, you lose. So, a quarter inch can make a big difference. It's a sport of enormous focus because the match is very fast, very short, and very decisive. So you start with the idea he was at Princeton, so you know he's smart; and he voluntarily went out for wrestling, so you know he's stunningly competitive. And you know that he has a disciplined, focused ability to think about things." The sport, Gingrich says, "tends to produce very confident people who don't mind being visible, because everybody can watch them, and ain't nothing between them and winning and losing."

And Rumsfeld knows—and the military he leads knows—that winning this war is going to be a long-term affair. As Vice Admiral Eric T. Olson, a career SEAL who rose through the ranks to become the number two officer at Special Operations Command, remarked to several Pentagon officials, "We are the ones who are fighting this war now, but we anticipate that this will be a conflict of some duration. The Americans in high school today are likely the ones who will see this through to the finish."

This book is not about the end to this new war, but its beginning. If Vice Admiral Olson is right, the final verdict will be celebrated—and written about—by the next generation. But the strategy, vision, and reshaped military will have been put in place by Donald Rumsfeld.

[CHAPTER 1]

RUMSFELD DECLARES WAR

WHILE THE PENTAGON BURNED, DONALD H. RUMSFELD SAT IN A VAULT-LIKE room studded with TV screens and talked to President George W. Bush. The setting was the Executive Support Center (ESC), where the defense secretary held secure video teleconferences with the White House across the Potomac or with ground commanders 10,000 miles away. The time was 1:02 p.m., less than four hours after American Flight 77 was steered by terrorists into the Pentagon's southwest wall.

When the plane first hit, Rumsfeld dashed to the impact site. In his shirt and tie, he helped transport the wounded. Finally convinced to leave the scene of terrorist violence, Rumsfeld entered the closely guarded ESC, where whiffs of burnt rubble penetrated the ventilation system. The screen in front of him was blank, but there was an audio connection with the president, who was at Barksdale Air Force Base in Louisiana.

"This is not a criminal action," Rumsfeld told Bush. "This is war." The word "war" meant more than going after al Qaeda in Afghanistan, the fault line of terrorism. After Rumsfeld used the word "war," Bush said he wanted retaliation.

This is the first time Rumsfeld's instant declaration of war has been reported, and it took America from the Clinton administration's view that terrorism was a criminal matter to the Bush administration's view that terrorism was a global enemy to be destroyed.

"That was really a breakthrough strategically and intellectually," recalls Douglas Feith, undersecretary of defense for policy. "Viewing the 9-11 attacks as a war that required a war strategy was a very big thought and a lot flowed from that."

Rumsfeld, as we'll see, wanted a war that was fought with ruthless efficiency: special forces, high-tech firepower, a scorecard for killing terrorists, a desire not to become the world's jailer (other countries could help do that), and a refusal to be stymied by bureaucracy. Here we'll look at how he put the pieces in place. In Chapter Two, we'll see how his strategy played out on the battlefields of Afghanistan and Iraq.

RUMSFELD'S TWO GENERALS

Rumsfeld's war plan immediately took shape. He shared his views in a meeting of his inner circle, the so-called Round Table group, which included Deputy Defense Secretary Paul Wolfowitz and the Joint Chiefs' chairman and vice chairman. This would be a global war, Rumsfeld said, and he planned to give Special Operations Forces (SOF)—Delta Force, SEALs, and Green Berets—unprecedented powers to kill terrorists. SOF missions lived or died on secrecy, so he would tolerate no leaks. Staff meetings that once attracted twenty or more bureaucrats were quickly shrunk to no more than ten. He publicly threatened criminal prosecution when "classified information dealing with operations is provided to people who are not cleared for that information."

Rumsfeld kept his eyes on two balls—one relatively small, the other as big as the globe. As most Americans know, he authorized General Tommy Franks to bring him a war plan for toppling the Taliban in Afghanistan, where Osama bin Laden operated. Less widely known—but perhaps far more important—is that he also summoned his top special operations officer, Air Force General Charles Holland, to draw up a blueprint for a broader war on terror.

Holland's Special Operations Command in Tampa, Florida, was a sleepy outpost at MacDill Air Force Base. U.S. Central Command (CentCom), across the street, got all the press. It fought wars. Holland's command, dubbed SoCom, merely equipped some 35,000 special forces soldiers. When they went into battle, combatant commands such as CentCom took control. Rumsfeld wanted that changed. Holland, however, was not a door-busting commando. He was a pilot who had flown the lumbering but deadly AC-130 gunships. Colleagues described him as courtly, polite, and soft-spoken. He was a compromiser, not a bureaucratic infighter like his boss, Rumsfeld.

Holland arrived for his first wartime face-to-face meeting with Rumsfeld on September 25, 2001. Also present at the meeting were the Joint Chiefs chairman, Air Force General Richard Myers, and vice chairman, Marine Corps General Peter Pace. Rumsfeld told General Holland he wanted SoCom to become a global command post. He asked Holland's opinion of where America could locate and strike the terrorists.

Aside from the obvious targets, like Afghanistan, Holland mentioned the so-called tri-border area of Paraguay, Brazil, and Argentina. Al Qaeda flourished in such no man's lands, where government authority was weak or nonexistent. Bin Laden had his eye on South America's lucrative drug trade. FARC, the left-wing Revolutionary Armed Forces of Colombia, had already displayed how an anti-government terrorist group could reap millions of dollars by controlling drug-producing land and setting up a distribution network. Al Qaeda operatives were starting to tap into the drug trade. Holland also mentioned the West African nation of Mauritania, where al Qaeda training camps would pop up, then disappear. But each time he broached a possible target, he also said he lacked "actionable intelligence," a phrase Rumsfeld did not like to hear. Rumsfeld told his commanders he wanted them to "lean forward" in the new war. That same day, Rumsfeld, who was deeply disappointed by Holland's caution, walked to the pressroom and announced, "The United States of America knows that the only way we can defend against terrorism is by taking the fight to the terrorists." It was a message for Holland and other commanders as well as the public.

Holland might lack "actionable intelligence," but Rumsfeld's Pentagon had no shortage of raw information. The data—Rumsfeld came to call them "scraps"—became so voluminous that his policy makers convened twice-daily meetings at 7:30 a.m. and 4:30 p.m. to try to make sense of it all. CIA-produced reports contained excerpts of intercepted conversations, the latest bin Laden sightings, and even the opinions of an Australian psychic. The CIA's information was augmented by special reports from the Defense Intelligence Agency and the National Intelligence Daily, or NID, a newsletter of both raw and confirmed data. Rumsfeld also saw the intelligence community's crown jewel, the President's Daily Brief, or PDB. Hand-carried by CIA officers, the short and super-secret document was delivered to the president, defense secretary, national security adviser, and a few chosen others—and then taken away.

Rumsfeld's Round Table immediately began to settle on strategy. Undersecretary of Defense for Policy Douglas Feith recalled later, "We developed what we called the territorial approach to fighting terrorism, which is instead of chasing every individual terrorist, you recognize that for terrorist organizations over a sustained period to do large-scale operations they need bases of operations. I use the term the 'quiet enjoyment of real estate.' It's important for them to have that quiet enjoyment because that's what allows them to recruit and to plan and to train, to equip themselves. There's a lot that flows from having a base of operations."

Afghanistan was the logical first step. But al Qaeda and its surrogates also thrived in border regions and ungoverned states like Somalia. Rumsfeld made a list: Yemen, where al Qaeda planned the October 2000 bombing of the USS *Cole*; the entire Horn of Africa, where terror cells moved money and men freely, and where the leaders of Kenya and Ethiopia told a senior American diplomat that their number one problem wasn't poverty, but preventing their predominantly or partly Christian countries from succumbing to Islamic militants; and the Philippines, where the Abu Sayyaf group of Islamic terrorists used kidnappings and deadly bombings to try to bring down the pro-American Filipino democracy.

Rumsfeld's next step was to host a stream of world leaders to convince them to let American personnel battle al Qaeda on their soil, among them Yemeni president Ali Abdullah Saleh. Saleh arrived in Washington in late November. Surprisingly, he agreed to let the CIA and Green Berets set up in his country. A promise of $400 million in aid helped. So had Bush's declaration on September 20 that countries had a choice to side either with America or with the terrorists. Put that way, President Saleh chose to stand with the United States.[1]

---

1. He had another motivation too. In secret diplomacy in 1994, the United States convinced the Saudis to stop backing Yemeni rebels who wanted to divide the country. Without Saudi support, the rebellion failed, and the Yemeni parliament elected Saleh president of all Yemen. Washington had already proven itself a friend, keeping the Saudis at bay, preserving a united Yemen, and making his presidency possible.

RUMSFELD VS. RICE

Rumsfeld's territorial strategy served not just for the war on terror, but for bureaucratic turf wars. By the time he was conducting the war in Afghanistan in October 2001, Rumsfeld was also fighting what he saw as a move by White House national security adviser Condoleezza Rice and her staff to gain power at his expense. Rumsfeld wanted direct access to the president without National Security Council (NSC) staff interfering in military decision making. Those decisions were the prerogative of the president, the defense secretary, and his combatant commanders. Rumsfeld did not want a replay of the Clinton era, when NSC analyst Richard Clarke ruled the White House on counter-terrorism issues and repeatedly challenged the Pentagon.

Retired general Wayne Downing, Bush's counter-terrorism chief on the NSC, was the potential new Richard Clarke figure. He floated a plan for making war in Iraq and sent out memos seeking a bigger voice in the global war on terror.

He got that role in a classified policy statement approved by Bush, National Security Presidential Directive 8 (NSPD-8). Rumsfeld saw this as a major power shift from the Pentagon to the White House. The directive made Downing, as national director for combating terrorism, the "principal" adviser to the president. But under federal law, Rumsfeld and the Joint Chiefs chairman are the principal military advisers to the president.

I can reveal that Rumsfeld dispatched a secret memo to Condoleezza Rice on November 1, 2001. "My understanding of NSPD-8 as issued suggests that it may cause confusion with regard to the statutory role of the chairman of the Joint Chiefs of Staff as the 'principal military adviser' to the president, the secretary of defense and the National Security Council," he wrote. "I am no lawyer, but it seems to me there is only one principal military adviser. Otherwise, the word 'principal' would have a brand new meaning. As we go forward on this terrorism effort, I think it is important that any confusion be untangled and corrected, at a minimum by confirming that DNSA-CT's [the NSC counter-terrorism director's] role is not intended in any way to detract from the chairman's role as the principal military adviser.

"Further, from my standpoint as secretary of defense, I find that the DNSA-CT's mandate could be read as infringing on the chain of command from the president and the secretary of defense to combatant commanders. It is dangerous—exceedingly dangerous—to suggest that there may be any additional players between the president, the secretary of defense and the combatant commanders in fulfilling war-fighting responsibilities, including mission planning and execution. I know this was done quickly for very good reasons and that we may not have provided you our considered views as you drafted the NSPD. Nevertheless, I think we should address these issues."

According to administration officials, Rice sent Rumsfeld a return memo saying she would fix the problem and that his concerns seemed an overreaction. It was another bureaucratic victory for Rumsfeld.

While Rumsfeld shored up his power, Joint Chiefs chairman General Richard Myers was also trying to protect his authority from encroaching bureaucrats. He wrote a confidential memo to Rumsfeld complaining that he was not included in the new White House Homeland Security Council (HSC). Rumsfeld, the memo shows, had tried to get Myers on board, but someone in the White House had blocked the appointment. "The omission of [the chairman] as a full member of the HSC prevents me from properly fulfilling my statutory role as principal military adviser to you, the president and the NSC on homeland security issues," the general wrote. "It also is difficult for the Joint Staff personnel to assist me in performing my statutory duties, since they are not invited to attend the numerous meetings of various [policymaking committees] we obtain information second-hand and without an opportunity to provide military input when an issue is first addressed."

As Rumsfeld and Myers fiercely protected their turf, Downing began to realize he was not going to play a co-equal role in the terror war—not when there was a master administration infighter like Rumsfeld. As a four-star general, Downing was used to big staffs and a big seat at the planning table. But as Bush's top adviser on counterterrorism, he had a small office, a small staff, and soon discovered that not he but Rumsfeld and Director of Central Intelligence George Tenet made the big calls on where to launch military strikes. Feeling he wasn't appreciated, Downing resigned in June 2002 after just ten months on the job.

COMMANDO COUNTRY

Rumsfeld was the undisputed man-in-charge in the new war on terror, and he successfully shifted the military from thinking in terms of big divisions charging across the European plains to instead focusing on operations emphasizing precise and deadly special forces backed by high-tech firepower.

In November 2001, Rumsfeld flew from Andrews Air Force Base to Fort Bragg, North Carolina, home to the lion's share of special operations troops. The Green Berets were ousting the Taliban from power in Afghanistan, and Rumsfeld wanted to thank their commanders personally. He also wanted to learn more about the corps of warriors he intended to rely on in the future.

At the Army's Special Operations Command, he greeted the "white" community—the Green Berets, psychological warfare specialists, and civil affairs officers. Rumsfeld then left public view and entered the "black" world of the "snake eater"—Joint Special Operations Command (JSOC). JSOC is a highly classified, fenced compound that straddles Fort Bragg and Pope Air Force Base, the commando launch point. The facility is wired with electronic and physical surveillance equipment. A spy could learn a lot about counter-terrorism tactics and intelligence by slipping inside JSOC. The buildings are mostly windowless. The roofs sprout masses of antennae. The back gate opens onto a quick roll downhill to the Yellow Ramp, the staging area for the Delta Force and SEAL teams at Pope Air Force Base. One building holds the Joint Communications Unit. Planners can talk to any deployed command instantaneously via secure satellite hookups. JSOC's warriors also move worldwide with their own intelligence support and specially configured task forces. Their intercept-proof computers can link up with the latest information from the CIA and satellite images provided by the National Imaging and Mapping Agency.

JSOC troops do more than just knock down doors: They secretly infiltrate countries. They were, for instance, in Baghdad before and during the war. They also regularly recruit local surveillance operatives and are America's experts at dismantling nuclear explosives. A former senior administration official told me that JSOC direct action missions are so sensitive they must be approved by the defense secretary and sometimes by the president. In the Horn of Africa, for example, every direct action must be approved by the president.

JSOC's hardscrabble commander at the time, Brigadier General Del Dailey, a Delta alumnus, was in Afghanistan setting up Task Force 11 to hunt high-value targets, such as bin Laden, when Rumsfeld visited JSOC. But he had plenty of other greeters among JSOC's complement of 1,500 warriors and support staff. Rumsfeld saw what few people, in or out of the military, get to see. All-purpose Delta soldiers and SEALs put on an exhibition of a hostage rescue, displaying some of their top-secret tactics. Then they executed a HALO (high altitude, low opening) insertion, the method for infiltrating enemy territory via skydiving. Next, Rumsfeld was led into an auditorium protected by bulletproof glass to watch a sharp-shooting exhibition. During the visit, five soldiers going through the rigorous training to earn the title "Delta," or "D-boys," were pulled from the course and brought over to meet their boss. Rumsfeld "was just totally impressed by those guys," said a special forces soldier.

Rumsfeld's new emphasis on special operations paid big dividends in Iraq as well as in Afghanistan. Task Force 20, a special JSOC unit, captured most of the Iraqi regime's high-value targets. A document stamped SECRET that went to the Joint Chiefs of Staff in summer 2003 praised the work of commandos in Iraq. "Maturation of special operations forces (SOF) and integration with precision airpower was a success.... War fighting potential of combining conventional and SOF capabilities as well as SOF-interagency coordination was exploited in OIF [Operation Iraqi Freedom] and has additional potential for use in future conflicts.... First coherent integration of SOF, conventional, allied and interagency organizations."

MONEY FOR HOSTAGES

Soon after Rumsfeld returned from Fort Bragg, he was embroiled in another dispute with the NSC that highlighted his preference for military, special forces solutions to law enforcement scenarios, especially ones that relied on ransom payments. Condoleezza Rice was proposing that the United States offer a ransom for the release of two American missionaries, Martin and Gracie Burnham of Rose Hill, Kansas, who were prisoners of the murderous Abu Sayyaf group in the Philippines.

In December 2001, Rice convened a meeting of the deputy secretaries of Defense, State, Justice, and Treasury in the White House Situation Room. The Pentagon was about to send a 1,200-soldier task force to the Philippines to train and guide the local army on how to fight the Islamic militants of Abu Sayyaf on their home turf of Basilan Island. Rather than rely on a military rescue effort alone, Rice wanted the FBI to dangle ransom money in front of the terrorists, whose modus operandi was to kidnap wealthy Westerners and win huge ransom payments. In some cases, Abu Sayyaf took the money and then brutally murdered the hostages anyway. Beheading by machete was a favorite method, and it made good TV to further terrify the countryside.

By spring 2002, the Filipino army had virtually cleared Basilan Island of Abu Sayyaf. But the fleeing militants, using their fleet of 400-horsepower cigarette boats to escape, took the missionaries with them.

What happened to the ransom plan? I obtained a highly classified White House document that shows for the first time that the Deputies Committee convened by Rice debated and then approved the idea of negotiating with Abu Sayyaf over its demands for $300,000 for the Burnhams' release. The plan called for an FBI agent, under deep cover, to handle the negotiations. I can report for the first time that the scheme went horribly wrong. Miscommunications between Washington and the FBI agent resulted in Abu Sayyaf walking away with $300,000 in taxpayer money without producing the Burnhams.

Rice titled her three-page ransom strategy, "Paper on Hostage Situation in the Philippines." It said, "Over the past six months, U.S. strategy to secure the Burnham's [sic] release has focused on supporting Philippine efforts to pressure the [Abu Sayyaf]. These efforts have been, for the most part, unsuccessful. The key obstacle to development of additional options to secure release has been the lack of actionable intelligence."

The deputies agreed on three goals: free the Burnhams, destroy Abu Sayyaf, and "contribute to the global campaign against terrorism."

"To that end, deputies considered an integrated effort, with the FBI in the lead. The purpose of this element of the strategy would be to buy time, improve the condition of the Burhams [sic] and acquire additional intelligence. Payment of ransom would not be part of the strategy except as a tactical lure to draw ASG [Abu Sayyaf] out as part of a release and arrest/destroy ASG strategy; deploying [Pacific Command] advisers to coordinate gathering of intelligence and develop follow-on options; and renewing the collection effort to develop actionable intelligence."

The deputies agreed on, and the White House approved, a four-point plan:

- Approve the immediate deployment of the CINCPAC [Pacific Command] advisers and coordinate with Adm. [Dennis] Blair for follow on actions to augment AFP capabilities.
- Convene the National Intelligence Collection Board to prioritize collection assets for the Philippines and coordinate deployment of those assets as required.
- Support FBI negotiating efforts. FBI will attempt to negotiate with the captors through the New Tribes Mission, the missionary group of which the Burnhams are members. Objective is to provide humanitarian assistance to Burnhams and buy time for both the intelligence picture and AFP capabilities to improve. Ransom would only be used as tactical lure in negotiations with ASG. The role of the FBI is being kept exceptionally close hold and only the country team and NTM [New Tribes Mission] is aware of their participation.
- Consider a presidential call to President Arroyo to thank her for her support and to reemphasize our goals to both rescue the Burnhams and destroy the ASG.

• Principals [secretaries of Defense, State, and others] are requested to review the paper and to inform me if there are issues related to the strategy that require attention in an upcoming PC [Principals' Committee] meeting. If no objections are raised, the paper will be considered as approved by principals.

The president approved the strategy. In early 2002, an FBI agent assigned to the U.S. embassy in Manila began making contact with representatives of Abu Sayyaf. The White House was playing a dangerous game, and things went wrong fast, according to a senior U.S. official. The terrorists demanded $300,000. The agent exceeded his authority and promised the money. This put the White House in a bind. If the ransom wasn't paid, Abu Sayyaf might kill the Burnhams. The FBI argued for paying the money. It promised the exchange would result in new intelligence on the group and the ability to track members. Aides say Rumsfeld at this point stepped in and voiced objections. Paying the ransom, he argued, was setting a bad precedent.

Rumsfeld was overruled. The FBI withdrew the money from a Federal Reserve Bank and recorded the serial numbers. Agents put the cash in a rucksack equipped with a tracking device. The FBI handed the money over to an Abu Sayyaf representative, who strapped the cash bag on a donkey and disappeared. Officials believe the Sayyaf member simply separated the money from the rucksack, making the homing device useless, and divided the money into small batches so that it was virtually impossible to trace. To add insult to injury, Abu Sayyaf did not produce the Burnhams. Instead, the terrorists asked for more money, saying the ransom was $30,000 short.

The White House refused to make more payments, in part because the U.S.-trained Filipino army was routing Abu Sayyaf so successfully. Finally, on June 7, 2002, a Filipino patrol found the terrorists' camp at Zamboanga del Norte. A horrendous firefight ensued. The terrorists shot and killed Martin Burnham and another hostage, Ediborah Yap, a Filipino nurse. Gracie Burnham survived.

COMMANDOS ON THE BENCH

In December 2001, the same month Rumsfeld and the NSC butted heads on ransom payments, a new figure started to appear regularly in the Pentagon: Richard Shultz, an author and expert on special operations. A spate of press stories had alleged that some in the Clinton administration wanted to deploy special operations troops to kill bin Laden, but, obviously, no such missions occurred. Rumsfeld's staff wanted Shultz to find out why, so that no similar inaction would hinder the Bush administration. Shultz received a top security clearance. He began interviewing current and former officials and poring over classified memos. Before the end of the year, Shultz had a rough draft of his findings and started briefing officials, all the way up to Deputy Defense Secretary Paul Wolfowitz. The Pentagon promptly stamped Shultz's report SECRET and filed it away. I obtained a copy. Shultz concluded that Clinton officials lacked the military knowledge and standing to challenge commanders who said they lacked "actionable intelligence" to go into Afghanistan after bin Laden. Shultz, a professor at Tufts University's Fletcher School of Law and Diplomacy, boiled down his secret brief to what he called ten "showstoppers":

- Criminalization of terrorism. "During the late 1980s, terrorism was defined as a crime. This had a profound impact on DoD [Department of Defense]. This reduced DoD to providing transportation for operations carried out by the Department of Justice. There was little opposition in DoD to this marginalization."

- "In the Pentagon of the 1990s no senior official deemed terrorism a clear and present danger, let alone a form of war. Even after bin Laden declared war on America and bombed U.S. embassies DoD continued to resist regarding terrorism as war." The report quotes General Peter Schoomaker, head of Special Operations Command from 1997 to 2000: "Rumsfeld might think we're at war with terrorism but I'll bet he also thinks he is at war within the Pentagon. The real war's happening right there in his building. It's a war of the culture. He can't go to war because he can't get his team up for it." (Rumsfeld called Schoomaker out of retirement to become Army chief of staff, after Schoomaker's interview with Shultz.)

- "The firefight in Mogadishu had a profound impact on the unwillingness of the U.S. to use SOF [Special Operations Forces] on offensive [counter-terrorism] missions for the rest of the decade. It reinforced an already jaded view. For the mainstream military the lesson of Somalia was that here was yet another example of those reckless SOF units attempting operations that end up in disaster."

- Somalia had a profound impact on the Clinton administration. Among the lessons it learned was that SOF units can get you into trouble. Recommendation: "If OSD [Office of Secretary of Defense] is to employ SOCOM [Special Operations Command] to conduct a global war on al Qaeda it must learn the right lessons of Mogadishu. Those lessons reveal how good SOF units are, even when policymakers misuse them. Imagine if they were employed properly in the war on terrorism."

- DoD has no authority to authorize covert missions. "Pentagon lawyers in the 1990s argued that DoD did not have the legal authority under Title 10." Title 10 is the part of the federal code that regulates the armed forces and the Pentagon. Rumsfeld overturned the Clinton policy of arguing in favor of Title 10 restrictions, and has decided that covert missions can indeed be authorized from the Pentagon.

- Risk aversion and failsafe options. "A lack of understanding of SOF CT [counter-terrorism] options by OSD leaders resulted in the conclusion they were too difficult to execute. That perception was magnified by a propensity to worry about risk."

- "The interagency process of the 1990s resulted in bureaucratic infighting over SOF CT options. DoD opposed the aggressive CT policy advanced by members of the interagency CSG [Counter-terrorism Strategy Group]. Such individuals were characterized as proposing ill-conceived ideas that would result in military disasters."

- "During the 1990s professional military status in the form of 'best military advice' contested CT proposals. This was fostered by senior officers highlighting their own military expertise and the policymakers' lack of it. Civilians, insecure in their knowledge of military affairs, were not willing to challenge the 'best military advice' of senior officers."

- "The footprint for proposed SOF CT missions turned big. This stopped several operations. It scared off policymakers. Small force packages would have had the same result because they would not be failsafe. It was a catch-22."

- "A lack of actionable intelligence was evoked often to stop the employment of SOF CT units. Special operators considered it one of the chief challenges for executing CT missions."

POWELL VS. RUMSFELD

With victory in Afghanistan under his belt, Rumsfeld spent January 2002 figuring out what to do with captured enemy combatants. He sent a memo to Douglas Feith, undersecretary of defense for policy, asking, "Why should we be the world's jailers?" Rumsfeld told aides he wanted the number of detainees kept small. He didn't want to burden America's troops with yet another mission subsidiary to war-fighting. A new prison built at Guantanamo Bay would hold fewer than one thousand detainees. The rest of the detainees could, in Rumsfeld's opinion, sit in foreign jails. President Bush and Rumsfeld agreed that the captives did not qualify as prisoners of war with rights guaranteed under the Geneva Convention. So the president created a new category: enemy combatants. Such combatants could be held indefinitely, and some would face trial in secret, without the full legal protections granted prisoners of war under the Geneva Convention.

Secretary of State Colin Powell didn't like the policy. A career soldier and Joint Chiefs chairman, he could find no precedent for not classifying battlefield captives as prisoners of war (POWs). He began lobbying Bush to reconsider. Powell's compromise: make them all POWs, then screen them one by one. If it turned out they were nothing more than terrorists, strip them of POW status. Rumsfeld opposed Powell. Rumsfeld wasn't shy about sending Powell memos, asking the secretary of state questions and making suggestions. In January, he signed a memo to Powell opposing POW status for captured Taliban and al Qaeda members.

Their rift broke into the open that month when the *Washington Times* published a story based on a confidential memo from White House counsel Alberto R. Gonzales. Gonzales told the president that an NSC meeting the following Monday would debate Powell's plan to give Taliban and al Qaeda detainees POW status. "The secretary of state has requested you reconsider.... Specifically, he has asked that you conclude that [the Geneva Convention] does apply to both al Qaeda and the Taliban. I understand, however, that he would agree that al Qaeda and Taliban fighters could be determined not to be prisoners of war (POWs) but only on a case-by-case basis following individual hearings before a military board." Once the memo appeared in the *Washington Times*, the White House tried to deny the memo's contents.

The next day, a Sunday, Rumsfeld convened a staff meeting at the Pentagon to discuss rules for running the fast-filling prison at Guantanamo. The topic turned to the *Washington Times* story. "That was a good one," Rumsfeld commented. Aides took the comment to mean he was glad Powell's position had been exposed.

But in public, Rumsfeld played the loyalist role. When a reporter asked that month if there was "distance" between him and Powell on the POW debate, Rumsfeld said, "There is none. The reports to the effect that Secretary Powell believes that they should be treated as prisoners of war is just flat untrue. I've been in ten meetings with him on the subject and he's never said that." But a Powell confidant subsequently told me that he had read a Rumsfeld memo opposing Powell's position, which was, in fact, that the detainees should be classified as POWs, at least until more was known about them.

That month, more Powell-Rumsfeld friction arose. Rumsfeld did not like Powell's habit of disclosing private conversations to author Bob Woodward. When Woodward interviewed Rumsfeld in January 2002 for a *Washington Post* series that would eventually become a book, Rumsfeld learned that people had spilled details on private NSC meetings. Powell and Woodward enjoyed a close source-author relationship. Much of Woodward's book *The Commanders*, for example, came from Powell in deep background interviews.

Rumsfeld did not play that way. He declined to discuss private meetings with journalists. He believed that if he discussed such encounters, his staff and commanders would be less candid. After September 11, 2001, he made this explicit in a gentleman's agreement with Tommy Franks: their conversations would be kept private.

"I'm not into this detail stuff. I'm more concepty," Rumsfeld told Woodward in their January interview. Woodward pressed for details. Rumsfeld stuck to "concepts." In between, he took the opportunity to chastise Woodward about *The Commanders*.

> Woodward: "This is a most serious history, really and I'm try-ing to do, and I talked to the president about this, and I'm going to do a book about his first year or first eighteen months, so I'll be back to haunt you."

> Rumsfeld: "I said I'm not even going to bother talking to you. My God, I wasted a whole bloody hour and a half with you one night, and you write this book *The Commanders*, and you didn't even use one thought."

Rumsfeld did not grant Woodward a second interview.

The White House, however, likes Woodward's reporting. They believe he is fair and thorough. Aides say Rumsfeld did agree to an interview for Woodward's next book, which will be on Iraq. But they say they do not expect Rumsfeld or his senior aides to divulge pri-vate conversations.

SUMMER OF DISCONTENT

By the spring, Rumsfeld was churning out action memos, dubbed "snowflakes," at such a rapid pace that he started burning out Under-secretary of Defense for Policy Douglas Feith's staff, which had to answer the majority of them. But Rumsfeld kept pushing. He had a global war to win. By June, Afghanistan's interim government was functioning amid an ongoing low-intensity conflict against Taliban holdouts. Iraq war planning had been started. But his ideas for hunting down terrorists worldwide still had not taken hold. And he let Feith know he was not happy.

"I think we need a scorecard for the global war on terrorism," said a confidential June 20 snowflake to Feith. "We ought to have a weekly report on the number of arrests and show the countries where they have been arrested, the number of detainees, the amount of money in bank accounts that has been frozen and the number of accounts, the number of sweeps in Afghanistan, number of MIOs [Maritime Interception Operations], the number of people trained in different countries, and progress in Afghanistan in terms of some measurements, like refugees coming in.

"We ought to get a series of indicators. Please have someone pull it together and see if we can't get the interagency group to do it. The president asked for this six months ago and it has never happened. Why?"

Less than two weeks later, Rumsfeld sent a snowflake to Feith asking, "How do we organize the Department of Defense for manhunts? We are obviously not well organized at the present time." Rumsfeld wanted action. He wanted it from, among others, SoCom General Charles Holland. Holland was reluctant, however, to turn SoCom into a global combat command; the military traditionally ran wars with regional commanders, not global ones. Stephen Cambone, a close aide to Rumsfeld, told colleagues, "Holland was given the keys to the kingdom and he didn't want to pick them up." Another aide told Rumsfeld, "You're going to have to put your finger in his chest and tell him what you want done."

On July 15, Holland returned to the Pentagon for another face-to-face with the boss. Holland again expressed caution about assuming new terror-hunt responsibilities. He didn't want to step on the toes of combatant commanders like Tommy Franks. Rumsfeld castigated the nation's top commando, saying he had made it clear to Holland and other four-stars that he wanted them "leaning forward," and Holland was not. Holland was ordered to come up with a plan of action.

I can reveal for the first time that Rumsfeld didn't wait for Holland's new plan, but on July 22 initialed a highly classified order to Joint Chiefs chairman General Myers, who was to turn the memo into a planning order to Holland. The Rumsfeld directive is just one page, but its impact was historic. In the directive, he changes the nature of special operations forces—and the Pentagon—giving special operations commanders the authority to plan and execute missions on their own with a minimum of bureaucratic interference. Some excerpts of Rumsfeld's order:

- The objective is to capture terrorists for interrogation, or if necessary, to kill them, not simply to arrest them in law enforcement exercise.
- The plan should identify the authorities needed for global operations and the steps necessary to acquire such authorities in advance.
- The objective should be that processing of deployment orders and obtaining other bureaucratic clearances can be accomplished in minutes and hours, not days and weeks. This will require prior briefing and preliminary pre-clearance, with final clearances subject only to the final details.
- Special Operations command will screen DoD for personnel —civilian and military—with languages, ethnic connections and other attributes needed for clandestine and covert activities. The results will be briefed to the secretary of defense.

- Gen. Holland will brief me on initiatives that can disrupt
  or destroy terrorist operations and additional assets that
  might be needed to pursue such initiatives.

Holland returned to the Pentagon on July 31 with a plan that became known as the "30 percent solution," because Rumsfeld wanted it done one chunk at a time. Holland wanted more men and money. He wanted diplomatic approval to go anywhere, anytime. And he wanted the always elusive "actionable intelligence" that decided whether a mission was successful. Rumsfeld wanted to make sure he got it.

FOX HUNTING

That summer, Rumsfeld's attention also turned to one of the most secretive units under Pentagon control. Code-named Grey Fox, the unit is made up of about two hundred army commandos working under "deep cover," using false identities and nationalities. They specialize in intelligence gathering and communications intercepts. In short, Grey Fox was just the sort of off-the-books organization Rumsfeld needed for his much-coveted "manhunts." But Grey Fox toiled under limitations. Officially, it was part of Special Operations Command. But the Army had the job of funding its equipment and personnel requirements. This meant its nourishment came from the conventional side of war fighting. Rumsfeld quickly signed the paperwork needed to give General Holland exclusive control. Eventually, Grey Fox was moved under Joint Special Operations Command, joining the Delta and SEAL elites. If Grey Fox was supposed to go out and find terrorists, why not put it with the people who would do the killing?

Seemingly mundane Army posts around the country hide some of the country's most covert activities. Fort Meade, Maryland, for example, a short ride from Washington on the scenic Baltimore-Washington Parkway, is home to the National Security Agency (NSA), America's highly sophisticated electronic eavesdropping center.

On Washington's southern flank, another Army base, Fort Belvoir, Virginia, is home to a number of low-profile logistics units and post-graduate schools. This is where Grey Fox makes its home. Grey Foxes carry miniaturized gadgets to intercept communications, talk on secure satellite hookups, and take pictures. If the coveted "chatter," the intelligence world's term for enemy communications, flows on underground fiber optics, Grey Fox knows how to penetrate them. The National Security Agency's vast array of electronic dishes can vacuum up streams of cell phone and email conversations. But for all of NSA's powers, its receivers cannot penetrate a land line. Someone or something has to execute a wiretap. Enter Grey Fox. Once Washington selects a target, Grey Fox commandos study satellite imagery or other intelligence to determine where the line is laid and where it can be tapped. They can enter the country legally or be inserted, parachuting in from high altitude. At the chosen spot, they dig up the cable and affix a gadget that relays the conversation to a satellite receiver.

The unit also has its own fleet of small jet aircraft at Baltimore-Washington International Airport. From there, the spies can be positioned around the world or inserted directly into the target country.

I can disclose here for the first time one Grey Fox mission in 2002. Its soldiers entered Somalia, where the Bush administration feared bin Laden was trying to establish a base of operations to replace Afghanistan. The soldiers, for all appearances local clansmen, located mid-level al Qaeda members attempting to establish ties with

Hibr, a dominant clan once led by notorious warlord Mohammed Farah Aidid.

Grey Fox then passed the mission off to one of America's strongest allies in the war on terror—the Arab nation of Jordan. King Abdullah II realized sympathies for bin Laden ran high in his kingdom. His late father, who was Western-educated and generally in favor of the West, had actually sided with Saddam Hussein in the first Gulf War. But the son, also educated in Western schools and trained at home in special warfare, aligned himself closely to Washington. King Abdullah knew that an unchecked al Qaeda would eventually swamp all the moderate Arab states, including his own kingdom. He authorized his intelligence service to play a major behind-the-scenes role. For example, he dispatched agents to Guantanamo Bay, Cuba, to interrogate al Qaeda fighters captured in Afghanistan and Pakistan. He rounded up militants in his country, interrogated them, and passed on their information to the United States and Britain. U.S. interrogators are known to threaten some detainees with shipping them off to Jordan if they don't cooperate. Like other Middle Eastern countries, Jordan uses physical means to coerce confessions and vital intelligence information.

In the case of Somalia, Jordanian agents entered the country undercover and quickly killed the terrorists located by Grey Fox. It was the kind of neat and clean operation Rumsfeld wanted carried out by Holland's men.

Grey Fox and Jordanian intelligence have forged a close relationship. Grey Fox operatives have taught the Jordanians some of their top-secret techniques and in return Grey Foxes hope for actionable Jordanian intelligence about al Qaeda's whereabouts.

In November 2002, shortly after Rumsfeld moved Grey Fox to Holland's control, it executed one of its most successful missions. I can report that Grey Fox has the technical ability to track and download information from a satellite cell phone. It can then use that information to "turn on" the phone without the target knowing it. The phone sends out a signal seeking a satellite hookup. Grey Foxes uses that signal to pinpoint the user's location.

Grey Fox's big success came in the assassination of al Qaeda planner Qaed Senyan al Harthi as his convoy moved across the Yemeni desert. Al Harthi planned the October 2000 bombing of the destroyer USS *Cole*. He had the blood of seventeen American sailors on his hands. A Grey Fox unit in Yemen was only too happy to turn on his cell phone. The signal pinpointed al Harthi's location within a five-yard radius. The numbers were passed to CIA operators in the States who controlled the Predator unmanned vehicle and its armament of two Hellfire missiles. The CIA scored a direct hit, killing al Harthi.[2]

The U.S. used communications intercepts to snag another big fish in August 2003 in Thailand. Its special operations soldiers, aided by the CIA, apprehended Hambali, the operations chief of the militant Islamic terrorist group Jemaah Islamiyah, and thus the "bin Laden of Southeast Asia," in Thailand. Hambali (also known as Riduan Isamuddin) is no small fry. His murderous group has recruited thousands of followers and is responsible for a string of deadly bombings, from the Philippines to a Bali nightclub where more than 190 were killed. Asian authorities accuse Hambali of planning all of them. "He is a close associate of September 11 mastermind Khalid Sheikh Mohammed," President Bush said after Hambali's capture in August 2003. "He is one of

---

2. It has not previously been reported that the CIA did not always control the Predator from a ground station at CIA headquarters in Langley, Virginia. When the spy craft first started flying from Uzbekistan over Afghanistan in pursuit of bin Laden, the CIA controlled it from a base in Germany. It was on one of these flights that CIA analysts believe they saw bin Laden in 2001 in a terror camp near Kandahar in southern Afghanistan. When the Air Force figured out how to arm the Predator with the assassin's tools of two Hellfire missiles, command was shifted to Langley. Washington wanted to avoid a tussle with the leftist German government over using its soil to launch strikes.

the world's most lethal terrorists." Hambali's dream is to use violence to create a massive Islamic state enveloping Malaysia, Indonesia, Singapore, Brunei, and the Philippines.

Hambali will now dream his dreams in prison. Here's how he was taken. As Hambali was known to move in and out of Thailand, the CIA located one of his wives in a town near the center of the country. The Thai government maintains easily crossed borders as a way to encourage economic development. The agency waited, watched, and listened. Sure enough, one day Hambali telephoned the wife. The communications intercept put his position in central Thailand. The Thai authorities working with the CIA moved in and took a startled Hambali into custody, wounding him with a gunshot in the process. His wife was released. The Thais whisked their prize to a Bangkok airport, then told the press he was taken to his home country of Indonesia. But when Indonesian authorities said he wasn't in their country, they were telling the truth. Washington wanted complete access to Hambali. At this writing, the U.S. is holding the terrorist in a Middle Eastern country, where officials are free to question him without legal constraints. An official told me that Hambali, thirty-six years old, has no chance of ever walking free again. He will either spend the rest of his life in prison or be executed.

Hambali is not the only terror master to be held by the U.S. in a third country. Abu Zubayah, bin Laden's top recruiter, was captured in Pakistan and is being held in an Asian territory. (A U.S. official asked me not to disclose where Hambali and Abu Zubayah are held for fear it would embarrass the host countries.)

COMMANDO MAKEOVER

As al Harthi's death warrant was being signed by Grey Fox in the Yemeni desert, Rumsfeld worked to make Special Operations Command even more lethal. His July 22 directive had given SoCom unprecedented power. Now Rumsfeld asked the Institute for Defense Analyses (IDA), a Pentagon-funded research group, for more ideas to invigorate SoCom operations. In a memo to Rumsfeld, aide Marshall Billingslea reported, "I explained to [IDA] that the purpose of the effort was to start with a 'blank sheet of paper,' and re-design USSOCOM to fight the war on terrorism." General Pete Schoomaker, former SoCom commander, came on board as a consultant because Rumsfeld liked the tough but intellectual ex-snake eater. When Schoomaker became SoCom commander in 1997, his briefings often included pictures of the charred, mangled aircraft smoldering in the Iranian desert after the disastrous Desert One operation of 1980. "Don't Confuse Enthusiasm with Capability," said the headline on his briefing slides. That sort of realism sat well with Rumsfeld, and the duo's plan to improve special operations capability bore fruit in due course.

In January 2003, as Rumsfeld's tenure reached the two-year mark, he appeared in the Pentagon pressroom to announce a revamped SoCom. Rumsfeld announced that in-theater Special Operations Command units (called T-SOCS) would from now on have authority to plan their own hunt-and-destroy missions, requisition the needed weapons and men, and run covert actions themselves. In this one giant unshackling of special operations forces, Rumsfeld had engineered their biggest reordering since Congress created U.S. Special Operations Command in 1987. Rumsfeld had put in place a whole new mechanism for hunting down terrorists. He abandoned the Clinton administration's decree that the military must have an official "finding" signed by the president—a step that meant congressional notification and increased the possibility of leaks—before taking any action. Now special forces on the scene could react immediately to track and kill terrorists.

By spring 2003, General Holland had won commitments from the Pentagon for five thousand new positions and $1 billion more a year, bringing his annual budget to $6 billion. He got new Chinook helicopters for the 160th Special Operations Aviation Regiment. Its ground-skimming helicopters insert commandos behind enemy lines. Super-secret JSOC would add hundreds of men and new communications gear.

But Rumsfeld demanded results for all this support. At a conference of combatant commanders at the Pentagon, Rumsfeld pulled General Holland aside and asked, "Have you killed anyone yet?" General Holland retired in September and was replaced by hard-bitten Army General Bryan "Doug" Brown, a snake eater by profession. At his installation, he said he knew al Qaeda agents were working on new murder plans. "Our job is to work harder." Donald Rumsfeld would make sure he did.

"We did not have what we now think of as SOF when I was secretary of defense in the seventies," Rumsfeld told me. "All of us watched what happened in Desert One.... But we have now done a series of five, six, or seven things that are quite significant in terms of trying to get this institution organized and trained and equipped." But one thing is certain. Rumsfeld remains far from satisfied with a Special Operations Command that is still not making use of all the tools and freedom he has given it. His question to SoCom's commanders remains the same: "Have you killed anyone yet?"

[CHAPTER 2]

TOPPLING THE TALIBAN AND SADDAM, TOO

TWO WEEKS AFTER SEPTEMBER 11, RUMSFELD WAS IMPATIENT. GENERAL TOMMY Franks had brought him a war plan for Afghanistan that called for more than two divisions of ground troops. Rumsfeld thought it too ground-heavy. The generals were beginning to learn that, while "everybody likes boots on the ground," as Rumsfeld put it, the new defense secretary was looking for more creative war plans. He wanted a fast flow of battlefield intelligence, precision air strikes, and light, lethal units on the ground. That was how to oust the Taliban and nab Osama bin Laden. Franks got the message.

But General Charles Holland, also present at this crucial September 25 meeting, pointed out that the CIA had not yet prepared the battlefield to introduce Army Green Beret A Teams. The war plan called for inserting them into Afghanistan to hook up with anti-Taliban rebels. The CIA's paramilitary force had made some headway with the Northern Alliance. But in the south, the CIA had not made sufficient contact with Pashtun tribal leaders—the agency had too few men in-country. Pentagon officials later accused the CIA of flat-out failure to prepare the southern battlefield. Holland's criticism of the CIA resulted in action from Rumsfeld. Within a year he had created his own intelligence shop, supervised by a new under-secretary of defense.

But Rumsfeld had a more immediate bureaucratic problem: CIA covert operations, under U.S. Title 50, required a presidential finding and notification of Congress. Should melding special forces with CIA paramilitaries in Afghanistan be subjected to this time-consuming bureaucratic procedure? Pentagon lawyers were unsure. The Pentagon began signing new deployment orders, switching Green Berets and SEALs from Special Operations Command to the CIA as covert warriors. Of the agency's 150-man paramilitary force, about half came from SoCom. When the decision had to be made about deploying them, Rumsfeld finally settled the debate by turning to his aides and saying, "Just send them in."

The CIA paramilitaries and special forces would set the stage, but how long would combat last? General Franks foresaw that it could last many months, and Rumsfeld worried about cold-weather war-fare. A team of ex-commandos quickly put together a briefing for him on how Afghanistan's subfreezing winter would actually help U.S. forces. Bin Laden's caves would emit a more intense heat signature for infrared sensors to detect, the briefers told Rumsfeld, and special forces could then guide strike jets to the target.

Special forces were still Rumsfeld's focus. His staff made the removal of the Taliban to get to bin Laden the campaign's primary political objective, and planned that this would be done "by proxy"—that is, mostly by indigenous troops assisted by U.S. special forces. Rumsfeld had convened a number of war sessions during which the Soviet Union's disastrous experience in Afghanistan was discussed. One of the lessons learned was that deploying tens of thousands of troops would look more like an army of occupation than an army of liberation, and would mean only more targets for the Taliban.

Rumsfeld's troop-light war plan was dictated by other factors besides the disastrous Soviet experience. No neighboring country provided the huge staging areas it would take to launch a ground invasion. Central Command would have to wait until it secured and rebuilt an air base at Bahgram, north of Kabul, before a large number of boots could hit the ground. Pakistan's Musharraf let CentCom use three bases in the south primarily for resupply, but not for ground troops or U.S. bombers. I can report that the general did, however, secretly allow the CIA to launch the Hellfire-armed Predator from one of those bases. It gave the agency a close-in launch point, which cut flight time to the target.

By early October, Franks had submitted a drastically scaled-back plan that met Rumsfeld's objectives. The secretary signed orders positioning three carriers off the Pakistani coast. They carried not only warplanes but also the Green Beret A Teams who would win the war. Lacking close-in air bases, the Air Force had to play from a distance, sending pilots on a twelve-hour round trip from Kuwait to their targets.

With war about to be launched in Afghanistan, Franks also set aside a team to dust off the war plan for Iraq. At the first NSC meeting after September 11, Rumsfeld had mentioned Saddam Hussein, along with the Taliban, as targets that had to be taken out to win the war on terror.

On October 7, 2001, President Bush signed the papers to begin hostilities against Afghanistan. The plan called for only about one thousand American troops to be deployed in-country. By early November, with the Northern Alliance bearing down on Kabul from the north, a southern front finally developed, led by men like Captain Jason Amerine, an A Team commander. Amerine flew by helicopter from the carrier USS *Kitty Hawk* to join up with tribal fighters led by future Afghan leader Hamid Karzai. Together, the Americans, code-named "Texas One Two," and the Afghans fought their way to the outskirts of Kandahar, the Taliban stronghold. Amerine later told me, "As far as actual Green Berets being the main effort, going in there and doing their mission, I don't think we had the opportunity to do something like this before Afghanistan. It became validating a way of fighting. In Vietnam, we became so sucked into the CIA world. In Afghanistan, I certainly wasn't run by the CIA. They gathered intelligence and sent up reports. I wasn't overly interested in what they were doing." Amerine, with an M-4 carbine strapped to his back and a secure radio in his hand, busied himself with fighting the enemy and calling in air strikes.

The Rumsfeld-Franks war plan ushered in other new twists. The carrier USS *Kitty Hawk*, its deck normally bristling with attack jets, became a floating base for Green Berets. The Predator spy drone suddenly emerged as a remote-controlled assassin, with the addition of sleek Hellfire anti-tank missiles. Months later, in Operation Anaconda, the last major offensive against large clusters of Taliban and al Qaeda, the Navy also found a new way to fight. It used its venerable P-3 Orion submarine hunter as a land surveillance aircraft. The plane's infrared optics could pick up all sorts of human movements that the crew would relay to friendlies down below. In Anaconda, some bright naval officer (no one seems to remember who) came up with the idea of putting SEALs on each plane. They watched the optics screen and immediately radioed what they saw to their special operations buddies on the ground. Al Qaeda had been adjusting. They hid under blankets when they heard the Predator overhead. But the keen eyes of Navy SEALs often spotted the slightest movements and allowed the allies to get the jump on the enemy in several firefights.

There were other new tactics. For years, the CIA has put damaged goods on the arms market, particularly the Soviet-designed SA-7 shoulder-fired missile. The idea is to discredit arms dealers and attach tracers to the weapons so terrorists can be tracked. Now, the intelligence community got more involved in the cell/satellite phone market. They "salted" phones with recognizable codes, and then flooded them into areas where al Qaeda buys its communications gear.

In the Afghan war's first month, a *New York Times* front-page article declared that the U.S. was in a "quagmire." Rumsfeld repeatedly ridiculed the story, especially after Kabul fell in early November and Kandahar followed a month later. Rumsfeld saw the war, far from being a quagmire, as the first necessary victory in the war on terror. "I firmly believe that this is the most important tasking the U.S. military has been handed since the Second World War," Rumsfeld said shortly before forces at Kabul surrendered. "And what's at stake here is no less than our freedom to exist as an American people. So there's no option but success."

As Amerine and other Green Berets moved toward Kandahar, press questions moved from the "quagmire" to whether Rumsfeld's troops were moving too fast. Rumsfeld was not afraid to respond in stark terms. At one briefing, a reporter asked for the "tactical rationale" for dropping cluster bombs. Critics said the spray of bomblets struck innocent civilians. Unexploded bombs could lie in wait to maim or kill children who disturbed them. General Richard Myers took this question, providing an air commander's view. You match weapon to target, while making sure to consult legal counsel on the laws of armed conflict. "We've worked this very, very carefully," he said.

Rumsfeld interjected. He was unapologetic. "They are being used on the front line—al Qaeda and Taliban troops to try to kill them, is why we're using them, to be perfectly blunt," he said. Later that month, a reporter asked him to justify attacking retreating troops. "It is a perfectly legitimate and attractive target, and we intend to take every opportunity to do that," he answered. When a reporter suggested that the entire Afghan attack was designed to kill al Qaeda members, the defense secretary replied, "Oh, you bet." He said, "The way to deal with [terrorists] is to go find them and kill them."

Americans became smitten with this new, plucky character on TV and tuned in by the millions. The writers at *Saturday Night Live* were watching too. Suddenly, a new character appeared: Donald Rumsfeld, impersonated by Darrell Hammond.

Rumsfeld: Remember what I said about your question the other day?

Reporter: That it was idiotic?

Rumsfeld: And?

Reporter: And that I am an embarrassment both to myself and to my newspaper?

Rumsfeld: That's right.

By mid-December, the biggest prize in the war seemed cornered in a large mountainous area along the Pakistani border. The *Washington Times* reported that commandos intercepted a voice in Tora Bora believed to be bin Laden directing his al Qaeda troops. Rumsfeld was traveling in the region at the time and expressed anger over the leak. When asked about it later by a reporter, he curtly said he did not comment on intelligence reports. At the Pentagon, planners told cable news outlets on background that they had the terror master cornered. But bin Laden slipped away through one of Tora Bora's thousands of escape routes into Pakistan's vast tribal no-man's land. Rumsfeld felt the first sting of concerted media criticism. He had too few ground troops in Afghanistan, the critics said, to block bin Laden's vanishing act.

Still, with the Taliban ousted and Karzai in power, Rumsfeld remained extremely popular. After testifying on Capitol Hill, he would pause and work the crowd of tourists along the rope line before getting in his limo. Bush was anxious to be seen with the wildly popular Rumsfeld. The president came to the Pentagon in January 2002 to sign a new bill to fund ongoing military operations. "I always love being introduced by a matinee idol," Bush joked, as he stood before a laughing audience of Pentagon workers. "Who would have thought it?" A month later, while talking to airmen at Eglin Air Force Base, Florida, the president referred to his defense secretary as "my administration's matinee idol for the seniors." On prime time cable, CNN's Larry King sat in Rumsfeld's conference room and said to him, "You now have this image called sex symbol. You are 'the guy.'" Rumsfeld was "the guy" who delivered victory.

THE TEAM

He wasn't alone. By January 2002, Rumsfeld had assembled the brainpower he needed to plot the global war. The three who proved most prominent were Deputy Defense Secretary Paul Wolfowitz, policy chief Douglas Feith, and Middle East expert William Luti.

Wolfowitz's academic background, cluttered desk, and occasional absent-mindedness belie a steely, ideological view of the world. His connections run deep through Republican national security circles, but he got his first Pentagon job under Jimmy Carter. It was an obscure post, deputy assistant secretary of defense for regional programs. But Wolfowitz's ambition and long work hours brought him notice. With Ronald Reagan's election, Wolfowitz won a senior State Department job, and was later named ambassador to Indonesia.

The appointment was provocative—naming a vocal Jewish supporter of Israel to be ambassador to the world's most populous Muslim nation. Wolfowitz's time there made him a strong advocate for establishing military-to-military contacts between the United States and Indonesia to fight Islamic terrorists there—something that hasn't yet happened because of human rights concerns.

The first Bush administration hired Wolfowitz as undersecretary of defense for policy, the number three slot under Defense Secretary Dick Cheney. When I interviewed Wolfowitz a month before Desert Storm, he talked about Saddam Hussein's brutality and what a better place the Middle East would be without him. That would become a constant theme.

Another constant theme is support of Israel. Sources have told me that Wolfowitz's advocacy of more economic and military aid for Israel even led to some grumbling among generals in the Pentagon that Wolfowitz put Israel's national security ahead of America's. These grumbles have some foundation, because to earn cash Israel will sell advanced military technology to American adversaries, including China. After the first Gulf War, the Pentagon received credible intelligence reports that Israel shared Patriot anti-missile technology, for a fee, with Beijing. A Rand study concluded that Israel was a backdoor route for foreign countries to obtain American weapons technology they could not acquire legally. Officials say that on some occasions Wolfowitz pushed arms transfers to Israel that were opposed by the Joint Chiefs. That did not make him popular.

Wolfowitz sat out the Clinton years as dean of the prestigious Paul H. Nitze School of Advanced International Studies at Johns Hopkins University. But he threw occasional bombs at the Democratic administration in op-ed columns, articles in stuffy foreign affairs journals, and in congressional appearances. In a 1996 piece in the *Wall Street Journal*, he accused President Clinton of ineptitude in allowing the Iraqi Republican Guard to invade the northern Kurdish region. He wrote of "betrayal" and "inept covert operations" and a modern-day "Bay of Pigs." "Saddam is a convicted killer still in possession of a loaded gun—and it's pointed at us," he wrote. This was a preview of the public statements that would come five years later to justify a war with Iraq. In another article, Wolfowitz pronounced Saddam a "war criminal." The first Bush administration, he wrote, made a "serious mistake" in leaving the dictator in power after the 1991 war.

Wolfowitz's rhetorical push to get Saddam reached a new level in 1998. William Kristol, editor in chief of the *Weekly Standard* and a leading neoconservative[1] in Washington, forged a new pressure group, the New American Century, which advocated a robust American presence worldwide. On January 26, 1998, a broad spectrum of conservatives signed a two-page letter to Clinton. The signers urged the president to dump the policy of containing Saddam. "The only acceptable strategy is one that eliminates the possibility that Iraq will be able to use or threaten to use weapons of mass destruction," the letter said. "In the near term, this means a willingness to undertake military action as diplomacy is clearly failing. In the long term, it means removing Saddam Hussein and his regime from power. That now needs to become the aim of American foreign policy." The eighteen signatures stood as a preview of the second Bush administration, then three years away. Endorsers included Wolfowitz; Richard Perle, who would chair the Defense Policy Board; John Bolton, destined to be the top arms control negotiator at the State Department; Zalmay Khalilzad, Bush's special envoy to Afghanistan; and Peter Rodman, now the Pentagon's assistant secretary for Asian affairs. Joining the group was a man not normally identified with the neoconservatives: Donald Rumsfeld.

Wolfowitz played a major role in forging candidate George W. Bush's national security views. He perched near the top of an eight-

---

1. There is no hard and fast definition of a neoconservative, but one can generally say that aside from being former "liberals who were mugged by reality," they tend to be strong supporters of Israel and of an interventionist foreign policy, often come from academic backgrounds, and are heavily represented in media and government.

member advisory group self-named "The Vulcans." Headed by Condoleezza Rice, the Vulcans immersed the lightly traveled Texas governor in a crash course on world affairs and military policy.

The Vulcans avoided appearing as job-seekers. At one point, Rice said on C-SPAN that it made more sense for her to remain as provost at Stanford University than to come back to Washington. But behind the scenes, the Vulcans jockeyed for position and sized up the competition. "People in the campaign took on this false humility, like they didn't want another job. But in the background, they were scrambling," said one adviser.

One Vulcan who sincerely wasn't angling for a job was Richard Perle, who was comfortable in his chair at the American Enterprise Institute, a Washington think tank and halfway house for neoconservatives, from which they can position themselves to enter or reenter government. A gourmet, Perle spends his summers at his home in the south of France. Perhaps because he had no designs on another Pentagon job, he was the boldest Vulcan, expressing aggressive opinions on how to get rid of Saddam Hussein.

Wolfowitz shared Perle's opinions and did want a job—the top defense post, if possible—but realized that Bush, an oilman and major league baseball owner by profession, was not interested in intervening around the world. Clinton's feckless interventionism was not something Bush wanted to repeat. Bush wanted a strong military, but he also warned of the perils of "nation-building." He complained that forces were stretched thin, and suggested he might pull troops out of the Balkans. Recognizing Bush's reluctance, Wolfowitz spoke of the need to remove Saddam, but did not press for an all-out war. He thus evolved into the Big Picture Vulcan.

"Wolfowitz had a philosophy that connected things," a Bush adviser recalled. "Trade policy. South Asia. Europe. The Middle East. Wolfowitz connected them all for Bush." He made trips to the then–governor's Texas ranch, thick briefing books in hand. He, Perle, Richard Armitage, another Vulcan member and a close friend of Colin Powell, convinced Bush to make the state of the Clinton military a pivotal campaign issue. After the election, Wolfowitz's slim chances to become defense secretary were dashed by Rumsfeld.

Rumsfeld was not a Vulcan, having played a small advisory role in the campaign. During the transition, Bush talked to Rumsfeld about what kind of defense secretary he needed. The president-elect was charmed by Rumsfeld's resolute manner. Both men knew evil when they saw it. They clung to old-fashioned values like family, hard work, and patriotism. And Bush settled on a defense secretary: Rumsfeld was the man he wanted.

I can report that Wolfowitz was not Rumsfeld's first choice for deputy. Rumsfeld wanted his old colleague Bill Schneider, but Schneider wanted to stay in the business world, and instead accepted the chairmanship of the Defense Science Board.

Douglas Feith, undersecretary of defense for policy, did not join Wolfowitz at the Pentagon until the summer of 2001. Educated at Georgetown and Harvard, he had started his government career as a special counsel to Richard Perle, assistant secretary of defense for International Security Policy at the Pentagon during the Reagan years. Perle masterminded the administration's hard-line arms control policies during Reagan's $2.4 trillion military buildup to confront the Evil Empire. Feith had a front-row seat as his mentor Perle slashed and burned his way through anyone who blocked pursuing the Cold War against Moscow.

Feith later won a small plum as deputy assistant secretary of defense for negotiating policy. He spent the next fifteen years at the international law firm of Feith and Zell. In his spare time, he churned out weighty policy articles, and contributed chapters to books on Churchill and on Israel's legal right to exist. When George W. Bush was elected, he sought a top-level Pentagon job. His first interview with Rumsfeld did not go well. Sources told me Rumsfeld wanted Schneider or another old friend, Carl Ford, who ended up at the State Department. Perle promoted his protégé, and Feith finally got the job as undersecretary of defense for policy. He oversaw a staff of seven hundred, the Pentagon's brain trust. Feith quickly became one of Rumsfeld's targets. The secretary chewed Feith out for poor staff work or verbal bureaucratese so often that, according to a colleague, "he woke up every moment with two thoughts in mind: What is the secretary of defense going yell at me for today, and how do I avoid it?"

Feith weathered the Rumsfeld criticism and actually proved adroit at maneuvering himself into the catbird seat. Rumsfeld convened morning meetings of his inner circle—the Wolfowitz-Myers-Pace gathering known as the Round Table. Trouble was, Feith was not a member. After September 11, he realized he had to gain entrance to this exclusive club or risk failure. Feith described his move to me. "I got together with the secretary and said, 'How can the policy organization better serve you?' I had a sense that we were not in on everything that we needed to be in on to be serving the secretary. And he said, 'You have to be lobbing ideas ahead of me.' And he raised a question, 'Can we move fast enough?' And I remember I said to him, 'I think we can move fast enough, but it's difficult to know whether we're lobbing an idea ahead of you or behind you if we don't know where you are at a given morning.'" Shortly thereafter, Rumsfeld admitted Feith to the Round Table. "That's the key institution in this building," Feith said. "We then became much more useful to this organization."

One of Feith's key post–September 11 decisions was to create a special intelligence team. Some CIA analysts believed that al Qaeda had no firm links to anti-Zionist terrorist groups like Hamas and Hezbollah. Feith thought there were links—all the way to Baghdad.

He put two policymakers in front of secure computers. They read years of intelligence reports: communication intercepts and human source reports that linked Baghdad to terror groups, including al Qaeda. Feith and other staffers believed the CIA had not done a good job of analyzing a decade of contacts and documenting the Baghdad-bin Laden link. His shop would do it for them. By the fall of 2002, the team produced a catalogue of contacts going back to the mid-1990s. In some instances, Saddam's bomb-making experts had traveled to bin Laden's farm in Sudan, where they presumably taught the latest in truck bomb technology. Over at Langley, mid-level CIA analysts were not happy with what they considered Feith's trespassing. In turn, some of Rumsfeld's staff got the impression that the CIA career employees didn't really want to fight a global war on terror. That fall, Rumsfeld and other top officials started talking about some of the team's findings. "We do have solid evidence of the presence in Iraq of al Qaeda members, including some that have been to Baghdad," the defense secretary declared. "We have what we consider to be credible contacts in Iraq who could help them acquire weapons of mass destruction capabilities." It would take a year for the full force of Feith's findings to reach the public.

In November 2003, a Feith memo to members of Congress was leaked to the *Weekly Standard*. The memo detailed what his team had found out. Bush backers cited it as further justification for war with Iraq. The secret report was one of the most useful services Feith performed for Rumsfeld.

Another key member of Rumsfeld's team is William Luti, who arrived in summer 2001 as deputy assistant secretary of defense for national security affairs. Luti is a retired Navy captain who tasted the Republican Revolution while a 1996 military fellow in the office of House Speaker Newt Gingrich. A product of conservative New Hampshire and South Carolina's tradition-bound military school, the

Citadel, Luti spent most of his naval career as a flight officer inside reconnaissance and radar-jamming jets. In Desert Storm, he was a crew member on the venerable EA-6B Prowler off the carrier USS *Kennedy*. The Prowler knocked down and confused Iraqi radars, dramatically cutting losses for allied fighter pilots who had to penetrate Baghdad's densely protected targets. "Luti is an iconoclast," Gingrich told me "Very intense. Very patriotic. Very impatient with bureaucracy. Very frustrated with the old order. Very pro-transformational."

Before the war, Luti attended the Fletcher School, tutored by professor Richard Shultz, who informs his students about the good that can come from exercising America's considerable military might overseas. Shultz, for example, believes Pakistani president Pervez Musharraf did not join Bush in the war on al Qaeda out of any beneficent reasons. Musharraf heard Bush's stirring speech to Congress nine days after September 11, when the president divided the world into two parts: those countries with the United States in the war on terror and those opposed. Musharraf also saw the naval armada gathering not far from Pakistan's coastline. A show of military power is why Musharraf joined the new war, Shultz believes.

As Rumsfeld's deputy assistant secretary of defense for national security affairs, Luti's domain spanned the Persian Gulf and Central Asia. With Russia tamed, those two regions now held America's chief adversaries, and Luti proved adroit at interagency combat with the State Department in forging harder-line policies against Iraq.

After September 11, Luti's importance grew. Feith carved out a new role for him by adding "special plans" to Luti's title. Luti got a promotion to deputy undersecretary, with an open route to Feith's office. His office of Special Plans produced the arguments for invading Iraq, as the internal debate with the State Department grew contentious. Like Rumsfeld, he went public in October 2002 on the Baghdad-al Qaeda connection, affirming that "Iraq's relations with al Qaeda go back a decade. They have harbored al Qaeda operatives in Baghdad and provided chemical and biological warfare training to al Qaeda."

TARGET IRAQ

A number of different classified war plans circulated in the Pentagon in 2002. According to Army sources, Feith's policy wonks floated the idea of toppling Saddam with two Army brigades, thousands of special operations troops, massive air strikes, indigenous rebels (primarily Kurds in the north and Shi'ites in the south), and defecting Iraqi army units. But Tommy Franks knew it would take more boots on the ground. He started by proposing a total force of more than 300,000. After meetings with Rumsfeld, the number of conventional troops went down and the number of special operations forces went up. Rumsfeld never dictated numbers, aides told me, but used questions to help Franks refine the plan.

One of Rumsfeld's most influential advisers on special forces and air power is retired General Charles Horner, who sits on the Defense Policy Board and was the top air commander in Desert Storm. He got to know Rumsfeld well when he served on a space commission chaired by the secretary in the late 1990s. Afghanistan, Horner told me, showed Rumsfeld how "small ground forces were very deadly if they integrate with air power." Another influential voice was an officer whose career Rumsfeld had to save.

Colonel Douglas A. Macgregor has bedeviled the top Army brass for years by advocating a totally revamped army. He wants its ten active divisions converted into fast-moving battle groups. They, in turn, would be tied electronically to mass inputs of information on the enemy. His 1997 book, *Breaking the Phalanx: A New Design for Landpower in the 21st Century*, was read avidly by reformers and think tank scholars. Macgregor teaches and writes at the National Defense University (NDU) at Fort McNair in Washington, D.C., and he readily granted press interviews to advocate his plan for a lighter, faster army.

As planning for Iraq become an open secret, Macgregor let it be known through back channels that he favored a smaller force than the one advocated by his ultimate boss, General Eric Shinseki, the Army chief of staff. Some in Rumsfeld's office wanted to bring Macgregor to the Pentagon to advise retired Vice Admiral Arthur K. Cebrowski, Rumsfeld's handpicked aide for transforming the armed forces to fit Rumsfeld's mold. The army brass didn't want that to happen.

So, in January 2002, Shinseki had Macgregor pulled from NDU and placed on the Army staff, where the generals could keep an eye on him. Next, someone on Shinseki's staff got the idea of sending Macgregor back to Belgium. He had been a war planner there during the 1999 NATO bombing of Serbia and was not due for another overseas billet. Macgregor's enemies assumed he would retire rather than accept the assignment and be separated again from his wife and two sons. But Macgregor had gained an important ally. Newt Gingrich showed Rumsfeld a copy of Macgregor's book, and the secretary liked it. A colleague quotes Rumsfeld as saying, "Why doesn't the chief of staff like this guy? He wants to do everything I want to do in the Army." When Gingrich learned of the Army's plan, he told Macgregor, "You are not going to Brussels and this is not going to happen." Not wanting to embarrass the Army completely, Rumsfeld did not put him on Cebrowski's staff, but moved him back to the National Defense University, from which in 2003 he put out a new book on reforming the Army.

Meanwhile, preparation for the real war moved forward. Rumsfeld and Franks commenced what would become scores of phone conversations, video teleconferences, and face-to-face briefings to settle on a war plan. Franks dusted off the existing plan, which had not changed much since Desert Storm: 500,000 total troops. But that idea was a non-starter. Rumsfeld told Franks that the American military, propelled by great advances in precision weapons, was ten times stronger than it had been in 1991. And, he added, Saddam's military stood at one-tenth its previous strength. "He's less strong, so we don't need the old plan," is how aides remember Rumsfeld's message.

At one point, Rumsfeld threw out a total troop number, somewhere around 150,000. He didn't necessarily believe that was the right force. But he wanted to spur debate. "Speed kills," Rumsfeld would say. It was his way of angling for a fast, agile force without imposing his own war plan. On the use of special operators, he never dictated a number or a specific mission, but he urged Franks to look at the lessons of Afghanistan and apply them to Iraq. "The secretary really turned the heat up to get these guys in on the ground," an official recalled. Aides remember Franks as so self-confident and well prepared that he took in all of Rumsfeld's questions unfazed. He went back to Tampa, reworked things, and returned to Washington. Sometimes just the two of them would work out ideas in private phone conversations.

On February 16, 2002, Bush signed a secret National Security Council directive establishing the goals and objectives for going to war with Iraq, according to classified documents I obtained. In March, General Tommy Franks put Central Command through a major Iraq war exercise code-named "Prominent Hammer." In April, he came to the Pentagon. For the first time, the Joint Chiefs, sitting in their secure lair, known as "The Tank," heard a detailed war plan. Franks's plan called for 200,000 to 250,000 troops and a two-front land war, with American troops striking from Kuwait and from Turkey. On May 11, Franks and Rumsfeld went to Camp David to brief President Bush. In summer 2002, Joint Chiefs chairman General Richard Myers issued detailed war plans to his combatant commanders and set up a special planning cell within the Joint Staff.

Rumsfeld moved to make sure Israel stayed out of the war. In July, the Joint Staff came up with a plan that would rely, in part, on briefing Tel Aviv beforehand on exactly how the invasion would play out. In return, the Israeli Defense Forces gave the Pentagon a detailed briefing on how they thought Iraq's military would respond.

On August 29, two weeks before he went to the United Nations to ask the Security Council to deliver a resolution endorsing force, President Bush approved the overall war plan.

In October, Franks conducted a series of secret war games, and began a piece-by-piece troop deployment to the Gulf—with Rumsfeld choosing which unit would go next. Bush delivered Rumsfeld another bureaucratic victory when the president signed an order making the Defense Department, not the State Department, the top dog in post-Saddam Iraq.

By January 2003, Franks's war plan, OpPlan 1003 Victor, was essentially in place. Its centerpiece: A fast-paced drive to Baghdad to oust Saddam as soon as possible. Invaders would bypass towns along the way, if possible. Also in January, Central Command delivered a highly classified document to the Pentagon entitled "Phase IV OPLAN: Reconstruction of Iraq." I obtained an exclusive copy.

The report is remarkable both for its rosy assumptions and for its emphasis on the need to reduce the number of American troops in Iraq once Baghdad falls. CentCom predicted large areas would not require occupation by allied troops. While the document predicted U.S. troops would remain in Iraq for four years, it also called for immediate force reductions.

There was at least one agency suggesting a dangerous post-Saddam era. The CIA circulated several analyses that warned "Ba'ath remnants might try to assume the role of opposition," that they "might destroy critical economic infrastructure," and that an armed opposition might arise if it appeared Washington was trying to make Iraq dependent on the West.

Retired Lieutenant Colonel Robert Maginnis was among a small group of TV military analysts who received an off-the-record briefing from Luti that February on post-Saddam planning. Maginnis, a Christian conservative, is friendly toward the administration, which provided him good access to Pentagon officials. "He clearly did not anticipate the levels of resistance," Maginnis said of Luti's briefing. "There was a general assumption on his part and on the part of others we would quickly win the hearts and minds. People would hardly resist. They refused to think about the Fedayeen. We asked hard questions and he didn't have good answers."

I asked Luti about charges that Feith's policy shop badly misjudged how Iraqis would greet the conquering Americans.

"We do assumptions-based planning," he answered. "We make assumptions based on intelligence and your gut. In a tyrannical society that is closed and we have a soda-straw view into it, you're making assumptions based on a soda-straw view. Sometimes you're going to be wrong. Now, the smart people have backup plans, or can be flexible enough on the ground to react quickly. And that's the genius of the American fighting man. That's the reason why we win wars, because our guy on the ground can make decisions for himself down to the NCO level. . . . They don't have to call home and ask for permission to do something."

He added, "Secretary Rumsfeld had us, the Joint Staff and the policy shop, look at all the things that could possibly go wrong. And on that list was Sunni-Ba'athists collapsing in the Sunni triangle and fighting us from there. Why do we get this bum rap that we didn't think about it?"

It turned out that toppling Saddam was the easy part. The mix of fast-moving troops, commandos, and air strikes worked even better than Rumsfeld thought it would. Baghdad fell April 9. It was a three-week war. The campaign now shifted to "Phase IV," the rebuilding of Iraq.

NOW THE HARD PART

During the war, the Joint Staff "crisis action teams" briefed Rumsfeld each morning on the war's progress. After April 9, the team's main focus became the hunt for weapons of mass destruction—President Bush's main public reason for going to war. The CIA picked scores of suspected weapons sites. As the war unfolded, however, site by site turned up empty of chemical or biological weapons. Each morning, the crisis action team had to report that another location was a bust. Rumsfeld grew angrier and angrier. One officer quoted him as saying, "They must be there!" At one briefing, he picked up the paper briefing slides and tossed them back at the briefers.

When retired Lieutenant General Jay Garner arrived in Baghdad as head of the Office of Rehabilitation and Humanitarian Assistance, which President Bush had established two months before the war, he quickly found out that General Tommy Franks and his staff seemed more interested in the hunt for weapons of mass destruction than in supporting his organization. He lacked telephones, office space, and transportation. He made one trip south to meet with Shi'ite leaders and could not get a helicopter ride back to Baghdad. He had to spend the night and wait for a ride the next day.

In mid-May, Garner—amid a growing, deadly insurgency against American troops—was replaced as America's top administrator in Iraq by L. Paul Bremer, a former ambassador and longtime associate of former secretary of state Henry Kissinger. Military officers say Bremer, a charismatic figure who sticks to talking points in press interviews, made a crucial early mistake when he disbanded the Iraqi army. Bremer did so because of its horrendous human rights record. But others, like Garner, thought keeping the Iraqi army garrisoned, but on the payroll, was a way to keep it from joining the resistance to America's presence in Iraq.

A similar question arose stateside when General Myers traveled to the Naval War College in Newport, Rhode Island, to deliver a confidential briefing to officers who would one day run the Navy. Much of Myers's talk was devoted to the impressive technical advancements that contributed to America's swift battlefield victory. But one of his talking points raised eyebrows at the Pentagon. *Lethality helped create enhanced combat power*, Myers's briefing chart says. *Focused on regime. Not annihilation of enemy army.* It was, however, some of these "enemy army" who reappeared later as Saddam's guerrillas assassinating American soldiers.

In June, Rumsfeld received a secret briefing from the Defense Intelligence Agency (DIA). It was not good news. The military was searching for an American navy officer who had not been seen since his F-18 left a Red Sea carrier in January 1991 to bomb targets near Baghdad. First classified as "killed in action," Captain Michael Scott Speicher later became "missing-captured." The Navy's about-face was based largely on the word of one Iraqi defector, a man assigned the code name "No. 2314" by the intelligence community. American soldiers had now found Speicher's initials scrawled on a prison wall, and members of Congress returning from Iraq reported promising leads. But the secret DIA report, of which I obtained a copy, said otherwise.

The report said No. 2314, a former functionary in Saddam's vicious Special Security Organization (SSO), was a liar. "No significant evidence of [Speicher's] status has been discovered," said the two-page report, dated June 23. "None of the information provided by 2314 has proven accurate."

The report lists a number of leads that hit dead ends:

- The defector provided the names of several physicians who he said had knowledge of Speicher's whereabouts. "All denied having any knowledge; two have passed a polygraph."
- The defector said his supervisor at SSO also knew of Speicher's imprisonment. But the supervisor denied this, passed a lie detector, and called No. 2314 a "born liar."
- The defector also said a psychiatrist at the Rashid prison worked there during Speicher's purported captivity. But the psychiatrist denied any knowledge of the pilot.
- U.S. Central Command recovered thousands of pages of documents related to allied POWs held by Baghdad in 1991 and later released. "To date, analysts have found only one reference to Speicher. The reference indicates he ejected and lists his status as 'unknown.'"

Subsequent to this report, a search team reached Speicher's crash site near the Saddam-friendly village of Hit. A U.S. official told me the team found no useable evidence. The source said No. 2314 passed a lie detector test administered by DIA, but that Saddam's men knew how to "trick" such exams.

The DIA report noted that an "alleged" flight suit, sponges, clothing, shoes, and manacles take from Hakimiyah prison were subjected to DNA analysis and came back negative. "U.S. CentCom has searched every known location associated with Speicher," the report concluded. "Other than at Hakimiyah prison, where U.S. forces found the initials 'MSS' on a cell wall, no significant evidence of his status has been discovered." Searchers were to return to the crash site in early 2004 when nomadic Bedouins camp in the area again. There is a slim chance the tribesmen may have seen something thirteen years ago.

MEA CULPA

In July, Rumsfeld went to Tampa to bid farewell to the retiring General Franks and to anoint General John Abizaid as the new chief of CentCom. The secretary had wanted Abizaid to run—and reform—the Army from within the Pentagon. But the well-educated Lebanese-American had his sights set on becoming a combatant commander. Rumsfeld had not been impressed by some of the senior Joint Staff officers he inherited. Abizaid, a former Joint Staff director, was an exception. Rumsfeld liked him for his smarts and his boldness. In the final weeks before the Iraqi war, Rumsfeld sent Abizaid to Qatar as Franks's deputy commander. Some in the Pentagon saw the repositioning as a way for Rumsfeld to keep an eye on Franks and make sure the push to Baghdad went as fast as possible.

Rumsfeld talked almost daily by phone or secure video link with his new CentCom commander. It was Abizaid who kept pushing Rumsfeld to internationalize the occupation force. He saw it as a way to allay Arab fears that America was colonizing Iraq. Rumsfeld sharply questioned the idea, but finally agreed. The problem then became finding countries that would send troops. Few did.

Rumsfeld repeatedly told reporters the Saddam loyalists in Iraq were not guerrillas. They were simply terrorists and criminals. "I guess the reason I don't use the phrase 'guerrilla war' is because there isn't one," he said. "It would be a misunderstanding and a miscommunication to you and to the people of the country and the world."

But his CentCom chief disagreed. That July, Abizaid appeared at a Pentagon press conference flanked by Larry Di Rita, Rumsfeld's spokesman. Abizaid said Saddam's forces were conducting a "classic guerrilla-type campaign." This was not merely his opinion, but the opinion of his aides who had researched the issue. Di Rita tried to change the subject, but the next day's press reports highlighted Abizaid's disagreement with Rumsfeld.

The two settled the dispute privately, an officer told me. Rumsfeld did his own research into the definition of guerrilla war and conveyed his findings to Abizaid via the Joint Chiefs chairman. It was not a rebuke, just a reminder that the defense secretary still thought he was right. Rumsfeld did not want to grant Saddam's henchmen the imprimatur of freedom fighters; Abizaid did not want to mislead his troops, who knew firsthand that they were facing a deadly insurgency. Rumsfeld settled on another classic military term to describe the fighting, one that everyone could agree on: low-intensity conflict.

Di Rita helped further defuse the tension by going to Rumsfeld and taking blame for the split. Di Rita told the secretary that he had failed to warn Abizaid beforehand that he was likely to get a question on whether Iraq was now a guerrilla war and that Rumsfeld believed it was not. When Di Rita fessed up to Rumsfeld, the secretary, who had coached his new spokesman on how to handle press questions, did not disagree.

Along with low-intensity conflict, Rumsfeld faced the challenge of rebuilding Iraq, and was assembling a massive spending bill— Iraq's Marshall Plan—the estimated price tag of which rose daily. The formerly standoffish secretary now went frequently to Congress for closed-door briefings and to lobby for the spending package. He urged lawmakers to travel to Iraq to see all the good things that were happening. By October, nearly one hundred members had made the trip. Rumsfeld sent out a confidential memo to his staff in July, saying, "We have to get a team that will start working Congress on Iraq regularly, every single day, so they pummel people with good information."

He took a personal interest in making sure that the secretary of veterans affairs, Tony Principi, got over to Iraq. "If he did," Rumsfeld wrote in another snowflake, "he would be able to come back and talk to the veterans in a very helpful way. He is going to have to be responsible for those folks when they get back."

Rumsfeld put Wolfowitz in charge of managing Phase IV's day-to-day operations. The public was learning of "improvised explosive devices"—remote-controlled, roadside bombs that were killing American soldiers. Wolfowitz rushed to Baghdad that July and reported back to Rumsfeld. They decided more troops were not the answer. Commanders said they had enough people to systematically root out every Ba'athist cell; it would just take time. Wolfowitz appeared in the Pentagon pressroom to brief the public. While Rumsfeld had refused to admit a war-planning mistake, Wolfowitz believed it was time to fess up.

"There was a plan, but as any military officer can tell you, no plan survives first contact with reality. Inevitably, some of our assumptions turned out to be wrong," he said. "Some conditions were worse than we anticipated, particularly in the security area, and there are three. No Army units, at least none of any significant size, came over to our side so that we could use them as Iraqi forces with us today. [The war plan had anticipated Iraqi soldiers fighting alongside the coalition.] Second, the police turned out to require a massive overhaul. Third, and worst of all, it was difficult to imagine before the war that the criminal gangs of sadists and gangsters who have run Iraq for thirty-five years would continue fighting."

Rumsfeld appeared before the same press corps a few days later and pointedly declined to endorse his deputy's assessment. "I have not had a chance to read the transcript [of the briefing] that Dr. Wolfowitz conducted down here," Rumsfeld later told reporters. Later in the same press conference, however, Rumsfeld inadvertently admitted he was well aware of what Wolfowitz had said. Asked about reconstruction in Iraq, he answered, "It's taken longer, as I believe Paul Wolfowitz mentioned, it's taken longer, for example to get it up to speed than anyone would have hoped."

Wolfowitz had laid out "what" the mistakes were. The answer to "why" came a month later. A team of senior Joint Staff officers scrutinized the war planning. By late August, the group produced a "final draft," stamped SECRET and titled "Operation Iraqi Freedom Strategic Lessons Learned." It said planning for post-Saddam scenarios had been rushed and insufficient. A key finding: "U.S. military and government viewed combat and stability operations as sequential efforts and did not address stability requirements as an integrated part of combat operations planning. Decision to form DoD Phase IV organizations was made in Oct. 02 but organizations were not formed until January due to [U.N. Security Council resolution] diplomatic debate in Nov. 02 and desire not to commit personnel to [combined joint task force IV] until a clear diplomatic mandate was established and Iraqi intention to disarm was assessed.

"Late formation of DoD IV organization limited time available for the development of detailed plans and pre-deployment coordination. Command relationships (and communication requirements) and responsibilities were not clearly defined for DoD organizations until shortly before [the war] commenced."

The secret report had some advice for the next war: "Establish Phase IV organizations and command relationships in time to plan, rehearse, prepare and deploy forward to fully integrate with joint headquarters prior to combat operations. Due to extensive IA [interagency]/coalition coordination requirements, must ensure Phase IV transition plan is complete prior to initiation of hostilities. Include coalition partners in stabilization and reconstruction planning prior to combat operations."

The report also concluded that the Pentagon's and CIA's search for weapons of mass destruction was poorly organized: "WMD elimination/exploitation on a large scale was a new mission area. Division of responsibility for planning and execution was not clear. As a result planning occurred on an ad hoc basis and late in the process. Additionally, there were insufficient assets available to accomplish the mission. Existing assets were not organized to perform the mission. Existing assets were tasked to perform multiple, competing missions, e.g. homeland security vs. OCONUS [outside the continental United States]."

The report recommended that combatant commanders, such as those in charge of Central Command and Pacific Command, develop a cadre of WMD experts as a separate cell. The strategic study found other flaws:

- The intelligence community, mainly the CIA and Defense Intelligence Agency, lacked expert analysts on Iraq. "Lack of expert Iraq analysts hindered the intel community's ability to properly analyze and disseminate products." In September 2002, the National Security Council took control of coordinating operations of the Joint Staff and the intelligence community. The NSC set up a new organization called the Executive Steering Group (ESG). It did not work as smoothly as hoped. "Some DoD-CIA disconnects occurred at the Strategic and Operational level. Because of the close hold on intelligence information, some significant planning issues could not be discussed at weekly ESG. ESG was primarily focused on near term issues, but needed to address long term issues as well."
- There were not enough intelligence personnel to collect intelligence in multiple theaters. "High demand for intel

personnel resulted from increased requirements in targeting, [battle damage assessment] analysis and imagery interpretation expertise at all echelons of command. Currently not enough intelligence support for multiple campaigns, theaters or service requirements." The report blames the shortfalls on the fact that the services "lack an integrated intel architecture and true interoperability among service intel systems and processes. Not enough battlefield persistent ISR [intelligence, surveillance and reconnaissance] assets." The report recommends that the CIA and Defense Department develop a joint doctrine to guide them when a "time sensitive target" arises.

On the positive side, the report states that Central Command greatly streamlined the targeting bureaucracy. The paper says that General Franks and Rumsfeld himself were involved in approving strikes on individual targets in the Afghanistan war. By the time Operation Iraqi Freedom came, new procedures and written guidance allowed commanders to approve a bombing target as soon as it came up. Joint operations, a pet project of Rumsfeld's, worked at its highest levels ever. "High degree of trust and confidence in and among Joint Staff, [the combatant command] and services in preparing for and conducting the fight," the report says.

After I wrote about some aspects of the report in the *Washington Times*, it became one of the most sought-after documents in Washington. Democrats wanted to use it to bash Bush. At House and Senate hearings, they asked a number of military and civilian officials to provide a copy. Rebuffed, the Democrats then turned to the legislative process. They introduced resolutions in two House committees, Armed Services and Foreign Relations, to order the Pentagon to produce it. Both resolutions failed on party line votes. Next, some Democrats appealed in writing to General Myers. They asked if the document could be brought to a secure briefing room in the House. There, members could read, but not copy it. Again, the Pentagon refused.

"While I appreciate your interest in obtaining the report, I must reiterate it remains a work in progress," Myers said of the "final draft" in a letter to Congressman Vic Snyder, an Arkansas Democrat. "We are still conducting critical staff interviews of those personally involved in Operation Iraqi Freedom planning process. It would be premature to release the study before their input."

Myers decided in September to give his civilian bosses some political cover. Democrats and the liberal media were pillorying Rumsfeld and Wolfowitz over the situation in Iraq. Before the war, Wolfowitz had testified that Iraqi oil would fund reconstruction. Now, the administration was close to presenting an $87 billion reconstruction price tag to American taxpayers. Sitting at the witness table before the Senate Armed Services Committee, Myers said, "It is a battle of wills. The terrorists have said, and think, they are going to win. They are absolutely wrong about that. They will not win. They can't win. We can't let them win, and we won't. We are going to win as long as we have the continuing will of the American people." Democratic senator Ted Kennedy of Massachusetts did not like a four-star general playing politics and playing on emotions rather than delivering the traditional military nuts-and-bolts explanation of policy. The war, Kennedy said, is "not about the will, the patriotism, the determination of the troops. We know that and you know it. And the parents in my state know it as well. . . . More than seven young men [from Massachusetts] have lost their lives. So we know about that."

More embarrassing was the CIA's leaking that some of its pre-war intelligence reports mentioned the possibility of an insurgency. Some at the Pentagon saw this as a "Cover Your Ass" maneuver, given that the director of Central Intelligence, George Tenet, was under intense media and Democratic attack. Despite the leak, Tenet maintained a professional relationship with Rumsfeld. The two lunched weekly, and Rumsfeld gave Tenet tips on baseline budgeting.

Tenet's mid-level analysts, however, were another story. Some on Rumsfeld's staff believed many of them opposed Bush and the war on terrorism. The leak, they thought, was not just a "Cover Your Ass" gambit but an attempt to undermine administration policy. Their suspicions grew stronger in November when details of the CIA station chief's field report from Baghdad leaked to the press. The report doubted the Bush administration's public claim that most Iraqis backed the occupation. Pentagon officials looked at the cable's list of recipients. The list was five pages long, all the way down to carrier battle group commanders around the world. Pentagon officials knew that the longer the list of addressees was, the better the chance for a press leak. Rumsfeld's people also remembered several CIA pre-war reports that had turned out to be wrong. One report said that if the military lopped off the head of the Iraqi police force, the rank and file would join the Americans. As it turned out, the police were rotten to the core and had to be rebuilt from the ground up.

Rumsfeld rarely criticizes another agency in public. But in September, as criticism of his postwar strategy grew, he felt compelled to do so. "There were some people who were quite optimistic that there would be a surrender of their army in a formal way," Rumsfeld said on PBS. "In fact, what happened was they didn't surrender. The intelligence was not perfect on that. They bled into the countryside." Rumsfeld then separated himself from those faulty intelligence reports. "Some people, as I say, did leave the impression that their view was that," he said. "My view was I didn't know. And I didn't ever give optimistic suggestions because I knew I didn't know." Moreover, some in the Pentagon believed the CIA was not giving the military the intelligence it needed to defeat the Iraqi insurgency. 2003 ended with this bureaucratic standoff. CIA analysts believe they had given the Defense Department sufficient warning to plan for a robust guerrilla war. Pentagon officials say the reports came only in bits and pieces. They, in turn, fault Langley for inaccurate predictions on Iraq's police force and army. Some defense advisers now believe the administration should have ordered up a National Intelligence Estimate (NIE) on post-Saddam Iraq. This process would have put the intelligence community's best minds together to focus on what became the most important—and challenging—part of Operation Iraqi Freedom.

On November 19, 2003, General Abizaid came to the Pentagon to brief Rumsfeld. The month would bring the deaths of over seventy soldiers. His ground commanders responded with yet another round of search-and-destroy raids. This time, they bombed the homes and businesses where Saddam's loyalists met and planned. To Rumsfeld's conference room came the secretary's inner circle: Wolfowitz, Feith, and Generals Myers and Pace. Abizaid talked of the secret tactics he was using to kill insurgents, one devised for Saddam's Sunni followers, the other for foreign fighters coming over the Syrian border. Near the end of the briefing, Rumsfeld asked Abizaid if he had enough troops. Abizaid, who is not afraid to push back at the secretary, said he did. On that point, history will judge.

RUMSFELD GETS HIS MAN

The phone on Rumsfeld's desk rang at 2:45 p.m. on December 13, 2003, just as he was concluding a Saturday staff meeting. The caller was General Abizaid from Qatar in the Persian Gulf. The two talked daily on a secure hotline through which either man could reach the other in seconds. Abizaid said he had good news, something

Rumsfeld needed. For months, the Washington press corps had blamed the defense secretary for poor post-Saddam planning in Iraq, saying that the United States was now trapped in a postwar quagmire it had not foreseen. *Time* magazine suggested he was "losing his mojo." A smattering of liberal Democrats called on him to step down.   General Abizaid had news that would put Rumsfeld's critics on the defensive. He told the defense secretary that a joint force of 4th Infantry Division soldiers and commandos had gone to a farm and apprehended three men. "We think one of them was Saddam Hussein," the general said of the number one target in the war, and added a few details of the capture and identification process, some of which would soon become public along with the photos of the captured dictator.

Rumsfeld immediately telephoned the president at Camp David. He relayed what Abizaid had said, but expressed caution. General Abizaid had told Rumsfeld, during the march to Baghdad, that the allies had killed Ali Hassan al-Majid, the notorious "Chemical Ali." Rumsfeld had announced this information to the press only to find out later that the information was wrong, that Majid had not in fact been at the site pinpointed by American bombers. Rumsfeld did not want to repeat that mistake.

Rumsfeld gave the president what details he knew of the capture. Saddam was dirty and living in a hole. "They feel they may have him," he told Bush. The president and defense secretary decided there would be no announcement from Washington. That privilege would go to America's top two leaders in Baghdad, L. Paul Bremer and Lieutenant General Ricardo Sanchez, when they believed they had a positive identification of the captured man being Saddam Hussein.

Rumsfeld canceled a planned squash game with his Pentagon associate Larry Di Rita and worked the phones. He talked to Director of Central Intelligence George Tenet, then took more calls from

Abizaid. Abizaid listed the evidence in a fax to Rumsfeld: eyewitness confirmation, a scar on his leg resulting from a bullet wound, a tattoo on his hand, and $750,000 in cash. Rumsfeld still expressed doubts. He told aides Saddam had dispersed body doubles who had undergone plastic surgery to look like the dictator. Uncertain about whether he had finally captured the Butcher of Baghdad, Rumsfeld left the Pentagon to attend General Richard Myers's Christmas party before going home to host his own annual celebration.

Early the next morning, Rumsfeld came to believe the manhunt was indeed over. It was the money. Why would a double be carrying so much cash? Also, by then, close associates like Tariq Aziz had looked the captive in the eye and said, "That's him."

By 5:30 a.m. Sunday, Washington time, Bremer and Sanchez believed they had enough evidence to make the announcement. Members of the Iraqi interim government were already leaking word to everyone, including the Iranians. Rumsfeld and his aides began calling senior congressional leaders to give them a heads-up. "Ladies and gentlemen, we got him," Bremer told a press conference in words sure to make good headlines. Saddam had surrendered meekly, rising from his cramped eight-foot-deep hold to announce, "I am the president of Iraq. I want to negotiate." Said the welcoming soldier, with typical American bravado, "President Bush sends his regards." Whisked to a holding cell, Saddam denied that he harbored weapons of mass destruction or knew the whereabouts of Captain Scott Speicher.

The next day, the secretary telephoned the seventy-six-year-old Republican senator John Warner of Virginia. Rumsfeld had talked to Warner at a Christmas party and had said nothing about the possibility of Saddam Hussein being captured. His relationship with Warner was already strained, and he did not want the senator to take offense because he had not confided in him at the Christmas party. Warner said he understood.

That taken care of, Rumsfeld glowed with satisfaction that the 4th Infantry Division and the CIA had done the kind of gumshoe detective work it took to obtain the elusive "actionable intelligence" he coveted. One CIA analyst said they had peeled the onion of Saddam family and tribal members. Near the core was a Ba'athist operative captured that Saturday in Baghdad. That man knew Saddam's location.

On Tuesday, December 16, Rumsfeld appeared in the press room, clearly in good spirits. He said the snatch of Saddam reminded him, "How important it is to take scraps of seemingly disparate information from widely different locations, piece them together, work them in a timely way, and then be poised, cocked, and ready to move in a matter of minutes or hours, not days or weeks, because time-sensitive targets don't wait."

The victory was sweet for Rumsfeld. He had seen bin Laden escape from Tora Bora into Pakistan. Taliban leader Mullah Omar had driven off from Kandahar in a Chevy Suburban. But now Rumsfeld had Saddam, and the added promise that the eight-month-long insurgency might begin to run out of gas.

And people in the administration who believed that winning the global war on terror depended on a politically healthy Rumsfeld saw an ebullient secretary walk into the press room to talk of finding Saddam Hussein in a dirty hole in the ground.

[CHAPTER 3]

RUMSFELD THE MAN

I F HISTORY HAS YET TO JUDGE RUMSFELD'S POST-SADDAM STRATEGY FOR IRAQ, it will certainly judge his seventy-one years on earth as an extraordinary life. He was born July 9, 1932, in Chicago's old St. Luke's hospital, the son of George Donald Rumsfeld, a real estate salesman, and Jeanette, a substitute teacher and stay-at-home mom. Rumsfeld spent his early childhood on Chicago's North Side before the family moved to the North Shore village of Winnetka.

"For a youngster, Chicago was enormous," he recalled to the *Chicago Tribune* in 1991. "You're so small, and it's so large. And the people, the vitality of the city, always struck me. The bustle and the movement, the smells, the sounds, the sights."

A rail line runs through Winnetka, taking people north to Milwaukee or south the twenty-three miles to Chicago. The trip dissects North Shore communities along Lake Michigan. Great Lakes is one, with its huge U.S. Navy facilities for training recruits, hospital corpsmen, and other sailor-technicians. Farther south, the train finds some of Chicago's affluent suburbs, like Lake Forest, Wilmette, and Winnetka. This is the environment where Rumsfeld soaked up old-fashioned values like hard work and vigorous play. His dad taught him business sense. His mother doted on him and his sister, Joan. His father also exposed him to military life, enlisting in the Navy when Don was eight. His assignments took the family across the country, from North Carolina to San Diego. His father was past draft age. "In fact, they didn't even want him, he was too thin," Rumsfeld told me. "They made him gain weight before they would accept him and we had to have a few more losses before they lowered the standards and took him in, but he finally got in. It was a big part of his life and a big part of my life."

Ned Jannotta, a Winnetka friend and high school classmate of Rumsfeld, said George was so honest he would point out flaws in a house to prospective buyers. "I think his father was a great role model in terms of ethics and treating people fairly," Jannotta recalled.

"He was a voracious reader and certainly that was an important learning experience for me to see," Rumsfeld said of his dad. "He was very energetic. He loved life. I remember him whistling all the time and he was upbeat. . . . He started working at a real estate firm when he was, I think, twelve or thirteen, as an office boy. Part time. But when I was a young kid and I would caddy at golf, he never had time to play golf because he worked day and night, seven days a week, but he would go out and play golf, nine holes at dusk, in about thirty-five minutes. He never took a warm-up stroke. He would just get on that course and hit the ball and go, and hit the ball and go. It was so much fun to be with him."

Rumsfeld has an ever-evolving list, called "Rumsfeld's Rules," of bon mots and proverbs—some his, some overheard or read. One entry quotes his father. "'If it doesn't go easy, force it.' —G.D. Rumsfeld's assessment of his son, Don's, operating principle at age ten."

Rumsfeld says his mom, a schoolteacher, stressed English. "She also was a reader and also had a lot of energy," he said, completing the gene pool that allows him to work double-digit hours every day. "Just a dear,

dear lady who wanted me to be a lawyer. I guess when she was growing up, being a lawyer was kind of something that one might aspire to."

After the war, young Don wrestled on the New Trier High School
team, became an Eagle Scout and class officer, and earned good
enough grades to gain academic and ROTC scholarships to Princeton. "In high school he was very concerned about keeping fit," his
mother told the *Chicago Tribune* some thirty years later. "He never
stopped thinking about it, and I think that's why he didn't smoke or
drink. He gave up Cokes and candy. He even gave up peanut butter
that he loved."

The friendships Don made at Winnetka's New Trier High School
lasted a lifetime. Ned Jannotta went on to Rumsfeld's first congressional campaign in 1962. Hall "Cap" Adams and John E. Robson,
both classmates, also volunteered in the campaign.

Jannotta went to Princeton while Rumsfeld finished his senior
year at New Trier. He and other alumni returned to Winnetka on
Christmas break and convinced the senior to join them in New Jer-
sey the next fall.

Today, co-ed Princeton upholds a twenty-five-year tradition.
Undergraduates doff their clothes and run naked through campus
with the winter's first snowstorm. The student newspaper publishes
pictures of the "Nude Olympics." Princeton's administrators have
tried to ban the run for years, but failed. But in 1950, the Ivy League
acreage was a languid, scenic, all-male bastion. No cars. No girls. "We
were children of the Eisenhower era," said classmate James M. Denny.
"A very different breed of cat." The counterculture lay at least a decade
away. There were no protests or illegal drug use. There was a tamer
version of the fraternity system, called "eating clubs," for juniors and
seniors. Sophomores jockeyed for membership in one of seventeen
clubs, while existing members recruited particularly smart or athletic
students. Rumsfeld was both and ended up in "Cap and Gown."

Rumsfeld majored in politics, wrestled, and captained the 160-pound football team, on which he played tackle. "In those days, it was all men," Jannotta says. "There were no love interests. No women close by and none of us had enough money to bring a girl down for the weekend. We didn't have much of a love life. I'd say zero. It was a pretty monastic environment."

Rumsfeld graduated in 1954. At age twenty-two, he fulfilled his scholarship requirement by going on active duty with the Navy. He followed Jannotta to flight school in Pensacola, Florida, earning his wings and then instructing new students in the T-34. Jannotta went to sea on the carrier *Intrepid*. He flew a land-attack plane whose mission was to drop atomic bombs at low levels. Rumsfeld's athletic prowess brought him the all-Navy wrestling championship. "For whatever reason, that sport worked for me," Rumsfeld told the author. "I wasn't very tall for basketball. I was quite small. . . . I played football and I did okay. But wrestling worked. I enjoyed it. I liked the competition and the discipline of it."

While at flight school in Pensacola, Ensign Rumsfeld took time out to marry his high school sweetheart, Joyce Pierson (both graduated in the New Trier class of 1950). A New Trier faculty member had matched them up for the junior prom. Rumsfeld told me, "I think the first time I had taken her out, the dean almost made me. She'd broken up with the football player she was dating and the dean—she was a class officer, I was a class officer—the dean said don't get a date because Joyce may need a date." Asked what it was about Joyce, the defense secretary said, "She's just a delightful person. . . . And of course luck. I mean, what do you know when you're seventeen, eighteen, nineteen, twenty. You get married when you're twenty-one, twenty-two maybe. It's good fortune that something like that works so well."

Their devotion survived Rumsfeld's attending Princeton and Joyce the University of Colorado. "It was long-distance maintenance," Jannotta said. "It wasn't easy, I'm sure." They exchanged vows in December 1954 in a Methodist church in Wilmette, Joyce's hometown. (The couple today belongs to the Fourth Presbyterian Church in Chicago.)

When he left active duty in 1957, Rumsfeld decided to see the political scene up close. (He remained a drilling Navy reservist for the next twenty years.) He and Joyce moved to Washington. He worked for two congressmen before returning to the North Shore in 1960 to do what many Capitol Hill aides eventually do: He plotted a political future. In the meantime, he earned his first substantial paycheck selling stocks at the investment banking firm of A.G. Becker.

In 1962, when his district's House member, Republican Marguerite Stitt Church, announced her retirement, Rumsfeld decided to run. He walked across the street to Jannotta's office and said, "I might go for this thing." The New Trier mafia, Ned Jannotta, Brad Glass, Hall "Cap" Adams, and others, rallied behind him even though they thought the whole idea was a 100–1 shot. George Rumsfeld had doubts too. "'There isn't a chance,'" Rumsfeld quoted his dad as telling him. "But the minute I decided to go, he went out and got petitions signed."

Rumsfeld had been a campaign manager on a congressional race in Ohio, but his friends knew little of politics. Nonetheless, Jannotta ran the campaign and Glass served as treasurer. New Trier friend John E. Robson joined the committee. Dan Searle, a wealthy pharmaceutical executive and active Republican, signed on as finance chairman. "Cap" Adams, who was making it big in the advertising business, volunteered to produce pamphlets and signs. And in the den of the Rumsfelds' modest home just outside Winnetka, maps of the thirteenth district replaced aerial maps from Rumsfeld's Navy flying days.

The North Shore's thirteenth district was then solidly Republican. Only the Jewish neighborhoods of Chicago's North Side, the Fiftieth Ward, voted Democratic. "We worked that ward," Dan Searle recalled. "We didn't win that ward but we worked it."

Rumsfeld was twenty-nine but looked like a teenager. "He had a brush cut," Jannotta said. "It was question of whether he looked old enough to vote." The shoestring campaign had the neophyte politician attending service organization meetings and women's coffees. At first, the candidate exhibited an unpolished speaking style. His friends rented a hall in North Brook, near Winnetka, and had him give a speech to about twenty voters. "He took criticism from his contemporaries," Jannotta said. "'Put your chin up. Get your hands out of your pockets. Smile.' We were sort of merciless."

Rumsfeld soon improved. "Don was a great campaigner," Searle remembered. "He talked to groups of a dozen at a coffee and he was good at addressing larger groups, and he didn't try and play games. He did not go to Skokie and preach one sort of line and then go to another city and preach something else." Rumsfeld beat fellow Republican Marion E. Burks in the primary and then easily won the general election against Democrat John Kennedy—a Winnetka businessman, not the president.

Searle recalls that the campaign cost a grand total of $50,000. "We never accepted a contribution beyond one hundred dollars," he said. That sort of thrift carried over to Rumsfeld's work in Congress. "Don was a great fiscal conservative. He wanted to get a bang for every buck the government spent. I never knew him to support any kind of a pork-barrel project. On the other hand, Don realized there were some citizens who were less fortunate than others and government had some obligation to help those citizens."

Among Rumsfeld's earlier supporters was future president Gerald R. Ford, who told me, "Early in my years in Congress I heard about a young candidate campaigning out in the Evanston area who was a good prospect. I went out to campaign for Don Rumsfeld when he first ran for the House." Ford and Rumsfeld soon got to know each other much better.

REPUBLICAN REBEL

Rumsfeld, barely thirty years old, began forming alliances and secretly whispering of leadership coups even before being sworn in. The Washington landscape had not changed much since Franklin Roosevelt created the Democratic majority. The House resided firmly in Democratic hands, while aging, dull leaders ran the minority Republican side. Congressman-elect Rumsfeld believed the GOP had been in the minority too long. It wasn't good for the two-party system, he told friends. Rumsfeld quickly befriended other young GOP turks, like Melvin Laird of Wisconsin, Charles Goodell of New York, and Robert Griffin of Michigan. "The minute I was elected, Bob Griffin grabbed me and said, 'Look, we're running Gerald Ford for conference chairman.... And we need you to round up the votes from the freshmen who have just got elected," Rumsfeld recalled.

Ford set out to defeat Iowan Charles Hoevan, the tame chairman of the House Republican Conference. Rumsfeld told Ford biographer James Cannon that the Republican rebels chose Ford because "he was a workman and very well liked. The goal was to become the majority party in the House and the question was: 'Is it possible to use the Republican Conference in a more creative way?'"

President Ford told me, "Don Rumsfeld was one of those who convinced me we had to change the leadership—and I accepted."

Six weeks later, the Rumsfeld-led rebels succeeded in electing Ford as the House Republican Conference chairman.

In 1964, Rumsfeld easily won his second of what would be four straight election victories. But the Lyndon Johnson-Hubert Humphrey ticket swept in a larger Democratic majority in the House. The turks assembled again. This time they urged Ford to take on Minority Leader Charles Halleck. Ford agreed, and the turks delivered, electing him House minority leader.

One of those lobbied by Rumsfeld was Howard "Bo" Callaway, a freshman-elect Republican from Georgia. "He was energetic, persuasive. He was by no means threatening," Callaway recalls. "Rumsfeld persuaded me we needed younger leadership, more aggressive leadership. . . . A lot of Republicans were pretty well convinced they would never in their lifetime be in the majority and they were working with the Democrats because they needed some things for their district. If you worked with the Democrats, they'd drop a few crumbs for you. A lot of people would say 'get along, go along.' I was not a 'get along, go along' person." Callaway, a West Point graduate who fought in Korea, later served as Army secretary under Nixon, ran President Ford's election committee in 1976, and helped build the Republican Party in Georgia.

While a fiscal conservative, Rumsfeld advocated bigger defense budgets and supported ending the draft and shifting to an all-volunteer military. He voted for both the Voting Rights Act and the landmark 1964 Civil Rights Act. He also voted in favor of the Gulf of Tonkin Resolution, giving Lyndon Johnson a blank check on Vietnam. Rumsfeld later said that was the vote he regretted most.

In 1969, Rumsfeld surprised colleagues by resigning from the House and joining the Nixon administration. His new job, running the Office of Economic Opportunity (OEO), seemed an odd fit. Robert Hartmann, then a Ford aide in Congress, recalled that conservatives thought Rumsfeld would work to abolish OEO, which had been established as part of Lyndon Johnson's "war on poverty." Nixon's domestic agenda, however, was only slightly less liberal than Johnson's. Rumsfeld not only kept OEO afloat, he seemed to thrive there, and made new friends across the political spectrum, a trait that marked his entire government and corporate career. But his most important new friendship was with a young Republican named Dick Cheney.

The two like-minded workaholics did not immediately hit it off. Cheney had applied for a job in Congressman Rumsfeld's office. "The true story of that first meeting is that I flunked my first interview," Cheney says today. "He thought I was some kind of airhead academic and I thought he was rather an arrogant young member of Congress. Probably we were both right." Cheney went to work for another lawmaker. When Nixon nominated Rumsfeld as head of OEO, Cheney, unsolicited, sat down and wrote a twelve-page memo to the nominee recommending how he should handle questions at the Senate confirmation hearing. After the hearing, Cheney was invited to talk to the OEO transition team about a job, and was then summoned to Rumsfeld's office. "He was in there all by himself, second day on the job. And he said, 'You, you're congressional relations. Now get out of here.' Now, mind you, he didn't say, 'Sit down. Have a cup of coffee. Would you like to come work for me?'... But that was, of course, just before he developed his suave, smooth, warm, fuzzy personality that we've all grown to love over the years."

Despite the rough start, the two eventually became fast friends and launched eerily similar careers. Both married their high school sweethearts, worked as congressional aides, held seats in the House of Representatives, served as presidential chiefs of staff, held the post of defense secretary, and ran major companies. Cheney, however, achieved something Rumsfeld coveted but never attained—the vice presidency. The vice president today readily acknowledges Rumsfeld's role in his life. His hiring at OEO "was a tremendously important event for me," he says. "The fact of the matter is, I like to joke about it. And Don Rumsfeld was probably the toughest boss I ever had. I worked for him two different periods of time, a total of about five years, and it had a huge impact on my life, literally changed my whole career. And much of what I've been able to do in the years since 1968—when I was kicked out of his office when I flunked that first interview—is directly due to the fact that he was willing to take a chance on me and give me some tremendous opportunity over the years. And I will always be grateful for his willingness to take a chance on an unknown quantity."

Rumsfeld hired brash left-wing lawyer Terry Lenzner—who later served as counsel on the Senate Watergate committee—in much the same way. Lenzner was working for the U.S. attorney's office in New York when another future Watergate prosecutor, John Dorr, called him and told him to get a foothold in Washington by applying for a job at OEO. Lenzner today runs a successful international detective agency. But in 1969, he had little job experience. Still, Rumsfeld liked Lenzner, partly because he had played varsity football at Harvard.

Lenzner was with Rumsfeld when anti-war protesters ran past OEO's downtown office at 19th and M Streets. "I remember standing on the roof with Don watching them run through the streets with helmets on and banners. There was a sense the country was about to lose control. But I think Don felt a confidence. There was no problem that can't be solved one way or another."

One day a demonstration hit even closer to home. During an OEO legal services conference, a band of Howard University law students burst into the room and refused to go until Lenzner agreed to give them a grant. Lenzner took the forty students down to his office to continue the debate. Once there, the students blocked Lenzner's exit, making him a prisoner in his own office. "I decided we needed to evict them," Lenzner recalls. "I tried to make my way out a couple of times and they shoved me back. A half hour later, there was a commotion at the door and in came Don. And he grabbed me by the arm and he said, 'We're getting you out of here.' I'm not sure they knew who he was but he started dragging me out the door and then they let him out.... I characterize it as extremely gutsy and putting himself at risk for one of his people. He showed a lot of courage and fortitude."

Complaints mounted against OEO as federal agencies and departments and state governors had to deal with a rising number of OEO-instigated lawsuits. Nixon's aides pushed Rumsfeld to fire Lenzner for not curtailing them. "Don said, 'This isn't really going to work. I'd like you to resign and if you don't resign, I'm going to terminate you.' I said 'Go ahead and terminate me.'"

Another friend was Ricky Silberman, whose husband, Laurence, was undersecretary of labor and would eventually become ambassador to Yugoslavia and a judge on the U.S. Court of Appeals for the Washington, D.C., circuit. "We had no money in those days," she says. "Joyce always was able to do fun things. Do things with class. Be cheerful. They would have a Sunday afternoon party in their tiny— and I do mean tiny—house in Georgetown, and the party consisted of beer and popcorn and everybody gathered in the backyard and had a wonderful time. No one but Joyce would have the creativity and nerve to entertain that way. She was entertaining people who were the highest levels of government."

The two influential couples continued their friendship over the next thirty years. "When one has dinner with the Rumsfelds, it's early. There is no lingering," said Ricky Silberman, who helped found the Independent Women's Forum and before that served as a chair of the Equal Employment Opportunity Commission for more than a decade. "Don is a person that goes to bed early. He gets up

early. He is the original Type A personality. The thing that is wonderful about Joyce is she has perfectly accommodated to his lifestyle
and wishes, while at the same time having a most interesting and
wonderful life of her own." Silberman says the Rumsfelds are "teetotalers or near teetotalers."

Rumsfeld left OEO in December 1970 to take another big-
government job: director of the Cost of Living Council. His job was
to oversee the board that imposed Nixon's ill-conceived program to
set wages and prices to control runaway inflation. "It was madness,
every day," recalls Judge Silberman, who as undersecretary of labor
frequently attended council meetings. Rumsfeld tells the story that
when Labor Secretary George Shultz offered him the job, he
answered, "But I don't agree with that stuff." Replied Shultz, "That's
why we're appointing you." The job came with the seemingly added
bonus of being a counselor to President Nixon. At age thirty-eight,
he shared power with H.R. Haldeman, John Ehrlichman, and John
Dean. Silberman remembers Rumsfeld firmly rejecting any price or
wage decision done to help Nixon politically. "I remember Don dis-
tinctly saying, 'I'm the only one who was an elected official at this
table and I don't think we should take politics into account,'" he says.

Nixon's landslide reelection in 1972 gave Republicans hopes of a
redrawn national political map. Only something cataclysmic—like
Watergate—could derail an emerging Republican majority. Luckily
for Rumsfeld, he chose 1973 to escape Washington and get some foreign policy experience as U.S. ambassador to NATO.

During Rumsfeld's ambassadorship, Ned Jannotta, his wife, and
their four children joined the Rumsfelds and their three children for
a European vacation. It was July, and the bulls were running in Pamplona when the two families arrived. The bulls run early in the
morning, announced by cannon fire. The main street is closed off,
so the only escape is to duck inside a building or cling tightly to a

wall. Rumsfeld was standing in the street when the shot was fired. From a second-floor balcony, Ned Jannotta looked down and spotted Rumsfeld against the far wall as the stampede rumbled closer. Rumsfeld reached for the hand of a man up above, then climbed up a drainpipe and clung to a "No Parking" sign as the bulls rushed by. "He's down in the crowd, mixing it up," Jannotta recalls. "What a sight. The ambassador to NATO holding onto a 'No Parking' sign. I wish I had a camera."

Rumsfeld told me the story, complete with a brush with death. "I went down in the street and I said, 'Heck, I can run with the bulls.' I ran for a ways, not very far, and they were catching up, and there were a whole lot of people thundering around me and behind me and I thought, 'This is kind of crazy.' I looked up and on the side of the wall coming out of two metal bars was one of these round one-way signs or no parking signs that they use in Europe. I jumped up and grabbed the lower bar and started pulling myself up and some Spaniard grabbed my legs and started trying to climb up on me. All of a sudden you look and an enormous bull fell. His back legs went out from under him. He's still on his front legs, and skidded up the cobblestone street right opposite where we were hanging. And he looked at us and he looked at the other side. There were a lot of people on the other side. And he got up and dashed right into all the people on the other side. They dragged people into the hospital."

With Nixon's resignation on August 9, 1974, Rumsfeld's life took its sharpest turn since the 1962 North Shore election. Vacationing with Joyce along the French Riviera, he read in the *International Herald Tribune* that Nixon might quit. He telephoned his NATO office, Ford aide James Cannon recounts, and discovered the vice president wanted him home—now. At Dulles airport, it was Dick Cheney who provided the wheels and a note from Ford asking Rumsfeld to head the transition team that would see power transfer from Nixon to Ford.

WATCH YOUR BACK

To call the Ford White House dysfunctional would be an under-
statement, not fully conveying the mistakes, backbiting, and betrayal
that characterized Ford's twenty-nine-month presidency. One scene
told it all. In January 1975, hours before the president was to give his
first State of the Union address, Rumsfeld (who was now chief of
staff), Cheney (deputy assistant to the president), NBC newsman-
turned-press secretary Ron Nessen, and Alan Greenspan (chairman
of the President's Council of Economic Advisers), were in Rumsfeld's
office trying to patch together the speech. Ford speechwriter Robert
Hartmann told me, "I was the only man who could write a speech
the way Gerald Ford talked." It was Hartmann who coined the
memorial line for the incoming president: "Our long national night-
mare is over." But on this day, few liked his draft speech, which
included an announcement of Ford's hastily put together economic
plan, "Whip Inflation Now" or WIN. Hartmann's dislike for Rumsfeld
grew so deep that he refused to attend the chief of staff's morning
meetings. Thus, he knew little of the president's new tax plan.
Nessen, in his gossipy memoir, *It Sure Looks Different from the Inside*,
described the speechwriting debacle:

> For the next eight hours, Rumsfeld, Cheney, Greenspan ...
> and I sat around the conference table in Rumsfeld's office,
> feverishly writing, rewriting, scissoring, pasting, editing and
> boiling down a State of the Union speech to rival Hartmann's
> effort. We munched cookies, peanuts and steak sandwiches,
> washed down with beer, as we worked, racing to complete our
> draft by 9 p.m.... The meeting degenerated into haggling over
> individual words. It dragged on until 3:30 in the morning. "I
> must say to you that the state of the union is not good," was
> one of Ford's lines.... Obviously, the long bitter struggles

required to produce a fireside chat [delivered days before] and a State of the Union address were not the way to write presidential speeches. It was a wasteful and divisive process.

The dysfunction was rooted in a confluence of warring factions that set up camp right outside the Oval Office. There were the Nixon holdovers, who still wanted to run the place, and the Ford aides, who wanted to uproot the Nixonites. And there was Nelson Rockefeller, who replaced Ford as vice president, and whose loyal, smart staff jockeyed for ways to empower their boss.

Ford saw Rumsfeld as a mediator. Before his appointment as chief of staff, "You could go to the door of the Oval Office and peek in," Nessen recalled in an interview. "And if [President Ford] wasn't busy you could go in to talk to him. Everyone had direct access to him. This was really an impossible way to run the White House." Rumsfeld, who became chief of staff in September 1974, tried to restore some sense of order to the chaotic White House.

In his new $42,500-a-year job, Rumsfeld set out to elevate Ford's stature and diminish those around him, especially Rockefeller and Henry Kissinger. Kissinger held not one, but two critically important posts: national security adviser and secretary of state. The national security adviser was supposed to be an honest broker who made sure the president heard all sides when devising policy. Serving in both jobs was a blatant conflict of interest that elevated the State Department. Rumsfeld opposed Kissinger's arms control efforts, disliked his close relationship to the press, and tried to permanently maneuver Kissinger out of the White House. In his no-holds-barred account, *Palace Politics*, Robert Hartmann said Rumsfeld disparaged both Rockefeller and Kissinger in leaks to the press via Nessen.

Aides noticed Rumsfeld did not follow the tradition of a chief of staff: working in the background, unseen. Rumsfeld liked the press spotlight, a signal to aides that his ambitions reached beyond a staff job. He tried to control the flow of information to the press. In July 1975, Rumsfeld became angered at Nessen for issuing news releases unilaterally. "It strikes me that we ought to establish a new rule that unless Rumsfeld, Cheney, Jones or Connor authorize the press office to actually, physically pre-release something, that it will not be done," Rumsfeld wrote to Nessen. [Jerry Jones and Jim Connor were senior aides.] "We ought to avoid instances where the president's flexibility is denied him as a result of the fact that somebody, through inadvertence, or misunderstanding or confusion, or direct order by one of the substantive offices, releases something to the press that ought not to be released. . . . If the press offices know that, then, conceivably we can avoid some problems." Three weeks later, Rumsfeld found it necessary to write Nessen a second memo on the subject. "From now on, we will have a policy whereby the press office will release nothing until it has been signed off on by Rumsfeld, Cheney, Jerry Jones, or Connor." After one of the two assassination attempts against Ford, Rumsfeld told Nessen he would brief the press.

Nessen recalls that in the summer of 1975, Rumsfeld was pushing Ford to launch a Cabinet shakeup. The chief of staff had advised the president to go to Camp David and think of big ideas to convey in the upcoming State of the Union address. Ford responded with a laundry list of legislative proposals. Normally an optimist, Rumsfeld fell into a funk. "At the end of three months, the Ford administration will either have the smell of life or the smell of death," Nessen quoted Rumsfeld as saying. "If it's the smell of death, this White House is going to be torn to pieces by the press, by the Democrats, even by other Republicans who will challenge the president for the nomination in 1976."

By October 1975, Ford decided on a wholesale housing cleaning— the infamous "Halloween Massacre." As he prepared to give the press the casualty list, Rumsfeld advised the president, "In your press conference tonight, Mr. President, try to act 'presidential,'" Hartmann quoted Rumsfeld as saying. "Don't go into long explanations of why you did this or that. Whenever you can, answer the question 'yes' or 'no.' Be decisive, in command. Be crisp and concise. Don't let them nickel and dime you to death." Hartmann said he advised the president to ignore Rumsfeld's media advice and "be yourself."

In the administration shakeup Rumsfeld replaced James Schlesinger, whose arrogance and professorial style grated on Ford, as secretary of defense. Director of Central Intelligence William Colby, who had thrown open CIA files to Democratic congressional investigations, shocking Ford and Rumsfeld, was fired and replaced by Ford's friend from congressional days, George H. W. Bush. Henry Kissinger lost his position as national security adviser to his aide, Brent Scowcroft. In another blow to Kissinger, the man he admired most in public life, Nelson Rockefeller, would be dropped from the ticket and eventually replaced by Senator Bob Dole of Kansas. Rumsfeld had won. He got promoted; Kissinger and Rockefeller were demoted.

In his 1999 memoir of the Ford era, *Years of Renewal*, Kissinger thoughtfully analyzed his competitive relationship with Rumsfeld: "With the passage of time, I grew more mellow about Rumsfeld's brilliant single-mindedness, especially after I left government and was no longer in his line of fire. He was tough, capable, personally attractive and knowledgeable. I came to believe that if he ever reached the presidency, he might be a more comfortable chief executive than Cabinet colleague—indeed he had the makings of a strong president."

Whether Rumsfeld instigated the Halloween Massacre is subject to debate. There is no "smoking gun" that he did. In fact, the evidence suggests that by the time Ford decided to shake things up, Rumsfeld thought it was too late. He advised against firing Schlesinger and stayed out of the debate on Rockefeller, since he was a possible successor to the vice president. Ford denied publicly that Rumsfeld urged him to dump Rockefeller. But Rockefeller did not believe him. A few years later, Rockefeller granted an interview to Hartmann, who used it to reconstruct a Ford-Rockefeller meeting. "I'm now going to say it frankly: Rumsfeld wants to be president of the United States," Rockefeller allegedly told the president. "He has given George Bush the deep six by putting him in the CIA. He has taken me out through this guy Bo Callaway. He was third on your list and now he has gotten rid of two of us."

As Ford's election chairman, Callaway had waged a public campaign to get rid of Rockefeller, because the party's conservative voters distrusted him. Callaway had sent a memo to the White House saying Rockefeller would be a huge problem. He called his committee the "Ford Election Committee," not "Ford-Rockefeller." Callaway told me he launched the anti-Rockefeller campaign based on his own political instincts and got no urging from Rumsfeld. "I think Rockefeller believed that he did, but he did not," Callaway says.

SOVIET THREAT

As defense secretary designate, Rumsfeld faced a relatively easy, two-day confirmation hearing before some of the Senate's most legendary members. As he sat at the witness table, he looked up at Senate Armed Services chairman John Stennis, Barry Goldwater, Robert Taft, Jr., John Tower, Strom Thurmond, Gary Hart, Sam Nunn, Harry F. Byrd, and Henry "Scoop" Jackson. Advised by hardliner Richard Perle, the Cold War Democrat Jackson emerged as the Senate's fieriest critic of Kissinger and détente. He also distrusted Rumsfeld, publicly criticizing his nomination to secretary of defense as nothing more than positioning Rumsfeld to succeed Rockefeller on the presidential ticket. "For the first time," Jackson said, "a president wants us to have our key national security institutions run by men whose paramount concerns are their own political futures—and his. . . . Let us be honest about it. Don Rumsfeld and George Bush cannot hold a candle to James Schlesinger and Bill Colby in terms of judgment, knowledge or intellectual ability."

Rumsfeld made courtesy calls on committee members. A White House memo shows that the administration viewed "Scoop" Jackson as the only potential opponent of Rumsfeld's nomination. Senator Sam Nunn was described as "pro-Schlesinger, but not anti-Rumsfeld. Is OK." Strom Thurmond: "Met in the presence of most of his senior staff and discussed South Carolina's role in the Revolutionary War." William Scott of Virginia: "Like some of the others, worried about DR's ability to stand up to HAK [Kissinger] on détente."

At the hearing itself, Rumsfeld assured Jackson he had not accepted the president's offer to serve as secretary of defense as a way to become vice president—but he refused to rule out accepting such an offer. "The long and the short of it is that I know Jim Schlesinger, I have admired him, I think he was a good secretary of defense, and I did not have anything to do with his departure," Rumsfeld testified. "Indeed, when asked by the president my views on what he was thinking, I gave him a view that was different from that which actually occurred." The committee voted to confirm his nomination, 16–0.

One of the first orders the new secretary gave after his November 20, 1975, swearing in was to turn up the lights inside the Pentagon. An ongoing energy crisis prompted the previous regime to dim the lights throughout the 17.5 miles of corridors, giving a downcast look to an institution already depressed by the Vietnam War. But Rumsfeld's real struggle involved the arms race. He enlisted Arthur Laffer as an ally, who in the Reagan years would be known as "Mr. Supply Side." The economist had left government to teach, but kept one foot in Washington through his frequent consulting work and had an office at the Pentagon not far from Rumsfeld's. The two became friends when Rumsfeld worked at the White House, having dinner together to talk economics and politics. "He was a normal human then," the economist said. "He wasn't this godlike figure that he is now. He was gracious enough to have conversations with me."

One dinner became somewhat historic. Rumsfeld, Cheney, and the economist dined at the Washington Hotel. President Ford had proposed a series of surcharges, or taxes, as part of "Whip Inflation Now." Laffer drew for the two his famous "Laffer Curve" showing how high taxes actually reduce revenues, rather than increase them. "If you tax people who work and you pay people who don't work, don't be surprised if you have a lot of people who don't work," was Laffer's message. Regardless, Ford stuck with WIN. There came a time when Laffer began advising a candidate more to his liking—the upstart Ronald Reagan, who loved tax-cutting. "I'm a Reagan guy, not a Ford guy," he says today. He met with Rumsfeld and Cheney, who by now was Ford's chief of staff, and told them he had to quit advising them. "Don looked at me and said, 'Your ignorance on politics does not detract from your competence on economics. We would still like to have you as our adviser.'"

At the Pentagon in 1976, Laffer applied his vast knowledge of economic trends to help provide the underpinnings for Rumsfeld's arguments on the Soviets. The CIA had arrived at a figure for Moscow's yearly defense budget by counting troops and equipment captured on satellite imagery. Laffer looked at the entire communist state's centralized economy and worked backwards, subtracting what he considered would be spending for various domestic programs and drawing an inference on what was left for the military. "Mine was less accurate but less biased," Laffer says. He concluded that the United States had been underestimating Soviet defense expenditures for years.

He had a loyal disciple in Rumsfeld. At a time when Watergate, a poor economy, and an energized liberal wing in Congress tormented President Ford and kept him focused on the political dangers of an election year, Rumsfeld focused laser-like on the Soviet threat. He was, in a sense, Reagan before Reagan came to Washington. If Rumsfeld had had his way, and more time, he would have worked for the kind of massive defense modernization Reagan commenced in the 1980s to defeat the Soviet Union. In one of his last press conferences before the 1976 election, with Jimmy Carter ahead of Ford in the polls, Rumsfeld stayed on message. "The Soviet Union today is clearly militarily stronger and busier than in any other period of its history. They devote more resources to defense than any nation in the world," he said.

Rumsfeld fought Kissinger relentlessly inside the administration, opposing the SALT II treaty and arguing that the administration should be vocal on pointing out the Soviet threat. The following exchange took place at a March 1976 NSC meeting.

> Kissinger: If we say the trend is going against us, that is bad enough. The impression that we are slipping is creating a bad impression around the world.
>
> Rumsfeld: But it's true.
>
> Kissinger: Then we have to define our goals. It is inevitable that our margin since '60 has slipped. Are we trying to maintain the same margin as we had in 1960 or to maintain adequate forces?
>
> Rumsfeld: But it is true. We have been slipping since the '60s from superiority to equivalence, and if we don't stop, we'll be behind.
>
> Ford: I don't think the president should say we are slipping.
>
> Kissinger: I think the posture to take is that Reagan doesn't know what [he is] talking about and he's irresponsible.

Rumsfeld's key achievement as secretary of defense was convincing a liberal-dominated Congress to approve an increase in defense spending. His strategy revolved around inviting groups of congressmen to the White House. Ford would put in a quick pitch for defense spending, then turn the presentation over to Rumsfeld, who tried to build a pro-defense majority of Republicans and Southern Democrats. In the end, the fiscal 1977 defense budget totaled $107.5 billion. A Pentagon history of the era says the number reflected a $5 billion increase from the 1976 plan. "It's one of the most brilliant examples of serious hard work and applied intellect on public policy that I've ever seen," Newt Gingrich told me of Rumsfeld's achievement.

Today, the bitterness of the Ford years has surrendered to sweet memories. The Fordites get together every year at the Capitol Hill Club near the House office buildings to talk over old times. At the 2001 gathering, Vice President Cheney introduced Rumsfeld, joking that he now outranked his mentor. It was too true. Rumsfeld had wanted the vice presidency in 1976, and again in 1980. Now, the man he had nurtured thirty years ago as a young Hill aide held the prize.

Former Ford press secretary Ron Nessen says someone approached him at one of the reunions and said wasn't it great that everyone got along so well back then. "I remember thinking, 'What administration was he in?'" said Nessen.

In his memoir, speechwriter Robert Hartmann derided Rumsfeld repeatedly, naming one chapter, "Rummy's Run." "Rummy regarded himself as something of a political genius," Hartmann wrote at one point, adding, "Don had some class. He was ruthless within rules." Today, the eighty-six-year-old Hartmann, who lives in a Washington suburb, admires Rumsfeld's handling of the war on terror, and told me, "I've revised my opinion and I'm a great fan of Rummy now.... I always liked him. But I was writing about what he did for Ford. Now I'm talking about what he's doing for this guy and he's doing good."

NUTRASWEET

After Ford lost the election, the forty-four-year-old Rumsfeld returned to the North Shore. He lectured at Northwestern University and occasionally at Princeton. But his immediate future lay in business. His old friend Dan Searle was struggling to keep his company up to speed in the increasingly competitive pharmaceutical industry. G. D. Searle & Company, headquartered in Skokie, had made its modern mark by developing birth control pills and a popular natural laxative, Metamucil. But in recent years, Searle's research and development branch had not produced one significant new product. Dan and his brother, William, had gone on a shopping spree in the 1970s, and much of what they bought lost money, for instance, a medical supply division. The firm's dream of selling aspartame, a revolutionary artificial sweeter, lay dormant. Bottling giants Coke and Pepsi desired aspartame (brand-named NutraSweet) because it didn't have saccharin's metallic taste. The Food and Drug Commission, after first approving aspartame, rescinded its approval. There were allegations that Searle had falsified test results. Detractors claimed aspartame caused everything from headaches to bowel distress. Dan Searle, his brother, and their brother-in-law ran the family-owned business. They collectively decided they needed new blood, a non-family chief executive officer who could objectively look over all Searle's holdings and make prudent profit-driven decisions. "We were spending more time trying to untangle family laundry than we were in turning the company around," Searle said.

Searle headed the search committee and drew up lists of attributes he wanted in a CEO. He also wrote down names of world-class leaders, both alive and dead, and studied their management styles. Rumsfeld, then defense secretary, was on Searle's list. He telephoned Rumsfeld to get his ideas, hoping he might want the job. The candidate expressed interest, and the winter after Ford's election loss,

Rumsfeld and Searle reached agreement on a five-year contract. Rumsfeld came to Skokie to sign it and asked for a copy. "He said, 'Where's the Xerox machine?' I said right out in the corridor. He said, 'Can you operate it?' I said 'No, can you?' Here was the CEO of one of the largest pharmaceutical companies and the secretary of defense and we did not know how to operate the Xerox."

I asked Rumsfeld why he chose to enter the corporate world rather than reenter politics. "Between late '57 and '77 I had done almost nothing other than government, and I had always been interested in business. . . . It just felt to me that I was happiest when I was learning and when I was reasonably central to something. I'd always worried about politicians who spent most of their time getting ready to be something as opposed to doing something. And I questioned whether that was a great way to live a life, getting ready as opposed to doing."

Rumsfeld had run the White House and the two million–person armed forces, but without sufficient time to make his mark. Now, he had his first company to oversee and plenty of time to chalk up tangible accomplishments. He studied Searle's structure and settled on a multi-pronged approach. First, he began selling off unprofitable divisions: twenty-five businesses with a combined worth of more than $400 million. He decentralized the Skokie headquarters, sending employees out to the branches where they actually did their work. He revamped the board of directors to bring in more non-family members. He greatly expanded the highly profitable Pearle optical division, opening new stores across the country. He recruited a renowned scientist to run the research division, removing any taint of corruption. The company had lost $28 million the year Rumsfeld arrived. By 1981, earnings topped $120 million on sales of $1 billion.

Looking at Rumsfeld today, as he stands at the Pentagon podium to denounce terrorists and rally the troops, it is hard to imagine that he is the man who brought the country NutraSweet. Rumsfeld created a team to work on the FDA. Scientists were recruited to testify about its safety. It did not hurt NutraSweet's cause that Ronald Reagan won the White House in 1980 and installed a new FDA chairman. The new official promptly approved aspartame as a tabletop sweeter and, later, as a sugar substitute in bottled drinks, which were the real moneymaker. Rumsfeld convinced Coke to switch from saccharin to NutraSweet. Pepsi quickly followed. The product spun hundreds of millions of dollars in profits for Searle by 1985.

"The way he does something is he studies something, gets to the common core of the problem, decides what to do, and turns it over to others to carry out," says William Greener, who was a press aide to Ron Nessen in the White House and then traveled with Rumsfeld across the Potomac to the Pentagon. "He judges people. He does it very carefully. He doesn't make snap judgments." When Rumsfeld inked his new corporate contract, one of the first men he called was Greener, to ask him to run Searle's public relations office. "He said he wanted us to be together again," said Greener, who is now in retirement in North Carolina.

Rumsfeld studied not only the company's books. He made a habit of eating lunch in the employee cafeteria. He'd just sit down with subordinates, uninvited, and start asking them what they did. Greener remembers one incident. "He said, 'What do you do?' and the guy told him and he said, 'Why isn't that being done in such and such a division so we don't have to worry about it in headquarters?' And then the guy said, 'But I wouldn't have a job.' I thought to myself, 'Man, you just made a mistake.' That wasn't the point." When an employee suggested posting the company's closing stock price each day, the chief rejected the idea. Greener quotes him as saying, "That's chasing the wrong rabbit. I don't want them concentrating on day-to-day fluctuations in the market. I want them concentrating on the long-range goals of what we were doing."

Rumsfeld normally reaches back into his past to staff whatever organization he's running with proven performers. New Trier friend John E. Robson followed Greener to Searle. The Yale- and Harvard-educated Robson, who had been chairman of the U.S. Civil Aeronautics Board under Ford, became Searle's number two executive. James M. Denny, a Princeton classmate who went on to get a law degree, became chief financial officer. Denny said Rumsfeld so worried about any appearance of impropriety that he sent the CFO a check every year for $1,000 to cover the cost of any company property he might have used outside work ."I can't remember Don ever doing it, but if he did the check would cover it," Denny remembered. "Don always bent over backwards to make sure they could never be any allegation of taint of conduct that would be less than 100 percent ethical."

Rumsfeld kept abreast of politics through his Republican contacts. He was developing a fast friendship with a new congressman who thought big thoughts, just like Rumsfeld. Congressman Newt Gingrich was in Chicago one day in the early 1980s. He made a side trip to the North Shore headquarters of G. D. Searle to seek Rumsfeld's advice on how to make the GOP the majority party. "He told me something that really truly shaped what I did," Gingrich recalled. "He said, 'For the American people to do something they have to believe that it's urgent, important and doable. If it wasn't important, they would never do it. If it wasn't urgent, they wouldn't do it right now. And if they didn't think it was doable, even if they agreed that it was important and urgent, they would feel sad about the fact that it wasn't happening, but they wouldn't waste their time.' He said that was the key characteristic of Americans. They have to believe all three for something to be doable."

In 1985, Searle's research budget was falling far behind spending by much bigger firms. Rumsfeld analyzed the situation and decided a moment of truth had arrived. Searle either had to get bigger itself by merging with another firm, or sell. Searle said the first option meant the family would lose further control anyway, so it hung up the "for sale" sign. Searle's stock hovered between $40 and $45 a share. Monsanto won the bidding war at $65 a share, or $2.7 billion, plus a debt of $500 million. "He probably could have made a decision that 'I'm going to sell the company,'" Searle says today. "He chose not to do that. At that point, he did what I think was exactly appropriate. He went to the major shareholders."

The Searles made about $700 million on the deal. Rumsfeld left the company a wealthy man for the first time. Denny says the sale did not require a proxy statement and there is no public document to show what Rumsfeld collected. "He made most of his money, as did all of us, when the company was sold," Greener said.

He and Joyce sold their Winnetka home shortly after the Searle transaction. They bought a spacious condo near the North Side, closer to an office he rented on La Salle Street, overlooking Lake Michigan. He made investments, advised entrepreneurs, and served on various boards, both corporate and civic. He returned briefly to the CEO chair from 1990 to 1993 at General Instrument Corporation, getting him back in touch with the military-industrial complex. His list of board positions included Gilead Sciences Inc., a pioneer in anti-HIV drugs founded by physician Michael Riordan, who recruited Rumsfeld and whom Rumsfeld eventually replaced as chairman of the board. Rumsfeld also served on the board of Amylin Pharmaceuticals and the Tribune Company, a media conglomerate that includes the *Los Angeles Times* and the *Chicago Tribune*. His nonprofit memberships included the Board of Trustees of the Chicago Historical Society, the Hoover Institution, the Rand Corporation, and the National Park Foundation. In the 1980s and 1990s, he got several invitations to take on high-profile assignments. But it was the big prize he thought about: He wanted back in the White House.

[CHAPTER 4]

RUMSFELD RETURNS

O N A CHILLY DECEMBER NIGHT IN 1983, RUMSFELD RODE IN AN ENTOURAGE moving from downtown Baghdad to the western end of the city, where Saddam Hussein awaited his visit. Rumsfeld's car was stopped several times at Iraqi checkpoints, where he and State Department officials Bob Pelletreau and Thomas J. Miller were asked to get out of the vehicle for a patdown. At one of Saddam's opulent palaces, Iraqis led the team into a large reception room featuring two large sofas. Iraqi handlers instructed the Americans on the mysterious protocol for meeting the leader: If Saddam sat on the far end of his sofa, Rumsfeld should do the same on his sofa. If the dictator sat on the near end, Rumsfeld should follow suit. Saddam suddenly appeared from a corner door. An Iraqi cameraman turned on his floodlight and rolled the film. Rumsfeld walked up to Saddam, who reverted to an old trick for the camera. He held his right hand low, near his side, in an attempt to coax Rumsfeld to reach down to take it. The resulting film footage would show the most senior U.S. official to visit Saddam bowing in homage. Rumsfeld would have none of it. He walked right up to Saddam. Inches away, he grabbed the hand, back straight, eyes staring straight ahead.

What took the pharmaceutical executive from the friendly confines of Skokie to the war-inflamed Middle East had begun two months earlier. A new radical group, Islamic Jihad, had executed a shocking truck bombing. On October 23, 1983, two Jihadists smashed a Mercedes Benz truck through the gates of a U.S. Marine barracks in Beirut, Lebanon, and then detonated a huge bomb, equivalent to 12,000 pounds of TNT. They killed 242 Marines. A stunned President Reagan searched for new options in dealing with Lebanon, which was roiled in a multi-front civil war, rubbed more raw by invading Israeli and Syrian soldiers and the presence of Palestinian terrorists. Druze fanatics and Hafiz Assad's Syrian army were eviscerating the Lebanese army. Druze soldiers regularly shelled Beirut from Chouf Mountain, to the point that Lebanese president Amin Gemayel's headquarters was reduced to a basement meeting room. Iran had formed and trained terrorists for the new Hezbollah ("party of God"), which attacked Israel from Lebanon.

Reagan needed an assessment of whether Lebanon was a hopeless situation, or if there remained some ray of hope that justified the remaining Marine peacekeepers' presence there. George Shultz, his secretary of state, favored a continued military presence. He convinced Reagan to recruit Rumsfeld as a special Middle East envoy to explore all possible peace options. The president agreed. On November 3, 1983, Rumsfeld appeared with Reagan at the White House, getting the requisite imprimatur of presidential authority.

A reporter asked Rumsfeld if he wasn't accepting a "no win" job. "I guess time will tell," he answered. He and Shultz headed to Foggy Bottom, the location of the State Department, to put together a team. Bob Pelletreau, the deputy assistant secretary of state for Near East affairs, recruited Thomas J. Miller, a young hotshot Foreign Service official who was languishing in congressional affairs. David L. Mack, another of State's Near East analysts, joined the team. (Pelletreau,

Miller, and Mack all went on to gain appointments to ambassador-ships. As of this writing, Miller is U.S. ambassador to Greece.) Rumsfeld handed them his handbook of "Rumsfeld's Rules" so they could understand his relentless drive and modus operandi. Shultz brought a Lebanese delegation over to State to meet the new envoy. "Don Rumsfeld comes from the heavy cream of American political leadership," Shultz told them. The Pentagon's top officer in Lebanon, then–Army Brigadier General Carl Stiner, augmented Rumsfeld's team. Stiner worked with the Lebanese army in an unsuccessful attempt to stave off the Druze militia and Assad's Syrian army. (Stiner later earned a fourth star and headed U.S. Special Operations Command before retiring.)

Rumsfeld launched a series of trips to the region, visiting the various heads of state. He knew, however, that any chance of peace resided in the presidential palace in Damascus, Syria, from which Hafiz Assad controlled a large force in Lebanon and pulled some of Hezbollah's strings. Assad treated the Rumsfeld team to numerous cups of strong black coffee as he lectured for hours on Syria's historical role. Lebanon was once part of Syria, he reminded Rumsfeld, as a way of justifying his occupation. "Secretary Rumsfeld took the view that the way to deal with Syria was to put pressure on it so it would be more amenable to some sort of a negotiated solution," Mack recalls.

During trips into bombed-out Beirut, the only relatively safe reconnoiter site was the ambassador's residence in Yarze, on the city's outskirts. Discussions were often interrupted by nearby Druze or Syrian artillery shells. The Americans took to ducking under tables and stairways. On one excursion into the city, the Rumsfeld entourage came under sniper fire. Bullets ricocheted off a nearby brick wall. Back in Yarze, the group paused for a backyard lunch. When Miller accidentally dropped a large wooden pepper mill, the shellshocked group instinctively jumped for cover.

From the start, Rumsfeld had inundated the team with snowflakes. After dealing with scores of memos, Mack caught onto the game. "We realized the purpose of snowflakes is to get people to come up with other innovative thinking," Mack says. "He doesn't necessarily think snowflakes are the best idea. He realizes some of them, or most of them, are not good ideas." Mack then decided to capitalize on what he knew about Rumsfeld. State wanted to improve the U.S. relationship with Iraq, which then was engulfed in what would be a eight-year war with Iran, the world's first radical Islamic state and the U.S.'s main worry in protecting the Gulf's oil-producing countries. Mack knew Rumsfeld wanted to put pressure on Assad. He also knew Rumsfeld as a macho guy, a former college and Navy wrestler who was not afraid to rattle an adversary. Mack penned his own memo to Rumsfeld recommending, "Let's drive Hafiz Assad crazy." His idea was for Rumsfeld to visit Assad's arch rival, Saddam Hussein. Rumsfeld liked the idea. "Rumsfeld asked me how would you go about doing this," he says. "One of my suggestions was maybe visit Baghdad." In December, he found himself in Baghdad meeting with English-speaking Tariq Aziz. "I don't think Rumsfeld charmed him and I don't think he charmed Rumsfeld," says Mack, who sat in. "I remember sitting there and Tariq Aziz smoking cigars and blowing smoke."

The meeting set the stage for the Saddam encounter weeks later. In Baghdad, Rumsfeld met again with Aziz, staying up until 3 a.m. Rumsfeld recalls, "I said something to the effect that it's a fact that a whole generation of Americans have grown up not knowing much about Iraqis and a whole generation of Iraqis has grown up not knowing much about Americans."

At the Saddam meeting, Aziz reappeared, this time as the interpreter who offered none of his own ideas. As Rumsfeld and Saddam sat on those two separate sofas about fifteen feet apart, the American asked the Iraqi for advice on Syria. Saddam gave a rambling answer. He said Egypt and his own country were temporarily not in their "natural state." Egypt was engrossed in making peace with Israel; Baghdad was pinned down in a war with Iran. This allowed Assad to fill the power vacuum. Saddam then put his hands together over his head to show how large Assad thought he had become. Saddam said that when Iraq could again play its natural role, Syria would revert to a minor player. As he said this, he brought his hands down to form a globe the size of a baseball. Saddam also brought up the fact that Washington had cut off diplomatic relations with Baghdad, a clear signal he wanted them resumed.

At another point, Saddam remembered his briefing from Aziz. "Out of Saddam's mouth comes this, 'You know, we've got a whole generation of Iraqis growing up and a whole generation of Americans growing up...'" Rumsfeld says years later, a bit amused.

"At one moment in the meeting he took me over to a window and pointed out at a tall building and he said, 'When the elevator doesn't work in that building which way do you think I look? I've got to look West. I need people who can help make this modern country of ours work.'"

I asked Rumsfeld what he thought of Saddam that year. "We were looking at it not from who do we want to be our new best friend but from the standpoint of geostrategic circumstances in that part of the world," he said.

Rumsfeld's visit did pave the way for restarting formal relations with Baghdad. But the two trips to Baghdad did little to worry the iron-fisted Assad, whose office featured a painting of Arabs defeating Christian crusaders in the 1187 Battle of Hittin. Mack and other diplomats believe Rumsfeld must have concluded that the U.S. military deployment was not suitable to chaotic Lebanon. Before Rumsfeld's mission ended in May, after six months, Reagan began

pulling out troops. Islamic Jihad turned to an even more brutal tactic: kidnapping and torturing Westerners. One of the first victims
was Beirut CIA station chief William Buckley. The fanatics tortured
him to force disclosure of his numerous informants in Beirut, then
they murdered him.

Rumsfeld's six months of grim shuttle diplomacy had its lighter
moments. Laurence Silberman entered the picture in the spring of
1984. Under Shultz's plan, Rumsfeld would work the Middle East
for six months, then give way to Silberman, who had left government work to join a private law firm. Both men were protégés of
Shultz: Rumsfeld had worked for him at the Cost of Living Council,
Silberman at the Department of Labor. Silberman felt he could be
frank with Shultz. He told him at the State Department during
Rumsfeld's mission that there were only two options for Lebanon:
bomb Syria, which controlled the terrorists, or pull out the troops.
"George at that point said 'That's the counsel of despair,'" Silberman
says today. "He wanted option three. There was no option three."

In April, Silberman joined Rumsfeld on a tour of the region. They
stopped in Riyadh, Damascus, Beirut, Jerusalem, Yemen, Baghdad,
and Sudan. In Saudi Arabia, the duo traveled to the home of King
Fahd. They found the huge man ensconced in his study, with the air
conditioner thermostat turned down to the mid-fifties. The principal subject was convincing the king to allow the pre-positioning of
military hardware in the event Iran launched an invasion. The issue
took hours to resolve. Dressed in lightweight summer clothes, the
two diplomats grew colder and colder and huddled together. Both
were then pipe smokers and asked the king if they could light up. He
said yes, and they proceeded to smoke bowlful after bowlful just to
keep their hands warm. "We were sitting there holding our hot pipes
in our hand," Silberman says. "I've never been so cold." A few hours
after the meeting, the Saudi foreign minister approached the two and

said the king had asked him a question: "The two Americans sat very close together. Are they gay?" The king was assured they were not.

Later, Rumsfeld and Silberman attended a lunch hosted by Fahd. The table was studded with mounds of food, including a large number of veal chops, which the king ate voraciously. In the next moment, the king delivered an unsolicited advertisement for Rumsfeld's favorite product—aspartame.

"King Fahd's sitting there," says Rumsfeld, "and all of his people are down the line, Crown Prince Abdullah and Prince Sultan, and the Foreign Minister Saud, and down here's our group. And they serve tea. I looked around for the sugar, for the Sweet and Low, Equal, because I think of it as aspartame. In Europe, it's called Candaral. And the King sees me looking around and the next thing you know he reaches in here, pulls out Candaral aspartame [and] passed it to me and then made a testimonial that his wife required him to use that because he wants to lose weight. He's lost X number of kilos. All I could think of was if I'd had a camera, what an ad. It was just wonderful. His government was in hysterics."

The trip eventually had Rumsfeld making another entry into warring Lebanon. He and Silberman met up with a Marine helicopter in Israel one night and headed for Beirut. When the men were handed bulletproof jackets, Silberman sat on his instead of wearing it. When a crew member reminded him to put it on, the future judge asked where the fire in Lebanon was coming from. "The ground," answered the officer. Replied Silberman, "You protect what you want to protect. I'll protect what I want to protect." The chopper set down in a pitch-black landing zone. As he stepped off under the whirling blades, Silberman found himself bodily picked up off the ground by men dressed in black, who proceeded to run across the rocky terrain. Silberman was sure it was Hezbollah or Islamic Jihad kidnapping them. He remained silent, thinking he would never see his wife and kids again. Then a black Cadillac appeared, studded in American flags, with U.S. ambassador Reginald Bartholomew inside. The "kidnappers" were members of the Army's then super-secret Delta Force. Because of the threat of snipers, the plan was to get the diplomats from aircraft to sedan as fast as possible. Rumsfeld knew about it, but purposely did not tell his friend. They had a good laugh later.

Mack remembered crossing paths with Rumsfeld at the airport in Tel Aviv. Mack was getting ready to go back into Lebanon; Rumsfeld was coming out. "He said, 'Over to you, Mack.' I thought to myself, he knows a loser when he sees it. He's not coming back."

Mack was right. In May 1984, Rumsfeld resigned and returned to the corporate boardroom in Skokie. Rumsfeld said he made no flat recommendation to pull out U.S. troops. "My recommendation was more analytical than a recommendation.... I clearly wished we weren't there. No question about that.... The first cable I sent back, as I recall, began with the words, 'I wish we weren't here.'"

WHITE HOUSE AMBITIONS

After leaving Searle in 1985, Rumsfeld pulled together his Winnetka-New Trier network for a new political project: running for president. Reagan was in his second term. The two Republican front-runners, Vice President George Bush and Senator Bob Dole, seemed beatable. Rumsfeld had been on the short list twice for vice president. But Ford and Reagan had turned to other candidates. This time he would control his own destiny by shooting for the top prize. He talked strategy with his friend Ned Jannotta while on vacation in the Dominican Republic. Kissinger, by now a wealthy international consultant and Republican Party elder statesman, joined them and expressed support. Rumsfeld also had a lengthy conversation with Silberman, by now a federal judge, who encouraged him. "I remember urging him to run for president," the judge recalled. "I thought he would make a great president."

Rumsfeld formed an exploratory committee and began criss-crossing the nation speaking to party faithful. He visited the early contest states, New Hampshire and Iowa. Searle started raising money, just as he had in 1962. "Cap" Adams handled advertising. But Rumsfeld's candidacy did not resonate. And the prospect of carrying a huge campaign debt of more than $3 million began to weigh on him. Campaign finance laws at the time prohibited a candidate from using his own money to pay off debts. Jannotta remembers discussing with his friend that the debt would mean small companies would not get their money for years. It's hard for a losing candidate to continually attract contributors to pay the debt off.

Edward Brennan, the Sears Roebuck chairman, had organized a big dinner in Chicago for May 6, 1987, to formally announce Rumsfeld's candidacy. More than $1 million in tickets had been sold, but Rumsfeld and Joyce decided to call the whole thing off. "I'd say he was very realistic," Jannotta recalled. "Personally he was disappointed. I think he thought he would be better than the other two." Said "Cap" Adams, "He didn't have much name recognition at the time. It was a money thing." On April 2, Rumsfeld sent a memo to supporters explaining the pullout. "For a dark horse, the probable imbalance of revenues and expenses early in the campaign raises the spectre of a deficit of several million dollars. Under current federal election laws, it is impossible to finance such a deficit through traditional sources. As a matter of principle, I will not run a deficit. Deficit spending plagues this country."

SAVING MISSILE DEFENSE

A 1998 phone call from Newt Gingrich's office marked Rumsfeld's reentry to Washington and into the good graces of Washington's new Republican majority in Congress. Rumsfeld accepted the chairmanship of a Republican-created, five-Republican, four-Democrat panel, the Commission to Assess the Ballistic Missile Threat to the United States. "We were looking for a strong team and I was a huge admirer of his and always thought he was a potential president," Gingrich said. "He was available. He was willing to do it."

Missile defense had become a core Republican issue. President Reagan had spent billions trying to develop a virtual shield against attack. His "Star Wars" rhetoric rattled the Soviet politburo, helping to hasten the "Evil Empire's" collapse. Since 1989, the argument for missile defense had focused on rogue nations like Iran, Iraq, and North Korea, which appeared bent on building an arsenal of ballistic missiles armed with nuclear, biological, or chemical warheads. History showed that such rogue regimes made progress acquiring weapons at a faster pace than the CIA predicted. North Korea, for example, did not spend a lot of time on testing and perfecting missiles. They tested once and then deployed.

Conservative Republicans saw the commission as a chance to debunk the CIA's latest national intelligence estimate (NIE) on missile proliferation. An NIE is the intelligence community's best judgment on a particular national security issue. This particular NIE said the U.S. had a safety net of fifteen years before a rogue nation could activate inter-continental ballistic missiles. If Rumsfeld's commission could compile the evidence to challenge that assessment, it would provide a boon to advocates of developing and deploying a missile defense. To his benefit, Rumsfeld's nine-member commission was tilted in his favor. There was his old friend Bill Schneider, Paul Wolfowitz, William Graham (an early "Star Wars" enthusiast), and Clinton's former director of Central Intelligence, James Woolsey. But in achieving what Rumsfeld wanted—a unanimous report—two members might put up objections. One was Richard L. Garwin, a renowned scientist who had advised Democratic administrations, and Barry M. Blechman, who ran his own consulting firm. Garwin and Blechman had long supported the Anti–Ballistic Missile Treaty. Liberals cited the thirty-year-old ABM Treaty with the Soviets as an impenetrable firewall between research, which the pact allowed, and actual deployment, which it did not.

Also working for the commission was Stephen Cambone, a young defense analyst at the Center for Strategic and International Studies. Introduced to Rumsfeld by Schneider, Cambone had passed the Rumsfeld test: he was smart and willing to work long hours on tough problems. "Rumsfeld forces you to make a decision about whether you will take the time and energy to be his guy. He forces you into it," said a person who worked on forming the commission. Cambone became the commission's chief of staff and helped the chairman get the right intelligence information.

Rumsfeld immediately cleared away some stumbling blocks. He made it clear that the commission was to assess the current missile threat, not recommend what to do about it. That approach won over anti-missile critics like Garwin.

The chairman then worked to get access to the CIA's most sensitive intelligence on a country's arms programs. Initially, CIA briefers passed out useless information. "When we started, they were trying to give us pap," recalled Blechman. "It was worse than a briefing for the Kiwanis Club. 'The Russian federation has a lot of missiles.' It was a joke." After one briefing, Schneider commented, "That briefer is a waste of food."

No expert on one country seemed to know what was going on in other countries. When a CIA expert delivered the assessment on

North Korea, the agency official who handled Iraq had to leave the room. It was classic "stovepiping." All sorts of critically important information flowing to the top was unseen by the hundreds of bureaucrats who were expected to report on global arms proliferation. "No one talked to each other," Blechman said later. "The briefer was quite sincere but did not know the whole story. As different briefers got up, different subgroups would have to leave the room. People were missing clues. It was disappointing."

Rumsfeld took his complaints directly to Director of Central Intelligence George Tenet. Soon, the commission not only got better information, it also got office space at Langley to view the crown jewels. "Rumsfeld pressed and pressed and pressed until we got the full story on these different countries," Blechman says. Woolsey took note of Rumsfeld's wrestling and football background and told me, "He runs an organization a little bit like a good athletic team captain.... On occasion, he would kid us and expect to be kidded back." He recalls Rumsfeld turning to him at one meeting, and jabbing, "You haven't said anything smart in three days."

Rumsfeld was merciless with briefers who do not know their subject. "He became nervous about the qualification of briefers," Schneider said. "So he made them show up with bios. You found political science majors talking about North Korean rocket motor technology. This did not wash with Rumsfeld, so he would dismiss the briefer."

Rumsfeld didn't stop at viewing CIA documents. The panel traveled to the Energy Department's Livermore laboratory, where an intelligence cell kept better information on proliferation than did the CIA. Rumsfeld also called in a parade of outside experts from aerospace companies, think tanks, and the scientific world. Members remember Rumsfeld reading all the material himself.

"Rumsfeld got very concerned about the intelligence community's lack of willingness to fill in the pieces of the jigsaw puzzle for which they didn't have direct evidence with judgment," Woolsey recalled. "That's what you've got to do." Rumsfeld culminated the commission's research by having the staff write a first draft of findings only. He then reworked it and unveiled the product. This approach avoided what could have been an agonizing, sentence-by-sentence, draft-by-committee process. "In terms of relevant policies," Blechman said, "Rumsfeld believes strongly, as I do, that proliferation is a foregone conclusion. It's just a question of when and the pace at which it grows." Only when the findings were agreed upon did the staff produce a 300-page report. In the end, all agreed on relatively simple, but important, language:

"The threat to the U.S. posed by these emerging capabilities is broader, more mature and evolving more rapidly than has been reported in estimates and reports by the intelligence community.... The warning times the U.S. can expect of new, threatening ballistic missile deployments are being reduced. Under some plausible scenarios—including re-basing or transfer of operational missiles, sea- and air-launched options, shortened development programs that might include testing in a third country, or some combination of these—the U.S. might well have little or no warning before operational deployment."

The commission recommended a second look at the NIE. In spring and summer 1998, during the commission's investigation and immediately afterward, two events happened that reinforced the notion of a dangerous, unpredictable world. In May, India conducted its first underground nuclear warhead testing since 1974—and did so while deceiving the United States, lying to the Clinton administration about its plans and preparing the site while U.S. spy satellites were not overhead. India's test prompted Pakistan to do the same. On August 31, a month after Rumsfeld released his findings, North Korea, as if on cue, test-fired its Taepodong rocket over Japan.

That the commission's recommendation was unanimous made it impossible to dismiss as politically partisan. "[Rumsfeld] figured out that a unanimous commission was worth everything because a unanimous commission meant that [liberal Democrats] are voting yes and it's impossible to discredit the report," said Gingrich. "Now, the report is more limited than Rumsfeld personally would have been. But by getting it unanimous it changed the landscape. It's an example of his ability to strategically understand what's necessary and then discipline himself to get it. What he wanted to do was get to the hardest unanimous report he could get to and that was an art form. I think it's a really great work of leadership."

Missile defense advocates now had an official finding on which to argue for accelerated missile defense deployment. And, Rumsfeld was back in the conservative fold.

LECTURING BEIJING

Rumsfeld was a jet-age business consultant in 1999 when he found himself at a series of banquets and government briefings in Beijing. He was part of a delegation headed by the American Foreign Policy Council and its head, Herman Pirchner, Jr. The delegation also included Rumsfeld's old friend Bill Schneider; Dov Zakheim, who was to become Rumsfeld's top budget officer in the Pentagon; and Sven Kramer, another Ford alumnus who would also enter the Pentagon with Rumsfeld.

At one banquet, the Chinese served a series of duck dishes, including duck feet in jelly. At this point, Rumsfeld held up a morsel, turned to one of his dinner mates and quipped, "My, this gives new definition to the world wide web." It was a classic Rumsfeld ad lib. What was also proved classic was the frankness with which he spoke on the trip. The Chinese are known for the precision with which they host such VIP visits. Pirchner put this one together as a preview for the Chinese of what a Republican national security team might look like if Bush or another GOPer won the presidency in 2000. As the group sat through scores of briefings, Rumsfeld listened carefully, and then made two important points. If Bush won, the U.S. would deploy a missile defense system despite any objections from Beijing. And, secondly, the ex–defense secretary bluntly told the Chinese generals and politburo members, if the mainland invaded democratic Taiwan, the United States would go to war against China in Taiwan's defense. (President Bush would later declare the U.S. would do "whatever it took to help Taiwan defend herself.")

During one Beijing meeting, the Chinese brought up an incident from earlier in the year, when a B-2 bomber, based on faulty intelligence, mistakenly dropped a satellite-guided bomb on the Chinese embassy in Belgrade. U.S. intelligence believed the building was a Serbian military logistics center. The communist Chinese government orchestrated protests that became a virtual siege outside the American embassy in Beijing, which led to a warning from the Clinton administration about the government endangering American lives. Rumsfeld sat and listened to the Chinese explanation for their conduct. Pirchner remembers Rumsfeld's response: "He noted that he had understood how decisions like this are made. 'I've been in rooms where decisions like this are made and you have choices. You can ignore the incident. You can pursue it in a very aggressive or diplomatic manner or you make it a big public event that will influence public opinion, presumably for some further domestic or foreign policy goal. We've watched how you've treated this incident and stand so instructed.'"

Pirchner sums up the encounter: "The message was they had orchestrated the demonstrations and that it was intended to make a change of public opinion of the United States in Chinese eyes."

Overall, Pirchner says, "The Rumsfeld you see at press conferences isn't very different than the one who traveled with us to China and other places. He's not a person who has multiple personalities. He's not a guy who puts on big fronts. What you see is what he is."

While being driven around Beijing, the delegation had noticed an exhibition hall that contained a commemoration of fifty years of Communist Party rule. Pirchner's group received permission to attend. They strolled through the large hall, gazing at artifacts of Mao's revolution and autocratic rule. One display caught Rumsfeld's special attention. It was a model of an island being invaded by Chinese warships, aircraft, and troops. It made a lasting impression on Rumsfeld that invading Taiwan and forcibly reuniting the island with the mainland is an open Beijing objective. He told me later, "The signal in the Taiwan portion of the pavilion to me was that the government of China was determined to bring back into China Taiwan, and the vehicle for doing it need not be peaceful. That is to say, you would not have had totally militaristic presentation with respect to Taiwan, with nothing else about it. There wasn't any other element of political or economic interaction."

That year, Rumsfeld took on another Washington job. He headed his second special commission in two years, this time to study outer space and U.S. satellite vulnerabilities to attack. During one closed session, he met his future Joint Chiefs chairman, Richard Myers. Myers was then Joint Chiefs vice chairman and a former commander of U.S. Space Command. Neither Myers nor Rumsfeld realized it at the time, but it was the pair's first job interview. Myers said something that clicked with Rumsfeld. He testified that he didn't care who managed America's network of satellites, the Air Force or the Navy. He just wanted the problems fixed. Rumsfeld, a stickler for joint operations devoid of inter-service jealousies, liked the answer. In 2001, when Rumsfeld was hunting for a new chairman, Myers got the job over his closest rival, Admiral Vern Clark, the chief of naval operations.

By the 2000 election, Rumsfeld had moved into the good graces of conservatives in Washington. He had joined neoconservatives in signing a letter to Clinton urging the forcible removal of Saddam Hussein. His ballistic missile threat commission had given missile defense advocates the underpinning to make their arguments. His trip to China had put the communists on notice of what they could expect from a Republican administration. If Bush were to summon Rumsfeld from his North Michigan Avenue office in Chicago back to Washington, the nominee would return with solid conservative credentials.

ACCIDENTAL SECRETARY

During the transition phase, after George W. Bush's election, Rumsfeld advised the president-elect on how to fill a Cabinet. He also came to Washington and socialized with old friends. He, Silberman, and Gingrich had dinner one night in Georgetown. Gingrich remembered thinking he was dining with the next director of Central Intelligence. The front-runner for secretary of defense was Daniel Coats. A lanky, hollow-faced lawyer who succeeded Dan Quayle to the Senate, Coats retired rather than face popular Democratic governor Evan Bayh in the 1998 election. Coats had served with distinction on the Senate Armed Services Committee. A devout Christian from a conservative state, he wasn't afraid to embrace politically incorrect positions; he had nearly single-handedly stopped Clinton in 1993 from lifting the ban on open homosexuality in the military.

Coats had landed at the prestigious law firm of Verner, Liipfert, Bernard, McPherson, and Hand. He had an office near former senator Bob Dole and former Senate majority leader George Mitchell. For the job interview, the Bush team—which was headquartered in the

Mayflower hotel—sent a blackened SUV to pick up Coats, who waited in his building's basement near a back exit. The SUV took a roundabout route to the Mayflower so as not to attract press attention. When Coats arrived at the hotel's alley entrance, a freight elevator stood ready to whisk him up to Bush's floor. But a nervous operator hit the wrong number. The doors suddenly opened to a crowd of reporters on patrol for any Bush Cabinet candidates. A handler stepped in to block the gaggle's view, and the elevator quickly ascended again. The interview lasted more than an hour, with Bush setting out his desire for a completely transformed military. Coats was candid. He volunteered his strengths—and weaknesses. He had strong ties to members of both houses of Congress. He knew the Pentagon. But he had no experience in running a government agency. He was not a detail man. He would leave nuts and bolts management to his deputy secretary. "My view of the role of a Cabinet official was not to get down in operational details," Coats told me later. Bush had a different vision for his first defense secretary. He wanted sweeping managerial and doctrinal changes, requiring a hands-on manager.

Enter Rumsfeld. His chairmanship of the ballistic missile commission had given him his first entry into candidate Bush's inner circle. In January 2000, Bush had invited him to Washington to brief him on missile threats. The setting was a private room at the Mayflower. "I met with him for hours just alone," Rumsfeld said.

Rumsfeld told me he never had a formal job interview with Bush. The president-elect sought his advice on the qualities needed to be defense secretary.

"He wanted to ask me questions about what I thought about the intelligence community and what I thought about defense and foreign policy areas. And not because I had any desire to come in or he had any desire to have me. I think that was out of the question. It wasn't on the radar screen." Rumsfeld met again with Bush, this time in Austin, Texas. Bush did talk jobs, but made no direct offer. Rumsfeld traveled to his ranch in Taos. A few days later the phone rang. It was his protégé, Cheney, offering him the defense job.

Gingrich analyzed the Bush-Rumsfeld marriage this way. "Bush is talking to a first-rate politician, who won elective office, who's been chief of staff to a president, who was the youngest secretary of defense in history, who had been CEO of a big corporation, very successful big corporation, so he could say to him, do you think you could redo the Pentagon? Well, this Rumsfeld spent his career preparing for this."

He added, "It doesn't hurt that the guy in charge of staffing the administration is Rumsfeld's former deputy. This is a small conspiracy."

[CHAPTER 5]

RUMSFELD THE MANAGER

"**M**Y GOODNESS GRACIOUS," RUMSFELD EXCLAIMED AS HE MET THE PENTAGON press on January 26, 2001, choosing an old-fashioned phrase that feigned innocence. At sixty-eight, Rumsfeld did not look much different than he had in 1976 as the nation's youngest secretary of defense. His hair was thinner, but still mostly black. The middleweight fitness of a Princeton wrestler still resided on a sturdy 5-foot, 9-inch frame. His spectacles of the 1970s—large, rimmed, tear-shaped—had given way to perfectly round, rimless glasses. His attire was timeless: the standard boxy, dark suit. He paid homage to a longtime friend and co–political conspirator in the audience. Reporters applauded as seventy-eight-year-old Melvin Laird, an old colleague in the House and a former defense secretary himself, stood up, his frame slightly bent. The press did not ask Rumsfeld about bin Laden or al Qaeda. In fact, during an all-day Senate confirmation hearing January 11, neither senator nor witness uttered those words, or mentioned Afghanistan.

The press conference over, Rumsfeld slipped on an overcoat and braved frigid winds on the Pentagon parade ground for an official welcome as the new defense secretary. The show included band music and spit-polished troops. It was the military's traditional first step in seducing a new secretary. But it took only a few days for the Pentagon bureaucrats to realize there would be no honeymoon with Rumsfeld.

The Pentagon workforce of 25,000 is made up of mostly conservative Republicans. They greeted the new Bush administration as conquering heroes; they were finally liberated from the Clinton administration and its politically correct social programs. When outgoing defense secretary William Cohen had honored Bill and Hillary at Fort Myer a month before, the Pentagon had had to send out a memo asking for "volunteers" to attend.

But the rank and file soon found out that the new guys on the block saw some of them as the enemy. Rumsfeld had been plotting a hostile takeover. Everyone knew Bush had given Rumsfeld orders to transform the military to prepare for new threats such as global terrorism and nuclear proliferation. What wasn't so well known was that the Bush people believed the generals and admirals had run the building under Clinton, and had run it timidly and badly. Rumsfeld vowed to take it back. Briefers, including Andrew W. Marshall, a seventy-nine-year-old Pentagon futurist with whom Rumsfeld had worked in the 1970s, told him the place was not open to new thinking.

Instead of summoning the brass who ran programs and operations—as they expected to be summoned in the first few weeks of January—Rumsfeld set up a series of outside panels with retired officers and industry leaders to give him new ideas on transformation. The brass referred to the groups as "The Filters," because they talked to the panels and the panels talked to Rumsfeld.

The secretary surrounded himself with trusted aides while the balky Senate Armed Services Committee considered his political appointees for confirmation. His old friend Bill Schneider ran up and down the third-floor corridor of the Pentagon with papers for him to sign. "It was my third hostile takeover," said Schneider, a veteran of the Reagan administration. Stephen Cambone prepared to be point man on the Quadrennial Defense Review (QDR). In another nine months, Rumsfeld would have to produce a QDR report for Congress dictating the number of troops, air wings, and divisions the country would have for the next four years. Marty Hoffman and Stephen Herbits, two friends from the 1970s, arrived to screen job applicants.

Herbits called Newt Gingrich at his K Street lobbying firm and told him to come over and help out. Gingrich, the architect of the 1994 Republican revolution in Congress, got a building pass and a parking space. Two rebel Republicans of different generations were now under the same roof in a common cause. Gingrich began going from office to office for impromptu brainstorming. "I just wandered around," he said. Rumsfeld put him to work with Richard Haver, his intelligence adviser, to produce a paper on future threats.

Rumsfeld was talking to everyone but the admirals and generals. "They squandered an opportunity to embrace the building," a senior officer told me two years later. "We waited for the cavalry. Mostly they didn't call us. They didn't play like we wanted. We were used to the Clinton administration. All they wanted us to do was keep quiet in public. No criticism." When Rumsfeld finally met with the chiefs to discuss the QDR, they complained it was the first time they had heard many of his proposals.

A civilian policymaker I interviewed told me of a "silent purge." As Rumsfeld's political appointees started trickling in, some workers suddenly found themselves transferred. Or they got the message and quit. One employee found out he had been tagged as a "State Department Arabist." "They had been thankful that Bush won the election," said a civilian who left the Pentagon early in the new administration.

"Then the new team arrived and it started to dawn on everybody that they were the enemy." Some employees started to lament Bush's victory and wondered why former senator Daniel Coats, once the front-runner for the job, was not the defense secretary.

Looking back on those first months, Gingrich said, "The truth is, Rumsfeld knew where he wanted to go. He was very impatient to get there. He didn't have enough people. There was a certain tension between the uniform services. . . . You're going to have tension with the senior military because they grew up in the system as it used to be." Still, Gingrich added, "He made a mistake in not including the chiefs early on. But in May that began to change."

Those first few weeks, Rumsfeld dealt with the big ideas of transformation and the minutiae of setting a routine. The Pentagon's outer ring windows are affixed with a yellow chemical film that blocks spies from using infrared devices to penetrate classified computers. Rumsfeld did not like the yellow tinge the window film cast over his spacious office. He had it removed. He does not use a classified computer in his office. Rumsfeld also ordered changes in the production of one of Washington's most widely read publications, "The Early Bird," a compendium of that morning's news articles and last night's TV broadcasts. Rumsfeld, an avid newspaper reader, wanted a hard copy in his limo when it picked him up at 6 a.m. So the "Early Bird" staff had to get in an hour earlier to meet the secretary's deadline. The Pentagon was slowly adjusting to Rumsfeld time. There was more adjusting to be done.

Unlike Cohen, Rumsfeld wanted the services to read him in early on significant programs. He wanted to know what the options were and who was consulted for advice. What he did not want was a service secretary coming to him late in the process for a "yes" or "no" decision. Rumsfeld also demanded thoroughly researched briefings; the use of exact English, devoid of acronyms; and absolute loyalty.

He shocked one three-star that winter by barking, "You don't know any more than I know," right in the middle of the officer's briefing. All of this was Rumsfeld's way of getting to the "ground truth" of an issue before he made the final decision.

CHINA CRISIS

In late March, Rumsfeld confronted his first international crisis and his first interagency tussle with the dovish State Department. A Chinese F-8 interceptor harassed a Navy EP-3 electronic aircraft as it eavesdropped and recorded conversations of the all-powerful People's Liberation Army. The reckless F-8 pilot purposefully bumped the EP-3, commanded by Lieutenant Shane Osborne. Heroically, Osborn kept his crippled, lumbering turboprop airborne while the crew destroyed sensitive equipment so that it couldn't be taken by the Chinese. Uninvited, he executed an emergency landing on China's Hainan Island. The Chinese pilot was not so skilled; his jet plummeted into the sea. The U.S. Navy flight crew spent two weeks in custody before Bush issued a statement apologetic enough to win their release.

Early in the crisis, Rumsfeld set out three major goals: Do nothing to hinder the State Department negotiations to free the crew. Review military-to-military contacts with Beijing. And fend off suggestions from the State Department's intelligence and research branch that the flights should be stopped or curtailed. Rumsfeld received immediate briefings on the mission's history. It was a fairly complex operation. The EP-3's powerful receivers reached deep inside Chinese territory to suck up streams of military conversations, radar signatures, and any other electronic spewing. The aircraft has sophisticated computer programs to instantly process and catalogue the intercepts. Higher up, a U-2 spy plane took pictures. And below, a Navy spy ship downloaded all the intelligence and sent it back to the NSA. Because it's a turboprop, the EP-3 has limited altitude and thus must come as close to the Chinese mainland as possible to intercept communications. State's intelligence people thought the excursions were becoming too dangerous and had antagonized Beijing. Rumsfeld lobbied the president to resume the flights once the crew got out. A senior Pentagon official told me that while China lost a fighter and a pilot, it gained an intelligence windfall. The American crew did not have sufficient time in the chaotic minutes between the collision and the landing to destroy many of the hard drives, where the eavesdropping computers store, process, and relay the intercepts to ships. The Chinese now know which emitters the U.S. targets and how it processes them. This enabled them to take countermeasures by making discussions on those nets more secure.

With no political appointees onboard, Rumsfeld turned to a long-term civil servant to keep him abreast of EP-3 developments. Daniel J. Gallington quickly got a taste of the piquant Rumsfeld management style. Gallington saw a genius at work, a shrewd CEO who used insults, humor, and penetrating questions to fetch the best data quickly. A thirty-eight-year government employee who was top legal counsel to the Senate Intelligence Committee, Gallington had worked for all sorts of Washington characters. They included fierce neoconservative Richard Perle and Caspar Weinberger, Ronald Reagan's bantamweight defense secretary. But none of these egos properly prepared him for Rumsfeld. Gallington arrived at the Pentagon on April 2, three days after the Chinese fighter rammed the Navy spy plane. He essentially became the secretary's policy chief, since Douglas Feith's Senate confirmation remained months away. Gallington, who greatly admires the man, remembers one of his first Rumsfeld encounters. "I went in to brief him and I had lots of details on what was going on. But he didn't seem at all interested in what I was saying.

I was troubled by that. I thought, 'There's something I'm not doing right here.'" He asked Rumsfeld, "Do you find any of this helpful? He said, 'Absolutely none of it.'" Gallington had never heard a superior dismiss his briefings quite so bluntly. Stunned at first, he replied, "We don't spend our time trying to irritate you. We're trying to help you. Can you give me some idea of what you want? He looked at me and said, 'I'm not sure what I want.'" With that Gallington returned to his office. He worked harder to provide even more details and options. He realized Rumsfeld had been out of government for three decades. He knew little about EP-3 excursions. He needed a baseline first, then more details. "I had learned right away, you need two things to work successfully with him," Gallington says today. "You need a good sense of humor and thick skin."

Gallington tried the comedian route once, only to see it backfire. He was preparing so many briefings for Rumsfeld he did not have time to order up printed graphics. Instead, he used a colored marker to create slides, then rushed back to the secretary's office. As he moved to the next slide, Rumsfeld remarked, "That's the dumbest thing I've ever seen." Gallington quipped, "'Wait until you see this.' And I flipped over to the next slide." There was no laughter. Rumsfeld told Gallington he was not there to entertain him. "I said, 'I'm here to brief you and I'm going to do it if it kills me,'" Gallington recalls. "He said, 'It may.'"

Gallington was swept up into Rumsfeld's ungodly working hours. His wife packed him a substantial lunch, enough food to munch on over fourteen hours as he sat at his desk. Still, the robust Gallington shed twenty-seven pounds in just three months, his weight dropping to 158. "I would not go home because anything was done. I would go home because I was exhausted," he said. Gallington became caught between two loyalties. Rumsfeld demanded fourteen-to-sixteen-hour workdays; Gallington's wife insisted he go forward with a promise to get a vasectomy. Gallington kept his appointment that day at Johns Hopkins. But instead of going home to rest, he went back to the Pentagon. He had brought along several chemical ice packs and placed them on his lap, one after the other, to soothe the incision as he worked.

Rumsfeld managed the EP-3 crisis detail by detail. His first countermove—and the signal to Beijing that a new guy was in charge—was to suspend all military-to-military contacts with China. Then he reviewed each program of U.S.-China military contacts—and there were hundreds of them. Gallington filled a thick binder with each program liaison and created a cost and benefit analysis for every program.

American officers got the message that Rumsfeld was in charge, and that contacts with the Chinese weren't a good idea. Chinese embassy military attachés in Washington had made a practice of passing out authentic Chinese whiskey when they visited the Pentagon, according to one three-star general who stopped accepting the gift. "It was horrible stuff anyway," he said.

The Chinese also got the message that Rumsfeld was going to be tougher than the Clinton-era defense department. "He wanted the PRC to understand that he, Don Rumsfeld, was managing the day-to-day military programs," Gallington says. "Some had been going on autopilot for years."

Two weeks after the EP-3 had made its forced landing, China released the crew. Several weeks later, the EP-3 flights resumed, as Rumsfeld wanted and the State Department didn't. The defense secretary had won his first battle with Foggy Bottom.

GUERRILLA WARFARE

It did not take long for an anti-Rumsfeld insurgency to organize in the Pentagon and across the river on Capitol Hill. By the spring,

Deputy Undersecretary of Defense for Policy Stephen Cambone was demanding force structure cuts, with briefing charts that showed how the Army could cut two divisions, about 40,000 soldiers. The Navy could afford two less carrier battle groups. Maybe the Air Force didn't need the new F-22 stealth fighter. "Why not a move to unmanned fighters?" Rumsfeld's people asked. No one was more vulnerable in these internal food fights than the Army. Outsiders, including Gingrich, were telling Rumsfeld that the Army was too heavy. It couldn't get to the fight. It needed a total overhaul. The Air Force was basically on the right track. It continued to push the envelope by inventing more precision-guided munitions, a Rumsfeld favorite. As an ex-Navy pilot, Rumsfeld knew the power of a carrier group, and Navy officers were confident they could convince him not to cut their eleven carriers.

But the Army was another story. General Eric Shinseki, a wounded Vietnam War hero, had already announced his version of Army transformation a year before Rumsfeld arrived. Some units would get lighter, but the basic mainframe would stay in place. When Rumsfeld and Shinseki met that spring, they talked past each other. The secretary wanted new ideas. Shinseki said he had put the Army on the right course. "It was a dialogue of the deaf," said a senior Army officer who was briefed on the meeting.

Shinseki had already gotten off to a rough start on the seemingly innocuous issue of hats. His transformation plan included a mandate for every regular soldier to switch his or her green cap for a black beret. The order stirred up a mutiny within special operations and airborne ranks. Heretofore, they were the only beret wearers. Congress got involved. Some lawmakers personally lobbied the president to intervene. To make matters worse, it turned out the berets would be made in, of all places, communist China. When Wolfowitz came onboard that February as the first Rumsfeld aide to win confirmation, the hat issue was so hot that Rumsfeld had to take him away from more pressing budget matters to manage the beret brouhaha. Finally, Wolfowitz and Shinseki announced a compromise. Army Rangers, the lone black beret wearers, would get new tan headgear. And no berets would be procured from Beijing. Thousands already bought were stuffed in a Defense Department warehouse in Pennsylvania.

Sensing that his plans were in trouble, Shinseki turned to Lieutenant General Kevin Byrnes to do battle with Deputy Undersecretary Cambone. The Army considered Byrnes one of its brightest stars. A product of public colleges, not West Point, Byrnes overcame his non-academy background to excel as an artillery officer, scholar, and teacher. He did a combat tour in Vietnam, attended two Army colleges, and commanded the vaunted 1st Cavalry Division at Fort Hood, Texas. At the Pentagon, he proved himself a master of bureaucratic infighting. Before going off to command the 1st Cavalry, Byrnes had survived a baptism by fire in the 1997 Quadrennial Defense Review. Then–Secretary of Defense William Cohen's people had wanted to trim two active Army and four National Guard divisions. It was Byrnes's job to protect them. He drew up analytical studies to show why a two-division loss would increase risk of combat deaths to soldiers and spread the Army too thin. In the end, Cohen backed off. The Army stayed at ten active divisions.

By the time Cambone arrived, Byrnes and the Army were well practiced in the QDR drill. But this time, the new boys on the block played rougher. They were under orders to rein in the generals, and Byrnes would find himself the target of a Rumsfeld lasso. Byrnes and Cambone had a number of heated exchanges. Byrnes argued that the Army had gotten even busier since 1997. He came to meetings prepared with charts and studies. Word got back to the secretary that Byrnes was uncooperative. Rumsfeld rarely forgets what he considers a slight.

Newly appointed Army secretary Tom White wasn't faring much better. When the Enron scandal broke, White was the only administration appointee who had been a big player there. Democrats pummeled the retired Army general with all kinds of accusations, none of which proved true. Then White got snagged in an internal investigation of his use of government airplanes. And the Senate Armed Services Committee publicly criticized him for not selling his Enron stock. Through all of this, White was trying to decide whether to support Shinseki or Rumsfeld in the battle over reforming the Army.

By May, Rumsfeld was hearing strong rumblings that Congress did not like his standoffish style. Lawmakers had a big stake in the $350 billion defense budget, but Rumsfeld's people were not consulting them. The politicians heard only lectures from the secretary about how Congress intruded into his affairs. Worse, some Republican staffers traveled to the Pentagon for job interviews and were told to get lost. The buzz on the Hill was that Rumsfeld dismissively referred to lawmakers as "hillbillies." Rumsfeld, through spokesmen, denied he used such a word. Trent Lott, the then–Senate majority leader who liked to play in defense issues, had had enough. He ordered his staff to schedule what is called a "Come to Jesus Meeting." The Republican Knights of the defense budget—Lott, Appropriations head Ted Stevens, and Armed Services chairman John Warner—would have Rumsfeld over to the Capitol for a little chat.

Rumsfeld has firm ideas about the chain of command. He believes that the secretary of defense—not Congress, not the Joint Chiefs, not the service secretaries—runs the Pentagon. Early on, he reached an accommodation with General Myers, the Joint Chiefs chairman. The Goldwater Nichols Act gave the chairman broad power to advise the president separately from the secretary. Myers, however, agreed not to go around Rumsfeld. Rumsfeld was not going to give any ground to Congress either.

Rumsfeld sat defiantly as Lott ticked off a list of grievances. Lott said that sources inside the Pentagon were telling him of an "us versus them" mentality among Rumsfeld's people. Rumsfeld aide Stephen Herbits, in particular, was telling job applicants of an impending "war with Congress." Lott warned that without cooperation, Rumsfeld had little hope of getting his reforms passed. Herbits, a gay rights advocate who contributed to Democratic political campaigns, was turning down too many good applicants. The list was long. Defense industry executives who backed Bush have no voice in the Pentagon. Congress was the traditional talent pool for a new administration. But these staffers felt insulted by Herbits during job interviews. Lott told Rumsfeld that his Pentagon was dysfunctional, and that he needed to conciliate Congress now before things got worse.

But he got no assurances from Rumsfeld. When the defense secretary left, the senators tossed around the word "arrogant" to describe their fellow Republican.

Lott attempted other maneuvers. He met with Powell Moore, Rumsfeld's top lobbyist, and complained of deteriorating Pentagon-Congress relations. He summoned Wolfowitz, assuming he would be more willing to work with Congress. And he quietly put a temporary hold on all Defense Department nominees. The list included Moore, Torie Clarke as Pentagon spokeswoman, Pete Aldridge as procurement chief, Charles Abell as a department personnel official, Dov Zakheim as comptroller, and William Haynes as general counsel.

None of these maneuvers worked; in fact, dynamics got worse. Rumsfeld decided to cut the fleet of B-1B bombers, but did not tell the affected congressional delegations. Bush flip-flopped on his campaign pledge to keep open the Navy's bombing range on Puerto Rico's Vieques Island. At the very moment Navy Secretary Gordon England was preparing to brief relevant lawmakers, the White House leaked the news to the TV networks. "They cut England off at the knees," said a congressional aide. Then came the Crusader debacle—terminating a jobs-producing program of building a new artillery vehicle just weeks after endorsing it in the president's budget.

Weeks later, I asked a longtime Washington lobbyist about Rumsfeld's relationship with Lott, Warner, and Stevens. "I don't think you will see them out socializing," the lobbyist said.

One of Lott's former aides did not fare any better. When the Pentagon telephoned Sam Adcock to set up a job interview, he though it was just another in a string of screenings that would eventually land him a senior post. When the interview ended, Adcock found out just how hard a brand of hardball the new Rumsfeld team played.

If anyone seemed a perfect fit for an incoming Republican administration, it was Adcock. He didn't need a road map to know every twist and turn the yearly defense bills took through the Armed Services and Appropriation committees. For years, he had worked for Trent Lott as his eyes and ears on defense. One of his jobs was to watch the Navy's shipbuilding budget to make sure Lott's home state of Mississippi and its largest employer, Ingalls Shipbuilding, received its fair share of contracts. In his spare time, Adcock worked for the Republican Party, both locally in Virginia and nationally where the party needed him. Adcock planted GOP campaign signs in his front yard every election season. Post-Lott, he worked for European Aeronautic Defense and Space Company Inc., a giant French-Italian arms maker. Like Ingalls, EADS wanted a share of the multi-billion-dollar Pentagon budget. It was Adcock's job to make that happen. By the winter of 2001, Adcock had the résumé to win a job as the Navy's assistant secretary for acquisition—the chief shipbuilder. But he ran aground once he met Stephen Herbits.

Herbits, who had had Republican connections in the past, had advised Rumsfeld in 1976 and had helped pick new people when Cheney became defense secretary in 1989. So in 2001, Herbits was

back in the fold as a per diem consultant in an office not far from
Rumsfeld's. But twenty-five years after he had first helped Rumsfeld,
Herbits had developed a new public profile. In an administration
stressing family values, Herbits was openly homosexual. He had
helped organize the modern gay rights movement, a particularly
anti-Republican crowd. He had made a small fortune as a Seagram
executive by finding ways to market liquor, especially to the well-
heeled homosexual community. Politically, Herbits opened his wal-
let for Democratic candidates. He even contributed to Al Gore's
recount effort in Florida. In other words, he had wanted Gore to win,
not Bush, the man who technically employed him.

This, then, was the face-off. Herbits, a Georgetown- and Tufts-
educated gay activist, versus Adcock, a Mississippi native and Republican conservative. Adcock did not know it then, but Herbits held a
special distaste for Lott. While Herbits championed gay rights, Lott
had helped defeat Clinton's bid in 1993 to allow open homosexuality in the military.

Herbits opened the interview by telling Adcock he had tried to
kill his application three times, but it kept coming back. "You've got
as much horsepower behind you as anyone I've come across," the
interviewer said. "But what you've got to ask yourself is: Why you
want to do that? The reason I say that is before you push to that point
you've got to understand how it's going to go." Herbits said if Adcock
persisted, he would probably get the assistant secretary's job. But
then came the hardball. Herbits said he would see to it that Adcock's
office was moved from the fourth floor to the basement. He would
have ethics lawyers force him to recuse himself from any shipbuilding issue. "You won't be able to play in the game," he said. Adcock
countered that the new Navy secretary, Gordon England, came
straight from General Dynamics, which builds ships. Herbits then
said Adcock lacked the operational experience, and that he would

help him get a lower-profile job and to come back and see him in three years. He said pressing for the job would hurt Lott, not help him. Adcock said Herbits was wrong. He had all the right experience to supervise acquisition. But, he concluded, "If I'm not wanted, I'm not going to push."

Adcock left the Pentagon angry and disgusted with his treatment. He began telephoning his supporters, including Lott, to tell them it was a no-go. Lott asked if it was "about me." Adcock answered, "My sense is it's not about me." Adcock figured Lott at some point must have called Rumsfeld. Days later, Adcock's cell phone rang while he worked in his downtown Washington office. It was Rumsfeld. The secretary said he understood Herbits had mistreated him. Adcock decided to take the high road. He declined to criticize the head-hunter, and told Rumsfeld he just wanted to contribute to the administration. Rumsfeld left it at that, though he later counseled Herbits to be more diplomatic in his interviews.

GUNS OF AUGUST

By August, with the QDR deadline bearing down, Rumsfeld settled on his two next steps to win troop cuts. On the first Saturday of the month, he convened a meeting of the three-stars he had shunned earlier. He offered them a secret deal, wanting them to confide in him. He asked them to spell out the programs they knew were expendable, but had defended because of political pressure from the Hill or from within the Pentagon. If the brass would identify these programs, Rumsfeld would take the blame for canceling or cutting them. "I will do it later and take the heat," the secretary said. "I can help you transform—get you out of political deals on stuff you don't want."

No one dared offer up any system of any importance. So Rumsfeld next went to the service secretaries and the Joint Chiefs themselves for a final showdown on the QDR. The setting was his conference room on a muggy August Saturday. One of Rumsfeld's rules is "Prune—prune business, products, activities, people. Do it annually." Rumsfeld was sure this rule would help cure what ailed the Pentagon.

Cambone was there, alongside Army Secretary Tom White, Navy Secretary Gordon England, and Air Force Secretary James Roche. Roche, like Rumsfeld, was a blunt-talking ex-Navy man, though he made it a point to tell people he was a Democrat, not a Republican. Rumsfeld had hand-picked each one principally because all three men had extensive experience running a business. Roche had been an executive with Northrup Grumman; England had been an executive with General Dynamics; and White had been, unfortunately, an executive at Enron. Rumsfeld wanted the Pentagon commanded like a profit-conscious corporation, from the top down. But the meeting, as one participant later described it, was "tortuous and painful." The troika of service secretaries had banned together to fight any more post–Cold War cuts. White, whose Army already had lost eight of eighteen active divisions since the Berlin Wall fell, said that if Rumsfeld's aides wanted to take another whack at the Army they should first scale back commitments. Soldiers were far-flung across the globe, stretched to the breaking point. That summer, Shinseki had told Congress the Army needed 40,000 *more* soldiers, not 40,000 fewer. "Given today's mission profile, the Army is too small for the mission load it's carrying," he said.

With the meeting going badly, Rumsfeld stunned those in attendance. He stood up and abruptly walked out of his conference room without saying a word. The service secretaries looked at each other, wondering if the meeting was adjourned. It was. A few days later, Rumsfeld tried a new tactic. He sent questions out to the services designed to get them to identify places in the world where they could make do with fewer forces. For example, could the Army defend

Europe with fewer heavy armored divisions? Did the Navy need a carrier battle group in the Mediterranean Sea full-time?

The answers were still being formulated on September 11, 2001. Days later, Rumsfeld produced a new QDR that kept the current force structure intact. But he created wiggle room for future cuts by changing the military's overriding mission. It was no longer structured to fight and win two regional conflicts simultaneously. Instead, it would win and conquer in one, while turning back, but not occupying, an enemy in the second.

POWER GRAB

As Rumsfeld completed his first year, he began to capitalize on the power he was accumulating. His nationally televised press conferences during the Afghanistan war had propelled him to mythic status among the American people. He was still not popular in Congress, but no lawmaker, except for an occasional complaint from Senator Warner of Virginia, challenged him. Rumsfeld dove into every issue, from officer promotions to the Pentagon's senior dining room operations. He started doing something unprecedented for a defense secretary. He interviewed officers up for two- and three-star promotions. Traditionally, only four-stars got such scrutiny. Rumsfeld's argument was that if he had to send their names to the Senate for confirmation, he should know for whom he was vouching. Service secretaries suddenly lost the prerogative of appointing senior staff. When Tom White wanted to name a three-star to run the Army staff, Rumsfeld had to approve the general. White told colleagues that if he had known about the Rumsfeld straightjacket, he would not have taken the job.

Rumsfeld also wanted more control over the network of dining rooms where top generals and officials ate. When he arrived, each service operated its chow lines as individual fiefdoms, with various rules and prices. A memo went out declaring, "The secretary of defense has expressed his desire to establish a Pentagon Senior Leadership Dining Facility (PSLDF) as the sole consolidated dining facility for senior leadership in the Pentagon."

With his first war victory under his belt, Rumsfeld had more time for play. He joined the Pentagon Athletic Club (POAC) and tried to break away three or four evenings a week for a vigorous game of squash, a lifetime passion. His usual partner was Larry Di Rita, an ex-Navy officer who had battled for conservative causes as a Heritage Foundation analyst before joining the staff of Senator Kay Bailey Hutchison and then Rumsfeld's staff at the Pentagon. One January day, a policymaker was in the POAC preparing for his match when Rumsfeld and Di Rita entered the locker room after theirs. The worker mischievously asked if the older secretary had held his own with the younger Di Rita. It's no secret that Rumsfeld does.

Rumsfeld still plays with the sport's "hard ball" even as the lords of the game are moving toward a softer ball that results in a slower-paced game. Rumsfeld is like a golfer who sticks to his persimmon woods when everyone else's bag sports titanium. "That's part of my problem," says Thomas Miller, the U.S. ambassador to Greece who teamed with Rumsfeld in the 1983 Middle East mission. "I play with the soft ball. I'm not making excuses. He did beat me."

Said his old friend Ned Jannotta, a frequent contestant at the Chicago Racquet Club, "When you play with him, you are lucky not having your head taken off with his racquet. The court is a finite place. If you are between him and the wall, Rumsfeld always fires away, even if you're in the way. Rummy is always very competitive." Another Rumsfeld opponent is Jannotta's son, Ross, who is some thirty-five years his junior. "Rummy likes to think he can beat my son with regularity," Jannotta says. "He said, 'I beat Ross. I beat Ross in two games.'" Of his friend's persona, he says, "Some people would read it as cocky. I would say it's confidence. He doesn't wilt from many things."

Jannotta said that as the hard ball became scarcer, Rumsfeld called the racquet club and asked them to find and acquire every hard ball it could find. The club came up with sixty dozen. "He said 'I'll take them.' So now he's got hard balls for the next forty years," his friend said. Asked about his new stash, Rumsfeld told me, "I hope I can use every one of them."

After the Afghan war, Rumsfeld and his staff made a series of decisions that endeared them to social conservatives and military traditionalists. In March, Rumsfeld approved a major downsizing of the Defense Advisory Committee on Women in the Services (DACOWITS). The Clinton administration had stacked the panel with scores of feminists, who repeatedly pestered the services to open more combat jobs to women. Elaine Donnelly, who runs the pro-military Center for Military Readiness, pressured the Rumsfeld team to rein in DACOWITS. It agreed, appointing all new members to a downsized board and writing a new charter that focused its mission on improving the quality of life in the military. Next, Rumsfeld's staff pressed the Army to take women out of a new unit called Reconnaissance, Surveillance and Target Acquisition (RSTA). Again, Donnelly was the primary mover. She argued that women's placement in RSTA violated the ban on women in land combat. In July, Bush political appointees in the Navy overturned a Clinton decision and approved a post-retirement promotion for Captain Robert Stumpf, a renowned F-18 pilot who flew some of the first missions near Baghdad in 1991. Clinton appointees had blackballed Stumpf because he had attended the 1991 Tailhook gathering of Navy pilots that was marred by lewd and drunken behavior, leading to a major political witch-hunt against pilots who were there. Though Stumpf had been cleared of all wrongdoing, the Clintonites still denied his promotion. The Bush administration undid that injustice.

Rumsfeld's second budget went over to the Hill in January 2002. The problem for some military reformers was that nothing was missing. Candidate Bush had promised to cut big weapons systems to capitalize on more advanced technologies in the next decade. But the new budget funded all the big systems inherited from Clinton. Cambone and Wolfowitz had been scrutinizing the Army's $11 billion Crusader artillery vehicle. Belatedly, they decided this would be *the* system to terminate, even as the budget sent to Congress endorsed it.

Wolfowitz summoned Army Secretary White to his office and gave him the news. White protested and was told the Army had a few weeks to do another study to justify the weapons. Meanwhile, over-exuberant Army staff sent out faxes calling on lawmakers to repeal the decision against the Crusader, an act of political insubordination.

"My goodness, no," Rumsfeld told reporters, when asked if he planned to fire White. Even the White House was forced to weigh in. "The president has confidence in Army Secretary White," declared press secretary Ari Fleischer. Days later, Wolfowitz certified the Crusader's termination. White was ordered to appear with the deputy secretary at a news conference to formally bury the project. He did as ordered. Later, the phone rang in White's office. Rumsfeld had watched the news conference on TV. He told White he did not like his performance. "Your body language was wrong," Rumsfeld said. "You are not sup-porting the decision." White responded that that was "nonsense." But Rumsfeld and his Army secretary were on a collision course.

Rumsfeld turned seventy that summer. He was both the youngest and oldest defense secretary in history. As an interview ended a few days before his birthday, I asked him if he had any special plans. His response was classic Rummy. He decided to imitate an old man: Hunching his body, he grabbed an imaginary cane and moved forward gingerly, adopting the cracked voice of the aged. "If I can make it home today," the voice said. The skit done, he said, "No, nothing special. I played squash last night, though." He said he had managed a tie against a much younger opponent, who happened to be sitting in on the interview.

For his wife, Joyce's, seventieth birthday on September 18, 2002, Rumsfeld surprised her by presenting her with a book written by none other than her husband. In his spare time, between conducting and planning wars, he had compiled family photos and written narratives to describe the scenes. He had it printed in brown hardcover and handed out thirty-five copies to his wife, their three children, and other family members. *Joyce Rumsfeld: A Joy to the World* shows the two dating at New Trier. "There was no commitment," it quotes Joyce as saying. "But there was never much doubt in my mind." There is a photo of Rumsfeld as a young Navy officer, a lit cigarette in his right hand, sitting with Joyce. There's one of a vacation in the Dominican Republic with Henry Kissinger. Rumsfeld wrote in the introduction, "It was conceived and fashioned with the hope that those who come along in the decades ahead will have some sense of what went before—that they will each have the opportunity to experience at least a peek into the life of their very special grandmother or great-grandmother."

Said friend Ricky Silberman, "Don told me, 'There will be many books about me and nobody is going to write a book about Joyce.' He put together a book with pictures. He wrote it himself. In the midst of all of this, I think it's the most touching thing I've ever heard. He had a million other things to think about and to do, and I know very few men who would have taken the time and effort to do something like that."

That summer, Rumsfeld skirmished with the Office of Government Ethics (OGE). He had amassed an enormous fortune over twenty-five years of running companies and investing his money. Some friends placed his fortune in the tens of millions. In the private sector, Rumsfeld could invest where he liked. Once in the administration, however, he had to divest millions of dollars in stocks before he could start participating in key defense industry decisions. He completed the divestiture, but not before firing off a letter to OGE complaining of "excessively complex and confusing" disclosure forms. It had cost him $60,000 in accountant's fees just to fill them out. He told reporters that June, "They're so complex that no human being, college-educated or not, can understand them. . . . It is a long, expensive, befuddling process. I haven't got time to go through and look at every single one of those things. I end up signing it with a prayer and a hope and explaining that I've hired people to help do this."

In late summer, Lieutenant General Kevin Byrnes left his E Ring office for a chat with the secretary. It's the kind of meeting that happens scores of times in a defense secretary's tenure. A senior officer and secretary meet privately, one-on-one, to discuss promotion and a next duty station. But this was no usual meeting. Byrnes had challenged Cambone during the QDR, and Rumsfeld remembered. The secretary unleashed a tongue-lashing.

The Army wanted Byrnes to get a fourth star. It suggested one of three jobs: commander of Army Europe, vice chief of staff, or chief of the Training and Doctrine Command, a prestigious post that guides all Army preparedness issues. But Rumsfeld did not want to talk future jobs. He wanted to scold. He told Byrnes he had not been a team player during the QDR. He had been very difficult to deal with. Byrnes did not give in. He offered no apologies. His job was to present the Army's honest point of view and that's what he had done. Rumsfeld said he did not know what his plans were for Byrnes. Stunned, the general got up and left. Back at headquarters, he told colleagues his Army career might be over. A Byrnes confidant told me, "Rumsfeld was looking for guys who say 'Yes, Mr. Secretary.' General Byrnes is not going to do that."

When the Army brass learned of the rough treatment given to Byrnes, it launched a rescue mission. Army Secretary White was not confident. He had seen Rumsfeld reject other officers' promotions and not change his mind. White had been particularly stung on the nomination for the next supreme allied commander of NATO, a traditional Army job, though the retiring NATO commander was an Air Force general, Joseph Ralston. White nominated General Montgomery Meigs. Meigs had spent a good portion of his career in Europe and was the Army's top commander there. Besides, 90 percent of U.S. forces in Europe were Army. Logic said it was the Army's turn to regain the NATO prize. But Rumsfeld surprised the Army by picking the Marine Corps commandant, General James Jones, who had no Marine troops deployed on the ground in Europe. Some Army officials muttered that Rumsfeld was determined to do things differently just to be different.

Nevertheless, White sprang into action. He got an audience with Rumsfeld and explained that the QDR process had been rough on everyone. White's suspicion was that Cambone had bad-mouthed Byrnes to Rumsfeld. He explained that Byrnes was only doing his job. He was a loyal officer committed to the inter-service cooperation Rumsfeld demanded. White delivered the same message to Wolfowitz. In the meantime, Shinseki and other generals talked to General Myers and General Pace of the Joint Chiefs, who seemed to support Byrnes. After a few weeks, Rumsfeld relented. He sent Byrnes's name to the White House as the next commander of Training and Doctrine Command.

A year later, I asked a Rumsfeld aide about the Byrnes episode. The aide readily admitted that Rumsfeld had been wrong. "That's the thing people don't often realize," he said. "If you can show the secretary he is wrong, he'll change his mind."

Fall 2002 brought a new round of battles. It was budget season again and Rumsfeld was always looking for cuts. The Army again came under scrutiny. This time Shinseki's pet project—the Stryker family of armored vehicles—was a possible budget cut. One of the Stryker family's strongest foes was Newt Gingrich, who sent an email to Rumsfeld's staff, Vice President Cheney's staff, and the Army, complaining that the Stryker was not suitable to ride in a C-130 transport plane. "Stryker should either be cancelled or limited to one test brigade that will never be air transported but that could be used to test the new electronics." Rumsfeld eventually rejected his friend's advice and approved new Stryker brigades.

The next month, Rumsfeld continued to consolidate power by sending out a memo that seemed innocuous but carried a powerful message. For fifty years, regional military chieftains had proudly borne the title CINC—Commander in Chief. This is the same description the Constitution affords the president. Rumsfeld does not like acronyms. He especially disliked CINC because it conveyed a certain all-powerful authority. His October 24, 2002, memo stated, "Effective immediately, the title 'Commander in Chief' shall be used to connote or indicate the president of the United States of America." He permitted "CINC" on existing stationery "until supplies are exhausted." Earlier that year, Rumsfeld had purged the culture of another term: National Command Authorities. He found the phrase too imprecise because it could mean himself or the president.

Undersecretary of Defense Douglas Feith found Rumsfeld's aversion to acronyms so intense that he started counseling his staff to use nothing more obscure than NATO. "He doesn't like abbreviations to obscure a message, so he's sometimes really hard on abbreviations," Feith said. "I came away from some additional sessions with him telling my people no abbreviations more obscure than 'U.S.' and maybe 'NATO.' If you have any question about it, spell it out. After a while, you work with him enough and you know which ones he's comfortable with, but he doesn't like the idea, even when he knows an abbreviation, he doesn't like the idea that someone presumes that he knows the abbreviation. So he will sometimes stop a new person and make him explain an abbreviation even when I think he probably understands what it is."

That November, Rumsfeld summoned Stephen Herbits from Miami Beach, where he lived when he wasn't advising the Pentagon on personnel issues. At the two-year point, some senior civilians typically leave. It wasn't well known at the time, but Rumsfeld was thinking of firing Army Secretary White and wanted prospective candidates.

Herbits's arrival opened old wounds. During his summer in Miami, he had given an interview to the *Advocate*, a gay-oriented magazine. He ripped not only Trent Lott, but also the president's brother, Florida governor Jeb Bush. Herbits called Lott "corrupt," and accused the majority leader of bringing the nomination process of defense appointees to a halt. "To me, it was just a staggering abuse of power," Herbits said. "Lott was wrong and corrupt and was willing to jeopardize national security for personal political gain."

Herbits complained that the president's brother had refused to meet with him to discuss an anti–gay rights referendum on the 2002 ballot. It ultimately failed. "I was so offended that I went to Rumsfeld and said, 'I have to go home because I have to protect my kids from the president's brother,'" Herbits said. Rumsfeld asked, "Your kids?" Herbits answered, "Not my birth kids, but my kids who are struggling with their sexual orientation and have no one to take care of them."

Once Lott read the article, his aides called the White House to complain. But Herbits stayed put.

I'M A CIVILIAN

Rumsfeld began 2003 with one of his most incendiary snowflakes. One of his targets had been the Joint Staff, the Joint Chief chairman's personal army of planners. Rumsfeld thought a lot of their work overlapped his own. He also did not like some of the senior Joint Staff three-stars he had inherited. Since the Joint Staff was normally a stop on the way to four-stardom, Rumsfeld interceded in the chairman's traditional role of picking the Joint Staff senior leaders. By January, he turned his guns on the Joint Staff's flow of paperwork. There was too much of it, he thought.

He dashed off a terse memo to the Special Assistant to the Secretary of Defense, Larry Di Rita. "Please pull together a list of all those documents we talked about yesterday that the Joint Staff, the chairman and the vice chairman seem to think they have to put out on vision, strategies and all that stuff," Rumsfeld wrote. "We ought to get our arms around them, compare them with what we put out overall and get a single DoD document rather than a Joint Staff document. It is just a lot of people spinning their wheels doing things we probably have to edit and improve." In one brief snowflake, Rumsfeld had managed to insult the military's best and brightest.

Later that month, when a reporter asked about persistent reports that he and his staff treated officers roughly, Rumsfeld exploded. "The Constitution calls for civilian control of this department," he instructed. "And I'm a civilian." He made no apologies for rejecting or rewriting strategy papers. "I have received on occasion from people— military and civilian—work that I was not impressed with, and have indicated that. And there have been times when I've sent things back six, seven times. Why? Well, because it strikes me that it's terribly important that we do things well and we do them right. And I have sent things back on the civilian side, and I have sent things back on the military side. And I will keep right on doing it." Then he felt compelled to justify his direct style: "We have done so much in the last two years. And it doesn't happen by standing around with your finger in your ear hoping everyone thinks that's nice."

Later that winter, Di Rita was hosting one of his regular morning meetings to take the pulse of the building and convey the secretary's thinking. Di Rita was moving up fast. A Naval Academy graduate, Di Rita had been recruited from the Senate to temporarily handle legislative affairs, which brought him into contact with Rumsfeld. The new boss needed an executive assistant. He interviewed Di Rita, who got the job. Di Rita showed a willingness to work "Rumsfeld hours" and play Rumsfeld hard in squash. When Torie Clarke resigned, Rumsfeld made Di Rita his chief spokesman, giving the ex-Navy officer wide powers as PR man and executive.

At the Di Rita meeting that day, one of those in attendance expressed anger at the Air Force chief of staff, John Jumper, for remarks he made in a trade publication about a space-based radar. The comments were off-message and not consistent with the president's budget, the official complained. Later, Rumsfeld hosted representatives from each service to prepare for his congressional testimony on the 2004 budget. When a three-star Air Force officer gave his presentation, Rumsfeld lit into him for Jumper's remarks. Some participants tried to shrink into the walls as the defense secretary lashed out at such disloyalty. His message, while directed at the Air Force, was really sent to the entire Pentagon: I don't like disloyalty. "What do I say when a committee asks about the inconsistency?" he asked. No one on the committee did.

Newt Gingrich concedes that his friend's style can go overboard. "He's intimidatingly smart," he said. "If he has any one weakness, it is that he doesn't realize that for most people his ability, frankness, mental capability, is intimidating, and even for four-star generals he's very intimidating. I think that one thing that made Tommy Franks so successful was that Franks figured out in the second or third meeting that we just got to go toe-to-toe and disagree bluntly or I'll never get anywhere with this guy. And as a result they developed a very good relationship."

January marked an influx of memos from Andrew W. Marshall. Marshall is the director of the Office of Net Assessment; his job is to look at world threats and think up possible counterweights. He had also been one of Rumsfeld's chief advisers in learning the ropes when the newly appointed secretary returned to the Pentagon. Marshall sent a confidential memo to Rumsfeld extolling a "portfolio approach to strategy." Instead of one defense strategy, planners could pick and choose depending on what they wanted to accomplish. But Marshall complained that the Pentagon wasn't signing on to the idea. "The most striking thing to me was how resistant the people in the study group (mostly drawn from DoD) were to looking at strategy as 1) constructing a portfolio (especially that top-level managers' approach to strategy might in any way be different than at lower levels), and 2) pursuing advantages rather than focusing entirely on reacting to threats." Marshall attached a copy of a paper prepared by his study group at the Naval War College in Newport, Rhode Island. "At present, the United States holds a pre-eminent position in military power that may last for several decades," the paper states. "It should be able, therefore, to use this period to develop and implement strategies that exploit and extend that advantage.... Perhaps no nation has ever had such reach and capability, and strategies should focus on extending that advantage for the long term."

The paper met with ridicule in some Pentagon quarters. "Why not have a thousand strategies?" said one officer. But Rumsfeld, the man who always likes to look forward, not back, expressed delight at the new idea and disdain for those in the Pentagon who balked. "I was struck by Andy's cover memo pointing out how resistant people are to looking at strategy in a different way," he said later in a snowflake to senior staff, "and pursuing advantages, rather than focusing on reacting to threats."

Rumsfeld continued to want to challenge the Pentagon's thinking, and one way he would do that would be to shake up the staff. That put Army Secretary Tom White back in his sights.

SHAKEUP

Senator Carl Levin of Michigan sealed White's fate during a committee hearing before the March 2003 invasion of Iraq. He pressed the witness, General Shinseki, to estimate the size of a postwar occupation force. "Something on the order of several hundred thousand soldiers are probably a figure that would be required," the soon-to-retire general replied. The Army had fought cuts during the QDR, and advocated more ground troops for the war itself. Now Shinseki was bucking Rumsfeld's people again at precisely the time the administration was trying to douse projections of a large, costly occupation. Wolfowitz counterattacked a few days later, before the House Budget Committee. This "is not a good time to publish highly suspect numbers," he declared, in an obvious rebuke of Shinseki. He called the general's estimate "wildly off the mark."

White, like Shinseki, a Vietnam War veteran, again had a choice of siding with his general or with Rumsfeld. He backed Shinseki. Both men's time was short.

White had seemed like the perfect match for Bush. He was a Texan, a West Point graduate, a corporate dynamo, and a close friend of Colin Powell, who as Joint Chiefs chairman had chosen White as his executive assistant. White won the Silver Star, one of the nation's highest military honors, for rescuing a fallen comrade in Vietnam. The citation reads: "Upon observing a friendly soldier critically wounded by enemy fire, Lt. White dashed through a deluge of enemy automatic weapons fire to the nearby assault vehicle, procured a stretcher and supervised the evacuation of the wounded trooper. Lt. White's actions contributed greatly to the overrunning and destruction of the enemy base camp."

With Saddam ousted on April 9, 2003, Rumsfeld felt the time had come to fire White. Shinseki's term as Army chief of staff would end in June. The defense secretary would finally have his own man installed, not a Clinton appointee. Rumsfeld summoned White to his office in late April and told him he wanted his resignation. White obliged. The two agreed on an open-ended departure date. White wanted to leave around the same time as Shinseki. But White did not even enjoy a dignified departure.

A week after Rumsfeld fired White, the "Early Bird" reprinted another column, by pundit Robert Novak, critical of the secretary. White came off as the hero, the defense secretary as an anti-Army ogre. A Rumsfeld aide showed up at White's office with a message: Pack up now. White never asked his friend Colin Powell for help. He left the building quietly.

I can disclose for the first time that White's firing likely saved one of the Army's most controversial policies: training men and women recruits in the same units and barracks. Pro-military conservatives blamed the practice for poor discipline and lewd behavior. After sex scandals broke out across the Army's network of training bases, the Clinton administration hand-picked a commission to examine training. To the Clintonites' surprise, its own panel, headed by former senator Nancy Kassebaum, unanimously recommended abolishing mixed-sex training at the recruit level. The Army promptly ignored the recommendation, arguing that the policy encouraged unit cohesion.

But Congressman Roscoe Bartlett, a Republican from Maryland's conservative western panhandle, didn't let the issue rest. And when

Shinseki got entangled in the beret flap, he saw an opening. He proposed legislation to force the Army to abandon the idea of universal berets. White telephoned to see if the seventy-year-old Bartlett would drop the matter. The congressman proposed a deal: You get rid of co-ed boot camp and I'll drop the legislation. White agreed. Bartlett got Congressman Duncan Hunter, House Armed Services chairman, on the line to verify the deal.

White ordered his Training and Doctrine Command at Fort Monroe, Virginia, to do another study. The report essentially backed the co-ed policy. But it did concede that the practice was "not efficient." The Army secretary now had some internal basis on which to cancel mixed-sex training. But by then, the Enron flap and internal disputes had so weakened him he did not have the standing to battle feminists in Congress. With Bush not interested in the issue, Bartlett lost his last chance to fulfill the Kassebaum commission's recommendations.

The same month he fired White, Rumsfeld faced a crisis at home. His beloved wife had to undergo an emergency appendectomy. As she recuperated at home, Rumsfeld's fourteen-hour days shrunk by a few hours. One of Joyce's jobs had always been to make sure her husband took time off, her indirect way of making sure his staff could also go home to their families. Now, there was another reason for the man she calls "Rummy" to be home.

In June, White returned to Fort Myer, adjacent to Arlington National Cemetery and all its heroes, to attend Shinseki's retirement ceremony. Shinseki looked out into the audience, saw his friend, and said, "Thanks for your unwavering support of soldiers and the Army, for your friendship, and for being here today. When they call the roll of principled, loyal, tough guys, you will be at the top of the list." It is tradition for the defense secretary to attend the retirement of a Joint Chiefs of Staff member. Rumsfeld did not. Nor did any of his senior staff. "Our mentors understood that mistrust and arrogance are antithetical to inspired and inspiring leadership," Shinseki said at one point in his speech. "The Army has always understood the primacy of civilian control. We reinforce that principle to those with whom we train all around the world. So to muddy the waters when important issues are at stake, issues of life and death, is a disservice to all of those in and out of uniform who serve and lead so well."

A "Rumsfeld Rule" reads, "Develop a personal relationship with the chairman and each of the Joint Chiefs of Staff. They are almost always outstanding public servants. In time of crisis, those relationships can be vital." In the case of Shinseki, Rumsfeld had violated one of his own commandments. Two headstrong and principled individuals never clicked.

In the meantime, Shinseki's men were purged. The vice chief, General John Keane, who declined the chief's job for family reasons, retired. But before he left, he informed about a dozen two- and three-star generals—protégés of Shinseki—that they would retire too. Instead of tapping a current Army leader to replace Shinseki, Rumsfeld chose Peter Schoomaker, the retired general who had helped him redesign special operations. Rumsfeld had won the bureaucratic battle, but it took only a few months before the quiet cry in the Pentagon became, "Shinseki was right." The unexpected postwar Iraqi insurgency was killing American soldiers practically every day. The Gallup polling organization pegged Rumsfeld's approval rating at over 70 percent when the Iraq war began. But by fall, only 48 percent approved of how he was managing post-Saddam Iraq.

In October, Rumsfeld organized a brainstorming teleconference with his nine combatant commanders. He sat in the Executive Support Center, where he had sketched an early war plan in his head on September 11, 2001. The commanders talked from their various headquarters around the globe. Rumsfeld took notes as the generals and admirals—now all of them his appointees, not Clinton's—talked about the future. How do we keep score in a war with an enemy for which we have no head count? We need more good intelligence on al Qaeda's whereabouts. Can we do Iraq, Afghanistan, and the global war simultaneously? Rumsfeld spat it all back out in a snowflake that went to Wolfowitz, Feith, Pace, and Myers. It was classic Rumsfeld, posing devil's advocate questions to stir debate. Someone leaked the memo to *USA Today*, and the media played the story as, "Rumsfeld has doubts on war," or "Rumsfeld doesn't think U.S. is winning."

The *New York Daily News* reported that Bush planned to fire Rumsfeld and Powell. The story seemed ridiculous. But Rumsfeld aides were worried enough to telephone Andrew Card, the White House chief of staff. He assured them there was no truth to the *Daily News* stories. Rumsfeld aides decided the stories reflected gossip from mid-level administration aides.

Some of Rumsfeld's handpicked men began to leave, returning to academia or industry or think tanks to recharge their batteries "Rumsfeld is burning out a lot of people," said Bill Schneider. "Not many of them can go the distance. The hours are killing people. A lot of people are seeking relief through retirement. They all love the jobs. It's just a killer."

Rumsfeld visited Schneider's Science Board for its fall meeting. Some members noticed he seemed a step slower, more subdued than at the previous meeting in the spring. But in public, Rumsfeld remained cocky, confident. He would send no signals of weakness to Iraqi insurgents.

He had a number of victories to brag about. Overseas, the Taliban and Saddam were out of power. At home, Congress handed him new flexibility on hiring civilian employees at the Pentagon so that he could get more uniformed personnel out of the office and into the field. Congress also passed President Bush's $87 billion peacekeeping package for Iraq and Afghanistan—on Rumsfeld's terms.

The Pentagon, by now, has adjusted to his style. Rumsfeld identifies a problem, picks the people to solve it, then micromanages them until he determines they are on the right track. An example is his reorganization of special operations. He pressed General Charles Holland over a ten-month span to do what he wanted. He then kept an eye on Tampa to make sure it was carried through. "In locker room terms, Rummy is a towel-snapper," said a department official who has briefed him scores of times. "If he senses in someone that they're equivocal or uncertain, he'll figuratively pop their butt with his towel to see if they'll stand their ground or fold. If you mumble or try to fake an answer, he'll kill you. But if you look him in the eye and say, 'I should know that, but I don't. I'll get you an answer,' you're going to be okay."

That might be another Rumsfeld rule.

[CHAPTER 6]

COMBATING FUTURE THREATS

PRESIDENT BUSH'S INAUGURAL ADDRESS FOLLOWED THE TRADITIONAL SCRIPT: paying homage to the outgoing president before mentioning the continuing national security threats and what he planned to do about them. "We will build out defenses beyond challenge, lest weakness invite challenge," he said. "We will confront weapons of mass destruction, so that a new century is spared new horrors. The enemies of liberty and our country should make no mistake: America remains engaged in the world by history and by choice, shaping a balance of power that favors freedom. We will defend our allies and our interests. We will show purpose without arrogance. We will meet aggression and bad faith with resolve and strength." Bush did not single out individual threats, but his aides realized they needed new strategies against bin Laden and Saddam Hussein, as well as against the nuclear programs of Iran and North Korea.

Waiting for the new president at the Pentagon was an extraordinary, massive, and classified paper on future threats stretching to the year 2020, prepared by the Defense Intelligence Agency. The DIA is the Pentagon's own CIA in miniature. It sends agents around the world to collect information. In Afghanistan, for example, military intelligence officers are assigned to Green Beret A Teams to help them develop intelligence sources in the various villages where Taliban members hide. The DIA also boasts an analytical staff. In late 1999, the staff produced a tour de force: more than 160 pages of classified material and predictions on where American threats lie for the next twenty years. I obtained a copy of "A Primer on the Future Threat, the Decades Ahead: 1999–2020." It is stamped SECRET. NO FOREIGN. The report is still actively used in the administration today by people who own the required security clearance.

THE REPORT

There are chilling predictions. The radical Islamic state of Iran will have nuclear weapons by 2008—with missiles capable of striking Europe. China will more than quadruple its arsenal of intercontinental ballistic missiles capable of reaching the United States. The report says Israel owns deliverable nuclear and chemical weapons. Warring neighbors Pakistan and India, the report predicts, will continue to entrench themselves in the world's nuclear club by building more nuclear-tipped ballistic missiles. The DIA provides a scenario for how a war between arch rivals Greece and Turkey will play out. The report also says a number of countries are in danger of collapsing, including our neighbor Mexico.

The report begins with an unclassified letter from then–DIA director Lieutenant General Patrick M. Hughes. "While the message is sobering," he writes, "my intent in preparing this primer is not to instill fear or foreboding. Rather, I hope that by identifying and discussing in realistic terms the emerging threat environment, such knowledge will help leadership better understand and prepare for it." Besides containing sensitive classified information on the arsenals of enemy and friend alike, the report emphasizes certain sections by including notable quotes from an unlikely cast of characters, such as this one from hockey legend Wayne Gretzky: "I skate to where the puck is going to be, not where it has been." A page stamped SECRET discusses "nation state trends."

> State failure will be more common in the developing world. In the future, demographic and resource infrastructure pressures—in concert with poor governance—will increase the likelihood of fragmentation. The economic interdependence that already exists worldwide has proven to be both a benefit and hindrance to state viability. Though not a given, economic failure could become a precursor to state failure. The collapse of some key "risk" states such as Mexico, Saudi Arabia, Colombia and Indonesia, would have profound implications for the United States.

This section of the report also worries about our neighbor to the north, Canada, and its preoccupation with the Quebec question: "Quebec separatist efforts to achieve independence will continue to preoccupy the Canadian government, possibly diverting attention from security issues and international commitments."

A subsequent page labeled CONFIDENTIAL predicts refugees may swamp some regions in the next twenty years. "A single Palestinian state would not be able to accept consolidation of all Palestinians. However, significant numbers would attempt to return, creating [a] potential destabilizing factor for the region.... Candidates for new, large-scale refugee waves in the approaching years include Mexico, Colombia, Cuba, most of Central America, Algeria, Central and West Africa, the Caucasus, and Central Asia." The DIA warns that two current problems—drug trafficking and terrorism—might combine to produce more failed states, requiring U.S. intervention. "Drug related corruption will reach epidemic levels in certain countries," it says on a page stamped SECRET. "This may require a more direct response from the United States to protect our national security...." International terrorism is expected to remain a problem through 2020. The report makes this chilling prediction:

> It is probable that terrorist organizations or individuals will employ a weapon of mass destruction against U.S. interests by 2020. Heightened publicity about the vulnerability of civilian targets, an increased interest in inflicting mass casualties, emergence of less predictable groups and greater availability of WMD-related production knowledge and technology have already drawn the attention of some terrorist organizations. Additionally, the hoax or blackmail value of WMD is a potentially powerful psychological weapon in itself, and its future use can be expected to increase in the future.

The report says the Soviets developed a new kind of nerve agent and that since the collapse of the Soviet Union, the proliferation of this agent to other countries cannot be controlled through the 1997 Chemical Weapons Convention. Chemical weapons are easier to obtain than some terrorists might realize. "Many of the components needed for chemical or biological agent weaponization are used in other types of weapons systems, many of which are available in the international arms market," the DIA says in a section labeled SECRET. NO FOREIGN. "Chemical and biological agents can be disseminated by tube and rocket artillery, ground and naval mines, aerial bombs, submunition dispensers for aircraft, and a wide variety of spray devices. An increasing number of countries are also capable of employing unmanned aerial vehicles, cruise missiles and ballistic missiles for chemical and biological attack. Terrorist use should also be anticipated, primarily in improvised devices, probably in association with an explosive." The report then goes on to list countries that have the ability to launch a chemical weapons attack:

Currently, those countries that have a delivery capability for both chemical and biological agents include Russia, Iraq, China and North Korea. Iran has a chemical weapons capability and probably a limited biological agent delivery means. Libya, Egypt, India, Taiwan, Israel, South Korea and Syria have chemical weapons capabilities. In addition, Pakistan, Sudan, Serbia and Croatia are believed to have programs to develop CW capabilities. Moreover, Libya, Syria and Pakistan probably can produce biological agents on a limited scale and presumably have some means of delivery even if not by military systems.

On the nuclear front, a page stamped SECRET says more countries will possess nuclear weapons in the next twenty years. A classified chart predicts that Iran will have ten to twenty weapons. China's nuclear ICBM force will grow from forty missiles to as many as 220. Rivals Pakistan and India will more than double their nuclear stockpile. Stalinist North Korea may have ten atomic weapons by 2020. Israel will maintain an arsenal of about eighty warheads.

The threat will grow as more nuclear technology is used. Several factors, including international counter-proliferation agreements, general counter-proliferation agreements, general public/political opposition, and the fact that nuclear weapons technology is expensive and difficult to obtain, will preclude the widespread proliferation of nuclear weapons. Nevertheless, the number of countries acquiring nuclear weapons technology and materials will slowly increase into the next century.... Germany and Japan, which have developed their technology base and fissile material production base in support of their civilian nuclear power programs, could develop a nuclear warhead within a year should the political decision be made to pursue such capability.

Even though America's adversaries will increase their nuclear arsenals, the DIA predicts that the U.S. will remain the world's pre-eminent power for the next twenty years. "No state will be able to match the combined political, economic, military, cultural and, to a large degree, technological power possessed by the U.S.," the report says. "The key 'peer' candidates all have long-term larger problems, and none has the capability or the will to usurp the U.S. over this time frame.... The United States will remain the sole superpower through its economic, political, military, cultural and technological superiority for at least the first quarter of the next century." Still, the report says a "camp" of unaligned countries will continue to try to limit U.S. power. This camp includes Russia, China, France, India, Mexico, Iran, and Iraq. "The French routinely are at odds with the U.S. approaches and solutions in Africa and the Middle East. France sees this as a clash over French interests and as American meddling. Russia and Mexico have a distinct fear of outside interference. Mexico will continue to remain sensitive to perceived U.S. encroachment."

RUSSIA AND NATO

The report not only predicts events over the next twenty years, but also discusses current conditions (as of 1999). While some of these conditions have changed, the report details, in a classified manner, troubling trends that continue today. For example, corruption and organized crime remain rampant in Russia today. The report is particularly critical of former Russian president Boris Yeltsin—at precisely the time President Clinton praised Yeltsin as his country's best hope. "The bloated state bureaucracy is basically parasitic, demanding fees for ordinary decisions," the DIA finds. "Corruption is systemic and corrosive. Yeltsin has used the collection of *kompromat*—compromising materials—to control government personnel. Major Russian organized criminal groups have ties

COMBATING FUTURE THREATS 151

to national and regional government officials." The DIA makes this prediction:

> As central control disintegrates, a civil war could erupt within the Russian Federation.... Whether the military—or the Russian Interior Ministry's MVD troops for that matter— would protect the government in a crisis is questionable.... The social fragmentation inherited from the Soviet era has deepened, in part because the Yeltsin regime has deliberately exploited it to retain power. The government has withheld resources from areas of prime social importance: education, science, medicine, health, and the environment.

Concerning the Russian military:

> Russia's conventional forces are dilapidated, reeling from years of neglect. Despite some progress in downsizing and restructuring the conventional forces, the military reform process remains in limbo.... Given the magnitude of the armed forces' problems and the paucity of resources available to deal with them, the condition of Russia's military will not improve substantially over the next decade and in some areas could get worse. At the extreme, Russia's military could even face institutional collapse, punctuated by military unrest, mutinies and violent political intervention.

This decline, the DIA predicts, "leaves Russia with extremely unattractive options for dealing with the regional conflicts, territorial disputes, peacekeeping operations and terrorist threats that it will most likely face over the next decade." Because of the decline, "Beyond the next decade, prolonged political and economic difficulty probably will yield a chronically weak military that could do little beyond defend Russia's borders." The Pentagon says Russia's strategic force will also decline, but it will deploy a road-mobile SS-27 by 2005. "The prospects for Russia's submarine force look bleak for the next decade," says the reporting, adding that the country's stocks of sea-based ICBMs will dip below 400. The DIA concludes its chapter on Russia with this chilling possibility:

> A large-scale environmental/humanitarian disaster could bring on a nuclear accident, testing the government's ability to respond.... Security deficiencies involving WMD have left these inventories vulnerable to inadvertent transfer, deliberate proliferation, and seizure. This raises the possibility that an adversarial state or group could come into possession of such weaponry.

Concerning Europe, the report predicts that France will link up with Germany as leader of the continent. "The Germans will continue to need the French in some measure to conduct actions and make decisions in the European context that they cannot make alone for at least the next five to ten years."

One of the report's most interesting sections deals with a potential war between longtime rivals Greece and Turkey, probably sparked by their conflicting claims to the Aegean island of Cyprus:

> Athens and Ankara will continue to be unable to resolve the practical and political issues in the Aegean that underlie the tensions between the two countries. Both prefer to avoid war. Nonetheless, a crisis involving Aegean sovereignty issues on Cyprus could erupt and escalate into an unwanted conflict because of perceived provocative actions or miscalculations. In the event of hostilities, Turkey and Greece expect and plan for a short conflict (3–4 days) and assume that the international

community would intercede by then to stop the fighting. Such a conflict, which probably would start in the Aegean, would be primarily an air and naval fight with a Turkish attack on some of the smaller Greek islands in the Aegean and possibly a limited ground operation in Thrace. A conflict that begins in the Aegean would not necessarily spread to Cyprus, but such expansion should not be ruled out. Turkey is expected to hold a quantitative and qualitative edge on force capabilities, though Greece will make modest improvement to its air and air defense capabilities. Greek military equipment acquisitions in the coming years will lessen the prospects of a catastrophic defeat at the hands of Turkey.

The DIA adds this cautionary note: "If Greece and Turkey enter into conflict, one of the greatest miscalculations by both parties could be on the speed of entry of the international community. Greek and Turkish perceptions hold that any conflict would be short, partly because of outside intervention. The potential exists that any hesitancy by the rest of NATO to intercede could increase and lengthen hostilities."

The Pentagon questions just how long the predominately Islamic country of Turkey can remain a secular nation. Turkey's military, by tradition, will step in to run the country if a leader or parliament moves to end secular, democratic governance. "It is questionable . . . whether this dominance [by the secular military] can last, especially if the religious fervor continues to grow." By 2020, all of Europe will become part of NATO, creating new problems. "Further enlargement could easily have the disadvantage of creating an alliance that is increasingly difficult to manage due to the increased multiplicity of views and concerns."

CHINA

China has set its military on two different courses, according to the classified document. On the conventional side, it plans to reduce its 2.5 million People's Liberation Army (PLA) by 20 percent over the next twenty years. Active divisions will decrease from eighty-five to seventy; the tactical air force of fighter bombers and interceptors will shrink by half, from 3,684 to 1,550. The attack submarine force will be cut almost in half, from sixty-seven to thirty-five. But Beijing plans big increases in strategic forces and will deploy its first ballistic missile submarine. And, it plans a four-fold boost in spy satellites, to fifteen orbiters. A graphic shows the number of Chinese ICBMs capable of striking the U.S. increasing from forty to 220 by 2020. Yet, the DIA concludes, "Nothing indicates China will field the much larger number of missiles necessary to shift from a limited, retaliatory strategy to a first-strike, war-fighting strategy."

NORTH KOREA

Rumsfeld has said he hopes the U.S. can achieve regime change in North Korea without a shot being fired. The DIA sees little likelihood of this velvet revolution happening in the next two decades. "Though the possibility of leadership change cannot be entirely dismissed, the regime, with its enhanced security apparatus, appears firmly in control. The likelihood that North Korea will initiate a war to reunify the peninsula is diminishing, but the possibility of conflict spurred by internal instability, miscalculation, or provocation is increasing."

On the WMD front, the North possesses not only two to four nuclear weapons—of limited nuclear yield—but it also has an offensive biological and chemical arsenal. "Despite limited intelligence on the status of its biological warfare capabilities, North Korea is thought to have developed agents including anthrax, plague, cholera and toxins.... The size of the North Korean chemical agent stockpile is unknown, but is estimated to be between 2,500 and 5,000 metric tons. Many of North Korea's chemical weapons are stored underground, including in railroad tunnels."

THE MIDDLE EAST

The DIA projects that nuclear-armed Israel will maintain a military advantage over its Arab enemies. "Israel will keep its qualitative military edge over its adversaries. Israel's substantial conventional military lead, coupled with its strategic capabilities, will deter its adversaries from launching military operations."

Iran poses the biggest threat to the Persian Gulf, now that the U.S. has ousted Saddam. The DIA lists a number of aggressive moves Tehran might make as it works toward establishing a nuclear arsenal by 2008:

> Iran should have a greater capability to disrupt the flow of commerce in the Gulf over the next decade, primarily through the use of mine warfare and integrated anti-ship cruise missiles. In fact, absent U.S. intervention, Iran could close the Strait of Hormuz to maritime traffic indefinitely.

The most troubling development is Iran's Shahab-4 medium range ballistic missile and Shahab-5 intermediate range ballistic missile.

> An operational [Sahab-5] system could have the ability to reach all of Europe. Though currently its program goals are ambiguous, Iran could pursue a "Shahab-6" ICBM platform, potentially achieving an initial capability before 2010 with external assistance.... If Iran were to acquire enough suitable fissile material on the black market, it could develop a nuclear weapon capability within the first part of the next decade.

On the biochemical front, "Iran is seeking self-sufficiency in dual-use BW [biological weapon] agent production equipment, CBW [chemical-biological weapon] protective clothing and medical protection against BW agents." The DIA concludes, "Iran is slowly, but steadily building an offensive capability far in excess of its mere defensive needs."

The DIA views the Saudi royal family as "weakened" and perhaps ripe for an Islamic revolution:

> Over the next five to ten years, the Kingdom of Saudi Arabia will experience a rapid succession of changes, but U.S.-Saudi relations will remain viable. The Saudi regime will increasingly feel the threat of prolonged economic constraints and internal demographic resource tensions. Weakened government finances and declining living standards will pose a challenge to the Saudi government. Under opposition pressure, the regime will likely try to distance itself from the United States on a variety of policy and military issues.

CUBA

The Pentagon holds no hope that opposition groups can topple the communist regime of Fidel Castro. "Cuba's division-riddled and personality-dependent domestic opposition groups are unlikely to gain much future leverage, even in a post-Castro Cuba. The Catholic Church will support democratic reforms, but not regime-destabilizing activities. Cuban exiles lack the military capability or political support in Cuba to destabilize the island, but their activities could provoke a U.S.-Cuban military confrontation." The intelligence report discloses that there is a schism between Castro and his military commanders, who want more rapid Western-style economic reforms. The Cuban army is so cash-strapped that it will prevent the dictator from sending them overseas in any significant numbers during the next decade. "However, Cuban security forces are likely to remain fully capable of

COMBATING FUTURE THREATS 157

maintaining internal stability in the face of any spontaneous or organized domestic unrest."

WEAPONS PROLIFERATION

The report warns that rogue nations will redouble their efforts to obtain anti-ship cruise missiles. Poorer countries like "their relatively low cost, and the improving capability to precisely strike targets at long range, while at the same time countering defensive systems." The DIA predicts that India will field its first ballistic missile submarine before 2020. More troubling, both Russia and China are working to deploy laser weapons capable of blinding American pilots. "Air defense laser weapons, capable of blinding pilots and aircraft optical sensors, and inflicting structural damage to weapons platforms, are likely to be deployed by 2020 by Russia and possibly China. Some pilot-blinding weapons may be deployed earlier."

Concerning ballistic missile proliferation, the DIA predicts Iran and North Korea will joint the "ICBM Club" before 2020. China will have two new ICBMs in ten years. On shorter-range ballistic missiles, the report says, "Egypt, India, Pakistan, Saudi Arabia and perhaps Libya will have deployed [medium-range ballistic missile] systems, and WMD payloads will be available in each of these countries. . . . India, China, North Korea, Indonesia and Turkey will develop or acquire new SRBM [short-range ballistic missile] systems." The DIA's chilling projection: "Future conflicts probably will involve the use of these weapon systems with WMD, including nuclear weapons."

In space, future adversaries will have the ability to knock out vital U.S. communications and spy satellites. Russia and China will be able to achieve this capability "through jamming equipment, ground station attack, concealment and deception, information operations, direct-ascent anti-satellite weapons and directed-energy weapons. By 2020, the number of countries with some capability to interfere with satellite operations almost certainly will increase."

Another major challenge for the United States is potential enemies hiding their military assets underground, where spy satellites and conventional bombs cannot penetrate:

The proliferation of underground facilities (UGFs) in recent years has emerged as one of the most difficult and significant challenges facing the U.S. intelligence community and is projected to become even more of a problem over the next two decades. Increasingly, rogue states and other nations of critical interest to the U.S. are digging deep into mountains and below the surface of the earth to conceal and protect key programs—particularly WMD and missile delivery systems—as well as leadership, command, control and communications.

The continuing growth of deep underground facilities in Iran, Syria, Libya, India and Pakistan and the initiation of deep underground facilities in Iraq—currently only known to possess shallow underground facilities—is expected over the next two decades. All these countries have burgeoning WMD and ballistic programs, and they continue to incorporate deep underground facilities into these infrastructures.

In a report section on future warfare, the DIA reveals how al Qaeda–linked terrorists planned the assassination attempt on Egyptian president Hosni Mubarak in 1995, when he visited Ethiopia during the Organization of African Unity meeting. The planning shows the patience and cunning of bin Laden's people. "Operational planning began in early 1994, when an advanced planning cell moved to Ethiopia. Members of this cell blended in with the local population, married local women, and found work in the local economy. Their mission was clear from the start: to identify the best location from which to launch a terrorist ambush against President Mubarak's entourage."

The report also reveals that the U.S. military is under continuing attack from computer hackers, some of them from rogue nations. This is the so-called "information offensive" (IO). It is being developed by at least nine countries outside the United States: Russia, China, France, Israel, Germany, Sweden, India, Pakistan, and Cuba. "In the realm of IO, military facilities will not be the only targets attacked by the adversary; much of the national infrastructure that directly supports military operations may be vulnerable. Cuba, for example, has an avowed mission to use IO against non-military targets for political revenge if necessary."

Under a section entitled "Outlook," the DIA sees at least one favorable trend. "China is still twenty years away from developing large-scale regional threat capabilities." But there are frightening scenarios: "Chinese economic collapse brought about by a crisis in currency and banking. . . . A conflict either in India-Pakistan; Iran-Iraq; Israel-other; or North-South Korea escalates. One or several of these states—or terrorists—break the nuclear taboo."

It is unclear how much of this report was absorbed by Bush administration officials before September 11, 2001. But it is a certainty that they have absorbed it now, and that Secretary of Defense Rumsfeld has his own new ideas on how to meet these threats, ideas that motivate his continuing mission to enlarge America's special forces, improve American intelligence collection and analysis so that it is "actionable," and streamline the American military for war-fighting in the twenty-first century. The snowflakes are still flying, and the formulation of strategy is still in progress to address the threats predicted in the DIA report.

HUMAN SPIES

These aren't the only threats, of course. Rumsfeld is well aware that the United States has to do a much better job of public affairs, especially in the Islamic world, providing an alternative to the message of radical Islam. More tractable, and more important, is improving America's intelligence capability.

Daniel Gallington, the man who once tried to amuse Rumsfeld with his hand-drawn slides, is now an analyst at the Potomac Institute in Northern Virginia. He has spent a long government career looking at how the United States, its allies, and its enemies collect intelligence. Gallington's conclusion is that as America's advantage in high-tech snooping has widened over the last three decades, its recruiting and nurturing of spies has declined dramatically.

But it is "human intelligence" (HUMINT) that provides the best intelligence. Spy satellites can show a convoy of trucks leaving an Iraqi factory. The spy can tell you what's in them. Intercepted al Qaeda communications can tell you that a big attack is planned. The spy can provide the when and where.

"We rely far too heavily on high-tech, and high-cost, collections, to the expense of more mundane collections," Gallington said. "We are sitting on the most reliable and diverse society in the world but yet unable to use it to our advantage. We spend far too much time at embassy parties reporting stuff that we are fed. We don't have the patience to put together, over a fifteen- to twenty-year period, a worldwide HUMINT network." Gallington told me we should study the Chinese, French, and British HUMINT systems. China is known to send hundreds of visitors here each year whose main purpose is spying.

Gallington has two recommendations. First, put more CIA officers in the field to recruit agents in the Third World areas, where al Qaeda itself recruits. "No one wants to go to the Third World," he said. "The better assignments are the cocktail circuits in Europe." Second, the CIA has to subdue its worries about the personal histories of reliable sources. "No one expects deceit to be according to Marquis of Queensberry rules," he said. "You don't invest in someone's character or politics or criminal record when you pay him for information. You should be able to use him as long as he is valuable, lock him up when he isn't, or take him out of the relationship when he becomes a threat."

Retired Air Force Lieutenant General Thomas McInerney, a decorated Vietnam War fighter pilot and prominent Washington TV pundit, said, "You've got to get embedded in the mosques. You've got to get moles inside." McInerney has thought long and hard about how to win the global war. He has come to the conclusion that President Bush needs to launch a major government reorganization that would put all FBI and CIA counter-terrorism personnel into a new, Cabinet-rank agency. "We just need an entirely different culture," the retired general said. "This is a race against time because the threat wants to put nuclear weapons into U.S. cities and detonate them. They are very bad people. They are the worst we have ever had in our history."

BOOTS ON THE GROUND

Another obvious area of concern for the secretary of defense is the size of America's military compared to the missions it has to achieve. The armed forces now stand at just over 1.4 million active duty personnel, down one million from the heyday of the Reagan buildup. Republicans complained that the force was stretched too thin in the 1990s, when Clinton sent it on more than fifty missions ranging from wars to peacekeeping to humanitarian operations. Units complained of a lack of spare parts and training hours. Some recruiting and retention goals were missed. Today, President Bush has the military on an even faster deployment pace. He is also using the National Guard and Reserves in the highest numbers since the all-volunteer force was born in the mid-1970s.

Michael O'Hanlon, a Brookings Institution analyst who worked at the Congressional Budget Office, has done a comparison. At its height, the Clinton administration had about 100,000 troops deployed away from their families and home bases. This included 30,000 troops in Korea, 25,000 troops in the Persian Gulf, 20,000 troops in the Balkans, and Navy and Marine units at sea. Today, more than 250,000 troops are stationed away from home. Most of the increase comes from the 130,000 troops that are in Iraq and the roughly 10,000 that are in Afghanistan.

O'Hanlon believes the United States needs to bolster its armed forces by adding 50,000 Army soldiers, about two divisions' worth, and have them in place by 2005. New troops are expensive; O'Hanlon's plan would cost up to $8 billion annually. But it would allow Rumsfeld to better rotate troops in Iraq. "It is unfair to the average soldier to send them back to Iraq only after one year at home," said O'Hanlon, one of Washington's most prominent defense intellectuals.

"Even in these difficult times," O'Hanlon told me, "you never want to deploy active duty more than every three years, and Guard and Reserve more than six years." O'Hanlon argues that unless the United States increases the size of its military, "you're going to risk breaking the all-volunteer force and draining away these extremely talented people who now make up one of the best institutions in the country and the best military probably in the history of the world. It's not something done lightly. You start to have insufficient numbers of people with the proper training and specialties."

O'Hanlon said that if this scenario plays out, the only answer will be to dig up the draft from its 1970s burial ground. "We would be going back on one of the major accomplishments of the second half of the twentieth century: building this great volunteer force. The great accomplishment of Reagan, Bush, and Clinton would be discarded."

So far, there is only anecdotal evidence of troops opting out because of the busy counter-terror war. The services said in 2003 that they met recruiting and reenlistment goals. One advantage was the weak economy. In the roaring 1990s, the airlines in particular drew away military pilots, forcing the Air Force and Navy to offer more money to keep air wings manned. The September 11, 2001, airline hijackings badly crippled the industry, which shed workers. Military pilots mostly stayed put. But the airlines began a robust recovery in 2003. If the economy continues its bullish ways, service recruiters might face their toughest quota test in a decade.

RUMSFELD'S ANSWER

I interviewed Rumsfeld on a Saturday in early October 2003. As the door swung open, there he was in his customary work position—standing at his desk, a lectern beside him to support the myriad of paperwork he devours in a fourteen-hour day. He handed me one such document, a nine-page "working paper version number five." It dealt with the pros and cons of increasing "end strength," which is the total size of America's armed forces.

"For the present, analysis by the Joint Chiefs indicates that the U.S. military currently has sufficient active and reserve forces to execute its assigned mission," Rumsfeld had written on page one. "Increased end strength has second and third order effects. The more end strength, the more force protection that is required; the more end strength, the more infrastructure that is required. The more end strength, the more pensions and health care that are required."

Rumsfeld considers the 2003 increase in deployments a temporary "spike" that will decline once Iraq is subdued and some of his initiatives take hold. One such initiative is to turn more security details over to the Iraqis. Also, he points out, advances in joint operations and technology are allowing combatant commanders to do missions with fewer people. "Our use of precision weapons, with greater accuracy, can maintain lethality while reducing both the operational footprint and the logistics tail, thereby reducing force requirements," he wrote. He concluded, "The task of DoD is to manage the force within acceptable levels of stress. Key measurements are recruiting and retention metrics. We must monitor all activities to see that we achieve solid progress on each of the above tasks, before taking the easy and more expensive course of increasing force levels."

Next, Rumsfeld handed me a four-page briefing chart that listed his goals for the time remaining in Bush's current term. It also included what he considers his top accomplishments as defense secretary. There are more than eighty, including the ousting of the Taliban and Saddam. Among the others:

- Restoring readiness funding depleted in the Clinton years
- Creating a new command, Northern Command, to protect the continental United States
- Withdrawing from the stale ABM Treaty, thus paving the way for deployment of a ground-based missile defense system in 2004
- Altering the two-war strategy to free up troops
- Canceling the Army's Crusader artillery system
- Personnel reform legislation that enables him to move some 300,000 uniformed personnel from desk jobs to combat-related posts
- Increasing and empowering special operations troops

Further light on Rumsfeld's thinking came out in November 2003, when he toured Asia. He plans to restructure the 37,000 American troops in South Korea, so that they are removed from the tense demilitarized zone and from South Korea's capital of Seoul to garrisons farther south. He also conducted a town hall meeting with Marines in Okinawa. Questioned about Iraq, he answered, "It's a tough business but it's an important responsibility. I just say when I visit the troops out there, they are proud of what they're doing. They're confident that what they're doing is the right thing. And they recognize the importance of succeeding. I do believe we will succeed."

He then turned to the global terror war and what it will take to combat future threats. "It's a different world today," he said. "We have to become much more agile. We have to be able to move in hours or days instead of weeks or months or years. We have to have a mind-set that is willing to continuously go to school on the terrorists just as terrorists are going to school on us, and watching what we do and we've got to be able to move inside of their decision cycles and react sufficiently fast given the difficulty of intelligence."

Rumsfeld's statements on the global war against al Qaeda and its subsidiaries often return to the "actionable intelligence" he needs to send Delta Force to kill terrorists. He also worries about the "unknowns," the lurking dangers no one foresees. He is a disciple of Roberta Wohlstetter's 1962 book, *Pearl Harbor: Warning and Decision*, which documents the colossal failure to connect the dots on the impending Japanese sneak attack.

At his Senate confirmation hearing nine months before September 11, Rumsfeld eerily suggested Pearl Harbor might be repeated.

"We all know that history is filled with instances where people were surprised," he testified. "There were plenty of signals, plenty of warning, plenty of cautions. But they weren't taken aboard. They didn't register. They weren't sufficient to cause a person to act on those.... We know that the thing that tends to register on people is fear, and we know that that tends to happen after there's a Pearl Harbor, tends to happen after there's a crisis. And that's too late for us. We've got to be smarter than that. We've got to be wiser than that. We have to be more forward-looking."

Four months later, he dictated a memo to his staff. It contained excerpts from the foreword to Wohlstetter's book, with comments from the defense secretary. "I was born in 1932, the Great Depression was underway, and the defense planning assumption was 'no war for ten years.'" He told his staff that weapons proliferation and new technologies "are putting unprecedented power in the hands of small countries and even terrorist groups, foreshadowing changes beyond any ability to forecast."

On September 11, 2001, America suffered her second Pearl Harbor. The man who warned of it at his confirmation hearing, and who was at the Pentagon when the terrorist-hijacked plane crashed into it, is on the job, fourteen hours a day, directing armies overseas, fighting the interior bureaucratic battles, and working to transform America's armed forces to ensure that it doesn't happen again.

[AN ASSESSMENT]

IN THE SAME SPIRIT IN WHICH HE DASHED INTO A NARROW PAMPLONA STREET to run with the bulls, Donald Rumsfeld's first instinct on September 11 was to dash from his office to see what had happened. He helped the wounded and surveyed the damage. He did not know whether there would be further waves of attacks. Yet, he stayed on the lawn amid the chaos. Rumsfeld is, then, a brave man and an impetuous one. As George Bush's secretary of defense he has brought these qualities, for better or for worse, to the Pentagon.

Rumsfeld's task of reconfiguring the military and fighting the war on terror is so immense that it will take the light of history to determine exactly what he finally accomplished and at what he failed. Brought in by Bush because of his managerial zeal, it turned out his zest for battle was the real quality the president needed. On September 11, 2001, Rumsfeld told his commander-in-chief we were at war. Since then, he has not lost one ounce of determination to win the global war on terrorism and to simultaneously transform the armed forces.

Rumsfeld knew early on that this war's scorecard would not involve just taking territory. It demanded killing. The best way to eradicate bin Laden's savage operators was to exterminate them. He bluntly talked of this required chore, and soon all his generals were talking about it too. The Clinton era's political correctness soon lost one of its euphemisms. "We would be happy to capture them," Rumsfeld said in December 2003 as he explained his war plan to reporters in much the same way he had after September 11. "We would be happy to have them surrender. And if they don't, we would be happy to kill them."

Rumsfeld came back to Washington at a time of nuclear disarmament. Yet, he fiercely went against the grain. He urged withdrawal from the dusty Anti–Ballistic Missile Treaty so his Pentagon could build the world's first missile defense system. After September 11, he further infuriated arms controllers by studying a whole new family of nuclear weapons. Bush's doctrine of preempting terror attacks meant he had to get at terrorists' hiding places. And, as the secret DIA threats report noted, America's enemies are increasingly turning to Mother Earth to hide weapons of mass destruction. So Rumsfeld wants ground-penetrating nuclear bombs to get at them, if necessary. In theory, the bomb would bore deep beneath the surface while keeping the complex warhead intact. The resulting 350-kiloton blast would obliterate the threat.

Rumsfeld also rewrote Washington press relations. Conservative Republicans generally absorbed the media's barbs at press conferences, and rarely returned fire. Rumsfeld barked back. On one occasion, he ridiculed a reporter's suggestion that the Washington press corps was representative of America. He has a reputation as a straight shooter. But in practice, he can be evasive, as when he misrepresented Colin Powell's position on prisoners of war.

His impetuous side will have him lashing out at a briefer or chewing out a commander. His critics say this approach can silence honest debate. Yet, he displays great affection for rank-and-file soldiers and sailors, gladly diving into their midst to shake hands and look them in the eye to say thanks. He can be stubborn. Even when his top aide, Paul Wolfowitz, admitted to miscalculations on post-Saddam Iraq, Rumsfeld refused to acknowledge any failings. In the face of rampant looting in Baghdad, he said the acts were an expression of liberation. They were, in fact, the acts of insurgents stealing a liberated country's wealth. He has stated he personally was not sure how Saddam Hussein's loyalists would react to the dictator's ouster. His critics say that, if this was his view, he should have pressed for more answers.

There is, however, a flexible side. If an officer pushes back with a good counter-argument, Rumsfeld will accept it. He came to town bent on teaching Congress that the secretary of defense runs the Pentagon, not Congress. His arrogance so offended Republicans that some decided not to challenge Democratic charges of incompetence. But he realized as the war got more complicated that he needed GOP help. He made the extra effort to keep lawmakers informed.

Of his accomplishments, this might be the most important: He has shown the militant Islamic world that George W. Bush's United States is not Clinton's. When Rumsfeld sends troops on an operation, they will not run when events turn sour. The Islamists will not be able to defeat America with hit-and-run tactics. Rumsfeld's troops will chase them, and kill them.

In assessing Rumsfeld, clichés work. His life is an "all-American story." He does not "suffer fools gladly." And, Donald H. Rumsfeld is "the right man at the right time." It is hard to imagine any other man to whom Bush could have turned to fight this war with more tenacity, panache, and, at the appropriate time, good humor.

He is America's man in the Pentagon.

[APPENDIX]

THE FOLLOWING PAGES PROVIDE AN INSIDE LOOK AT RUMSFELD'S INTERNAL BATTLES and management style. There are also secret planning documents, a confidential study of President Clinton's non-use of special operations forces, and excerpts from a lengthy Defense Intelligence Agency report on threats facing America from 1999 to 2020.

SECRET NOFORN//X1

<u>O:</u> CJCS

<u>HRU:</u> DJS, VDJS, DJ3, VDJ3, DDRO

<u>UBJECT:</u> Personnel Recovery (PR) Efforts in Support f Capt Speicher (U)

. (U) <u>Purpose:</u> To inform CJCS of the status of efforts ɔ locate and return Captain Speicher as of 23 June 03.

ı. (U) <u>Investigation:</u>

• (S) The recovery effort is led by USCENTCOM and the POW/MIA Cell. The cell is comprised of approximately 15 personnel at DIA augmented by personnel at NIMA, CIA, and NMJIC. Additionally, there are currently six cell personnel operating in Iraq.

• (S) 22-23 May 03, POW/MIA cell debriefed and polygraphed source 2314. 2314 is an Iraqi defector and former SSO officer who claimed to have seen Speicher as recently as 1998.

  o (S/NF) USCENTCOM has debriefed several doctors whom 2314 indicated should have knowledge of Speicher. All denied having any knowledge; two have passed a polygraph exam.

  o (S/NF) USCENTCOM debriefed Suleman, 2314's alleged supervisor in the SSO. Suleman denied any knowledge of Speicher and passed a polygraph. He called 2314 a "born liar".

  o (S/NF) Cell members recently interviewed a psychiatrist, whom 2314 identified as working at the Ar Rashid prison during the time of Speicher's alleged captivity. He denied any knowledge. Cell plans to administer a polygraph.

• (S) None of the information provided by 2314 has proven accurate. Cell has asked CIA to conduct an

SECRET NOFORN//X1

A secret Defense Intelligence report to General Myers that brands as a liar the Iraqi defector who says he saw Navy Captain Scott Speicher alive in Iraq in the mid-1990s.

Date: 23 June 2003

independent polygraph of 2314. Expect this to take place in approximately two weeks.

- (S) Forensic analysis of items recovered from Hakimayah prison is on-going. USA CID is examining several items including sponges, clothing, shoes, and manacles. Process consists of cataloging, chemical and DNA analysis and will take weeks to months to complete.

- (S) Forensic analysis of the alleged Speicher flight suit is pending. The Armed Forces DNA Identification Laboratory is currently occupied with remains identification and has been unable to complete the flight suit examination.

- (S) DOCEX is ongoing. USCENTCOM has recovered thousands of POW related files. To date, analysts have found only one reference to Speicher. The reference indicates he ejected and lists his status as "unknown".

- (S) US Forces attempted to reach the Speicher crash site last week, however, enemy fire forced the US convoy to turn back. US Forces plan to make a second attempt but have not yet scheduled a date.

- (S) Cell plans to debrief an ethnic Iraqi US citizen recently liberated from Abu Ghurab prison by US forces. This individual reported to US Marines that he heard Iraqi guards discussing the "US pilot".

- (S/NF) USCENTCOM has searched every known location associated with Speicher. Other than at Hakimiyah prison, where US Forces found the initials "MSS" carved in a cell wall, no significant evidence of his status has been discovered.

(U) Recommendations: None. FYI.

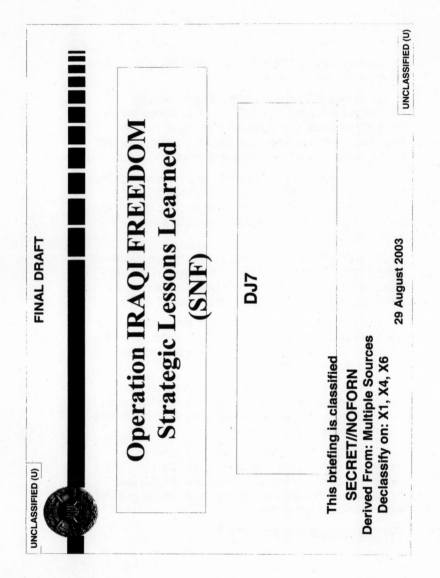

FINAL DRAFT

Operation IRAQI FREEDOM
Strategic Lessons Learned
(SNF)

DJ7

This briefing is classified
SECRET//NOFORN
Derived From: Multiple Sources
Declassify on: X1, X4, X6

29 August 2003

Six pages from a secret staff report for the Joint Chiefs that criticizes
Pentagon planning for post-Saddam Iraq.

SECRET/NOFORN (SNF)

FINAL DRAFT

Chronology

Event	Date
Al Qaeda strikes WTC & Pentagon	11 Sep 01
CJCS issues WARNO to COCOM to Cbt Terrorism	19 Sep 01
JS Coord Cell activated	20 Sep 01
SecDef issues "Strat Guidance for Campaign against Terrorism	3 Oct 01
OEF initiated against Taliban and al Qaeda	7 Oct 01
NSC issues NSPD US Strategic goals & obj in Iraq	16 Feb 02
Exercise PROMINENT HAMMER I	12-13 Mar 02
Camp David Briefs	11 May 02
UK & Australia Planning Conference	28 Jun 02
CJCS issues PLANORD for possible opns against Iraq	9 Jul 02
JS J5 Interagency (IA) Pol-Mil Cell created	10 Jul 02
IDF briefs US- Iraq War implications (US begins planning to keep Israel out of war)	30 Jul 02
Exec Steering Group (ESG) Initial Meeting	12 Aug 02
CDRUSCENTCOM discussion on assembling UK forces in Turkey	13 Aug 02
CJCS briefs Iraq Pol-Mil Strat Plan: Northern Front considered critical	22 Aug 02
Prep for SecDef KSA visit: OSW, overflight, CAOC, intel	27 Aug 02
POTUS approves Iraq goals, objectives and strategy	29 Aug 02
POTUS UN speech	11 Sep 02
CJCS issues PLANORD for training FIF	12 Sep 02
POTUS issues NSS	17 Sep 02
PROMINENT HAMMER II	25-26 Sep 02

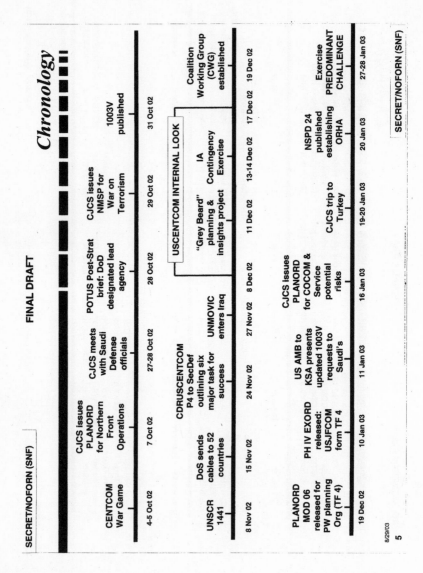

Chronology

FINAL DRAFT

SECRET/NOFORN (SNF)

SECRET/NOFORN (SNF)

8/29/03

5

SECRET/NOFORN (SNF)

FINAL DRAFT

Chronology

Date	Event
1 Feb 03	FIF Training begins in Hungary
5 Feb 03	SecState UN presentation
12 Feb 03	Saudi's agree in principle to PSAB requests
14-15 Feb 03	OIF brief to Key Israeli Leaders
16 Feb 03	EUCOM (CENTCOM controlled) info sharing in Tel Aviv begins
1 Mar 03	Pakistanis capture #3 al Qaeda (KSM) FIF deployed CENTCOM AOR
17 Mar 03	POTUS issues 48 hour ultimatum

Date	Event
18-20 Mar 03	ELABORATE CROSSBOW I Seminar
19 Mar 03	Operation IRAQI FREEDOM begins w/ strike against Hussein
20 Mar 03	CJCS/SecDef policy message to keep Israel out of war Ground war begins
25-26 Mar 03	Exercise ELABORATE CROSSBOW
31 Mar 03	FIF training suspended (76 grads)
5 Apr 03	US units enter Baghdad suburbs
6 Apr 03	US planes land at Baghdad airport
15 Apr 03	Major Cbt Opns concluded

Major combat operations

Date	Event
1 May 03	POTUS declares major combat opns over – stability & security phase
7 May 03	L. Paul Bremer appointed special envoy
7-8 May 03	Exercise ELABORATE CROSSBOW II
12 May 03	Terrorist attack 3 western compounds in KSA
12 May 03	"Mayor of Baghdad" asked to step down
13 May 02	L. Paul Bremer arrives in Baghdad
22 May 03	UNSCR 1483 passed lifting sanctions

8/29/03
6

SECRET/NOFORN (SNF)

FINAL DRAFT

Planning & Transition to Post Conflict Operations

- **Finding:** Planning began early and simultaneously throughout Interagency (IA), DoD, & CENTCOM, but was not fully integrated prior to hostilities. The transition to Humanitarian Assistance (HA) and Phase IV Stability Operations (SO) was blurred with simultaneous combat and stability operations limiting the coalition's opportunity to sequentially establish Phase IV organizations and procedures. Phase IV objectives were identified but the scope of effort required to continually refine operational plans for defeat of Iraqi military limited the focus on Phase IV.

- **Context:** OIF experience indicates HA and SO are likely to coexist during phases of combat operation. SO and HA operations must be integrated throughout the planning process .

- **Why it happened:** US military and government viewed combat and stability operations as sequential efforts and did not address stability requirements as an integrated part of combat operations planning. Decision to form DoD PH IV organizations was made in Oct 02 but organizations were not formed until Jan due to UNSCR diplomatic debate in Nov 02 and desire not to commit personnel to CJTF IV until a clear diplomatic mandate was established and Iraqi intention to disarm was assessed. Late formation of DoD PH IV organization limited time available for the development of detailed plans and pre-deployment coordination. Command relationships (and communication requirements) and responsibilities were not clearly defined for DOD organizations until shortly before OIF commenced.

- **Recommendations:**
  - Incorporate stability operations (with resources required) into deliberate war plan process. Conduct strategic war gaming for Phase IV and integrate requirements into OPLANS (include as part of Annex V requirements in war plans). Include level of preparation for Phase IV as a decision criteria for initiating combat operations.
  - Establish Phase IV organizations and command relationships in time to plan, rehearse, prepare and deploy forward to fully integrate with Joint Headquarters prior to combat operations. Due to extensive IA/coalition coordination requirements, must ensure Phase IV transition plan is complete prior to initiation of hostilities. Include coalition partners in stabilization and reconstruction planning prior to combat operations.
  - Expand Joint doctrine on transition from combat to Stability Operations; incorporate Stability Operations into JNTC requirements and Joint Exercises.

8/29/03

12

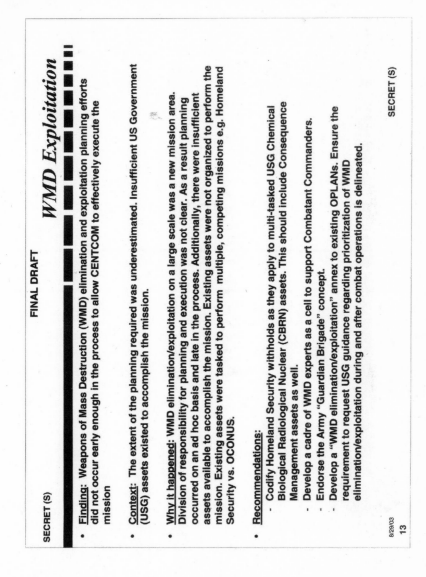

SECRET (S)

FINAL DRAFT

WMD Exploitation

- **Finding:** Weapons of Mass Destruction (WMD) elimination and exploitation planning efforts did not occur early enough in the process to allow CENTCOM to effectively execute the mission

- **Context:** The extent of the planning required was underestimated. Insufficient US Government (USG) assets existed to accomplish the mission.

- **Why it happened:** WMD elimination/exploitation on a large scale was a new mission area. Division of responsibility for planning and execution was not clear. As a result planning occurred on an ad hoc basis and late in the process. Additionally, there were insufficient assets available to accomplish the mission. Existing assets were not organized to perform the mission. Existing assets were tasked to perform multiple, competing missions e.g. Homeland Security vs. OCONUS.

- **Recommendations:**
  - Codify Homeland Security withholds as they apply to multi-tasked USG Chemical Biological Radiological Nuclear (CBRN) assets. This should include Consequence Management assets as well.
  - Develop a cadre of WMD experts as a cell to support Combatant Commanders.
  - Endorse the Army "Guardian Brigade" concept.
  - Develop a "WMD elimination/exploitation" annex to existing OPLANs. Ensure the requirement to request USG guidance regarding prioritization of WMD elimination/exploitation during and after combat operations is delineated.

SECRET (S)

8/29/03

13

1

PHASE IV OPLAN:
Reconstruction of Iraq

7. Three pages from U.S. Central Command's secret plan for post-Saddam Iraq. It shows that the top listed task after liberation was to find weapons of mass destruction. A time line predicts that after four years most American troops will be gone.

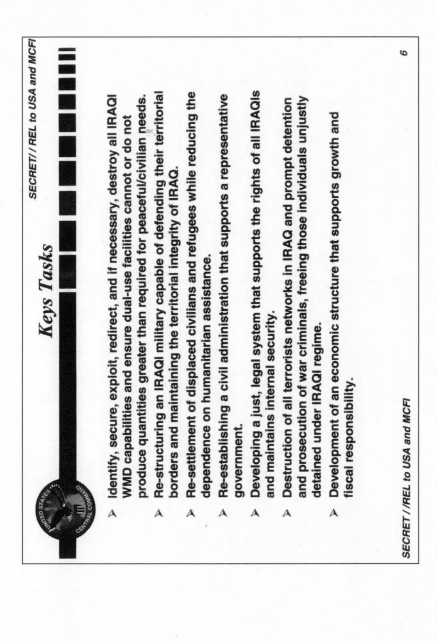

Keys Tasks

➤ Identify, secure, exploit, redirect, and if necessary, destroy all IRAQI WMD capabilities and ensure dual-use facilities cannot or do not produce quantities greater than required for peaceful/civilian needs.

➤ Re-structuring an IRAQI military capable of defending their territorial borders and maintaining the territorial integrity of IRAQ.

➤ Re-settlement of displaced civilians and refugees while reducing the dependence on humanitarian assistance.

➤ Re-establishing a civil administration that supports a representative government.

➤ Developing a just, legal system that supports the rights of all IRAQIs and maintains internal security.

➤ Destruction of all terrorists networks in IRAQ and prompt detention and prosecution of war criminals, freeing those individuals unjustly detained under IRAQI regime.

➤ Development of an economic structure that supports growth and fiscal responsibility.

6

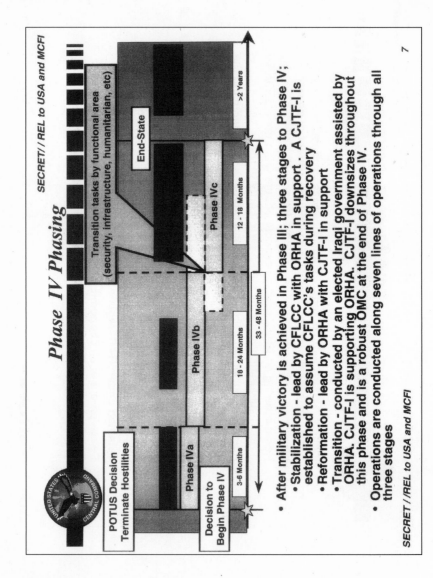

Phase IV Phasing

Transition tasks by functional area (security, infrastructure, humanitarian, etc)

POTUS Decision Terminate Hostilities

Decision to Begin Phase IV

Phase IVa	Phase IVb	Phase IVc	End-State
3-6 Months	18 - 24 Months	12 - 18 Months	>2 Years
	33 - 48 Months		

- After military victory is achieved in Phase III; three stages to Phase IV;
  - Stabilization - lead by CFLCC with ORHA in support . A CJTF-I is established to assume CFLCC's tasks during recovery
  - Reformation - lead by ORHA with CJTF-I in support
  - Transition - conducted by an elected Iraqi government assisted by ORHA. CJTF-I is supporting ORHA. CJTF-I downsizes throughout this phase and is a robust OMC at the end of Phase IV.
- Operations are conducted along seven lines of operations through all three stages

7

July 1, 2002   5:45 PM

TO: Doug Feith

FROM: Donald Rumsfeld

SUBJECT: Manhunts

How do we organize the Department of Defense for manhunts? We are obviously not well organized at the present time.

Thanks.

DHR:dh
070102-35

Please respond by ___08/02/02___

Seven of Rumsfeld's "snowflakes" that show his direct management style. He dictates such orders into a cassette recorder, then initials or signs the typed memo.

June 20, 2002   7:44 AM

TO: Doug Feith

FROM: Donald Rumsfeld

SUBJECT: Scorecard

I think we need a scorecard for the global war on terrorism.

For example, we ought to have a weekly report on the number of arrests and show the countries where they have been arrested, the number of detainees, the amount of money in bank accounts that has been frozen and the number of accounts, the number of sweeps in Afghanistan, number of MIOs, the number of people trained in different countries, and progress in Afghanistan in terms of some measurements, like refugees coming in.

We ought to get a series of indicators. Please have someone pull it together and see if we can't get the interagency group to do it. The President asked for this six months ago, and it has never happened. Why?

Thanks.

DHR:dh
062002-9

Please respond by _____ 07/09/02 _____

June 3, 2002   1:26 PM

TO: Service Secretaries
           Under Secretaries

FROM: Donald Rumsfeld

SUBJECT: Wasteful Spending

This recent report about wasteful spending bothers me and I know it does you, too.

I sure hope that when you have all investigated the problems here, that we don't decide there is no one to be held accountable. These sound like very poor decisions, and we are never going to change the culture around here without imparting the appropriate sense of urgency about our responsibilities as stewards of taxpayer money.

Please look into this and into our spending practices generally and let me know what course of action you recommend.

Thanks.

Attach.
  Hoffman, Lisa; Scripps Howard News Service, "$24,000 Sofa Among Luxuries Bought by Army and Air Force," *Seattle Post-Intelligencer*, 05/30/02

DHR dh
060302-29
....

Please respond by   07/12/02

THE SECRETARY OF DEFENSE
1000 DEFENSE PENTAGON
WASHINGTON. DC 20301-1000

OCT 2 4 2002

MEMORANDUM FOR SECRETARIES OF THE MILITARY DEPARTMENTS
CHAIRMAN OF THE JOINT CHIEFS OF STAFF
UNDER SECRETARIES OF DEFENSE
DIRECTOR, DEFENSE RESEARCH AND ENGINEERING
ASSISTANT SECRETARIES OF DEFENSE
GENERAL COUNSEL OF THE DEPARTMENT OF
    DEFENSE
INSPECTOR GENERAL OF THE DEPARTMENT OF
    DEFENSE
DIRECTOR, OPERATIONAL TEST AND EVALUATION
COMMANDERS OF THE COMBATANT COMMANDS
ASSISTANTS TO THE SECRETARY OF DEFENSE
DIRECTOR, ADMINISTRATION AND MANAGEMENT
DIRECTOR, PROGRAM ANALYSIS AND EVALUATION
DIRECTOR, FORCE TRANSFORMATION
DIRECTOR, NET ASSESSMENT
DIRECTORS OF THE DEFENSE AGENCIES
DIRECTORS OF THE FIELD ACTIVITIES

SUBJECT: The Title "Commander in Chief"

Effective immediately, the title "Commander in Chief" shall be used to connote or indicate the President of the United States of America. Further, this memorandum discontinues use of the acronym "CINC" (meaning "Commander in Chief") for military officers. Attached is a list of new titles to be used.

Utilization of current material (signs, stationery, etc) for military officers that indicates the title "Commander in Chief" is permitted until supplies are exhausted, or until the next regular maintenance period during which signage may be changed without any undue additional cost to the taxpayers.

Attachment:
As stated

January 3, 2003   9:20 AM

TO: Larry Di Rita

FROM: Donald Rumsfeld ꓚ -

SUBJECT: List of Documents

Please pull together a list of all of those documents we talked about yesterday that the Joint Staff, the Chairman and the Vice Chairman seemed to think they have to put out on vision, strategies and all that stuff.

We ought to get our arms around them, compare them with what we put out overall and get a single DoD document rather than a Joint Staff document. It is just a lot of people spinning their wheels doing things we probably have to edit and improve.

Thanks.

DHR:dh
010303-19

● ●

Please respond by   01 /24 /03

SECRET

July 22, 2002   7:18 AM

TO: Gen. Myers

CC: Gen. Holland
             Doug Feith
             Gen. Pace

FROM: Donald Rumsfeld   *D. R.*

SUBJECT: Terrorist Organizations

Please issue a planning order to Gen. Holland to develop a plan to find and deal with members of terrorist organizations. The plan should reflect the following general guidance:

- The plan should be developed using an iterative process, allowing for periodic reviews and guidance by you and me before doing all the work necessary to complete a final plan.

- The objective is to capture terrorists for interrogation or, if necessary, to kill them, not simply to arrest them in a law enforcement exercise.

- The plan should identify the authorities needed for global operations and the steps necessary to acquire such authorities in advance.

- The objective should be that processing of deployment orders and obtaining other bureaucratic clearances can be accomplished in minutes and hours, not days and weeks. This will require prior briefing and preliminary pre-clearance, with final clearance subject only to the final details.

- Gen. Holland will be responsible for conducting operational preparation of the battlespace required in this aspect of the war against terrorism.

- Special Operations Command will screen DoD for personnel—civilian and military—with languages, ethnic connections and other attributes needed for clandestine and covert activities. The results will be briefed to the Secretary of Defense.

- Gen. Holland will brief me on initiatives that can disrupt or destroy terrorist operations and additional assets that might be needed to pursue such initiatives.

Please have Gen. Holland brief us on the initial "30 percent solution" by August 1, 2002.

Thanks.

DHR/dh
071602-1S

SECRET

June 30, 2003

TO: Senior Level Review Group

CC: Andy Marshall

FROM: Donald Rumsfeld

SUBJECT: Portfolio Approaches to Defense Strategy

Attached is a memo from Andy Marshall about the Summer Study Report. I found it very interesting and thought it might be helpful if the SLRG discussed it at a future date.

I was struck by Andy's cover memo pointing out how resistant people are to looking at strategy in a different way and pursuing advantages, rather than focusing on reacting to threats.

Attach.
 1/30/03 Marshall memo re: Summer Study Report

DHR:dh
063003-61

```
SECRET                                                        9171


                      THE WHITE HOUSE
                         WASHINGTON
                      December 13, 2001



MEMORANDUM FOR  THE VICE PRESIDENT
                THE SECRETARY OF STATE
                THE SECRETARY OF THE TREASURY
                THE SECRETARY OF DEFENSE
                THE ATTORNEY GENERAL
                CHIEF OF STAFF TO THE PRESIDENT
                DIRECTOR OF CENTRAL INTELLIGENCE
                DIRECTOR, FEDERAL BUREAU OF INVESTIGATION
                CHAIRMAN OF THE JOINT CHIEFS OF STAFF
                ASSISTANT TO THE PRESIDENT AND WHITE HOUSE COUNSEL

SUBJECT:        Paper on Hostage Situation in the Philippines  (S)


The Deputies Committee met last week and reviewed efforts to
secure the release of two American citizens held hostage in the
southern Philippines by the Abu Sayaf Group, a terrorist
organization with known links to al-Qaida.  The attached paper
summarizes the DC-approved strategy.  Principals are requested to
review the paper and to inform me if there are issues related to
the strategy that require attention in an upcoming PC meeting.
If no objections are raised, the paper will be considered as
approved by Principals.  (S)


                              Condoleezza Rice
                              Assistant to the President
                                for National Security Affairs



Attachment
Tab A     Philippine Hostage Situation


cc:  National Security Advisor to the Vice President
     Deputy Secretary of State
     Deputy Secretary of the Treasury
     Deputy Secretary of Defense
     Deputy Attorney General

SECRET
Classified by:  Condoleezza Rice
Reason:  1.5(a),(c),(d)
Declassify on:  12/9/11
```

A secret three-page memo signed by Condoleezza Rice that sets the Bush administration on a course to pay $300,000 to Abu Sayyaf terrorists for the release of two American hostages.

9171

Philippine Hostage Situation

BACKGROUND:

American citizens Martin and Gracia Burnham were taken hostage
on May 27, 2001 in the southern Philippines by members of the
Abu Sayyaf Group (ASG), a group known to have links to al-Qaida.
On November 26, video obtained by a Filipino journalist was
broadcast indicating clearly that the Burnhams are in very poor
physical and psychological condition. (S)

Over the past 6 months, U.S. strategy to secure the Burnham's
release has focused on supporting Philippine efforts to pressure
the ASG. These efforts have been, for the most part,
unsuccessful. The key obstacle to development of additional
options to secure release has been the lack of actionable
intelligence. (S)

In early November, CINCPAC presented a set of recommendations to
the Philippine Government on ways in which PACOM could assist
the Armed Forces of the Philippines in developing their anti-
terrorist capabilities. A key component of CINCPAC's
recommendations was deployment of advisors to augment U.S.
collection capability and assist the AFP in integrating
intelligence into their operational planning against ASG
targets. On December 5, President Arroyo approved this element
of Admiral Blair's proposal. (S)

Accelerated Strategy:

Deputies reviewed the current situation and agreed that U.S.
goals were to:

- Free the Burnhams
- Destroy the ASG
- Contribute to the global campaign against terrorism. (S)

To that end, Deputies considered an integrated strategy to
expedite the Burnhams' release. The strategy focuses on:

- Pursuing a consolidated negotiating effort, with FBI in
  the lead. The purpose of this element of the strategy
  would be to buy time, improve the condition of the
  Burhams and acquire additional intelligence. Payment of
  ransom would not be part of the strategy except as a

tactical lure to draw ASG out as part of a release and
arrest/destroy ASG strategy;

- Deploying PACOM advisors to coordinate gathering of
  intelligence and develop follow-on options; and

- Renewing the collection effort to develop actionable
  intelligence. (S)

Deputies agreed to:

- Approve the immediate deployment of the CINCPAC advisors
  and coordinate with Admiral Blair for follow on actions to
  augment AFP capabilities.

- Convene the National Intelligence Collection Board to
  prioritize collection assets for the Philippines and
  coordinate deployment of those assets as required.

- Support FBI negotiating efforts. FBI will attempt to
  negotiate with the captors through the New Tribes Mission,
  the missionary group of which the Burnhams are members.
  Objective is to provide humanitarian assistance to Burnhams
  and buy time for both the intelligence picture and AFP
  capabilities to improve. Ransom would only be used as
  tactical lure in negotiations with ASG. The role of the
  FBI is being kept exceptionally close hold and only the
  Country Team and NTM is aware of their participation.

- Consider a Presidential call to President Arroyo to thank
  her for her support and to reemphasize our goals to both
  rescue the Burnhams and destroy the ASG. (S)

SECRET

SECRETARY OF DEFENSE
1000 DEFENSE PENTAGON
WASHINGTON, DC 20301-1000

TO: Honorable Condoleeza Rice

CC: Vice President Richard B. Cheney
             Honorable Colin Powell

FROM: Donald Rumsfeld   NOV 0 1 2001

SUBJECT: National Security Presidential Directive/NSPD-8 (U)

(S) I am told that National Security Presidential Directive/NSPD-8 established the National Director and Deputy National Security Advisor for Combating Terrorism (DNSA-CT) as the President's "principal advisor" on matters related to combating global terrorism, including military operations. Apparently, NSPD-8 provides that the DNSA-CT coordinates U.S. activities in deterrence, detection, and disruption of terrorist activities, destroying terrorist organizations, incident and consequence management overseas, and military cooperation programs.

(S) My understanding of NSPD-8 as issued suggests that it may cause confusion with regard to the statutory role of the Chairman of the Joint Chiefs of Staff as the "principal military adviser" to the President, the Secretary of Defense, and the National Security Council. I am no lawyer, but it seems to me there is only one principal military adviser. Otherwise, the word "principal" would have a brand new meaning. As we go forward on this terrorism effort, I think it is important that any confusion be untangled and corrected, at a minimum by confirming that the DNSA-CT's role is not intended in any way to detract from the Chairman's role as the principal military adviser.

(S) Further, from my standpoint as Secretary of Defense, I find that the DNSA-CT's mandate could be read as infringing on the chain of command from the President and the Secretary of Defense to the Combatant Commanders. It is dangerous – exceedingly dangerous – to suggest that there may be any additional players between the President, the Secretary of Defense, and the Combatant Commanders in fulfilling warfighting responsibilities, including mission planning and execution.

(U) I know this was done quickly for very good reasons, and that we may not have provided you our considered views as you drafted the NSPD. Nevertheless, I think we should address these issues.

(U) I have asked Jim Haynes to take a look at this and get together with Al Gonzales and John Bellinger to see if we can't promptly determine exactly how things ought to be, and come back to us with a proposal for clarifying the respective roles.

Derived from: NSPD-8
Declassify on: 10/8/11

SECRET

X01845 /01

A secret memo from Rumsfeld to Condoleezza Rice protesting a confidential presidential directive that would eat into the defense secretary's powers in war on terrorism.

The unauthoriz ed disc losure of c lassifi ed information ma y be pr osecuted under Section 793 and Section 798, Title 18, USC, and is punishab le by fine of not more than $10,000, imprisonment of not more than 10 y ear s, or both.

SECRET NOFORN

JULY 1999

A PRIMER ON THE
FUTURE THREAT

THE DECADES AHEAD: 1999-2020

SECRET NOFORN

Excerpts from a 160-page secret DIA report that shows President
Bush inherited a dangerous world in January 2001.

governments — insurgents and to a lesser extent narcotics trafficking organizations — and that generated by external elements, most notably Islamic extremists. Although these elements are expected to focus on Israeli or other Middle Eastern targets, the Americas also provide a potential avenue to the U.S. homeland and an external source of income.

(S) **Asian** terrorism will be rooted in religious extremism and ethnic differences. In some cases, governments will use terrorists or insurgents to further territorial goals in neighboring countries. Unstable countries like Afghanistan will provide safe havens for extremist and terrorist groups.

(S) **African** terrorism in general will be generated by ethnic differences and will be a subset of insurgencies or separatism. Transnational terrorist organizations will

(U) U.S. Embassy bombing in Nairobi.

find Africa a favorable environment in which to operate, as poor security and unstable governments persist.

Long Term Outlook

(S) New developments in technology will be used primarily to improve methods of delivery or concealment of terrorist weapons. The emphasis will be on simplicity, effectiveness and limited risk to the terrorist, his organization or sponsor. Terrorists increasingly will use information operations to collect intelligence and potentially to attack infrastructure.

(S) It is probable that terrorist organizations or individuals will employ a weapon of mass destruction against U.S. interests by 2020. Heightened publicity about the vulnerability of civilian targets, an increased interest in inflicting mass casualties, emergence of less predictable groups and greater availability of WMD-related production knowledge and technology have already drawn the attention of some terrorist organizations. Additionally, the hoax or blackmail value of WMD is a potentially powerful psychological weapon in itself, and its use can be expected to increase in the future.

WMD PROLIFERATION

(U) Proliferation by adversaries and noncompliant partners will lead to enhanced warfighting capabilities that will complicate U.S. contingency planning. U.S. forces may have to engage in warfare in which advanced

(U) UNSCOM inspectors arrive in Iraq.

196 RUMSFELD'S WAR

conventional weapons and WMD are used directly against U.S. forces, and on access and embarkation points. Conflict between other nations or groups in which such weapons are used may also affect subsequent U.S. involvement.

Chemical/Biological Weapons (CBW)

(U) The 1972 Biological and Toxin Weapons Convention (BWC) remains in place, and the Chemical Weapons Convention (CWC), which entered into force in April 1997, is gaining wide acceptance. Nevertheless, some countries will maintain covert chemical and biological warfare capabilities. Many countries possess the infrastructure to develop chemical and biological weapons, and those lacking an indigenous capability can purchase it. Furthermore, chemical and biological warfare programs can be concealed within legitimate dual-use R&D and industrial operations.

(U) Agents such as sarin and mustard, now the mainstay of chemical warfare arsenals, will continue to be a threat in the near term, and the persistent nerve agent VX will enter the operational inventories of more countries as their programs mature. An increasing number of countries with biological warfare programs will be able to develop infectious agents such as anthrax and plague, as well as toxins such as botulinum and ricin, for weaponization. U.S. forces, deployed in either military or peacekeeping roles, could be exposed to these agents.

(S/NF) Agent delivery development programs will continue to focus on microencapsulation, particulate aerosol (dusty) preparations, and other agent formulation components that enhance effectiveness. New types of agents, such as modified infectious organisms, low-molecular-weight physiologically active substances that disrupt body function, and synthetic/modified toxins, are also in development. A new generation of nerve agents developed originally by the Soviets pose a significant problem

because they are resistant to current Western countermeasures, and are not effectively captured by the CWC.

(S/NF) Many of the components needed for chemical or biological agent weaponization are used in other types of weapon systems, many of which are available in the international arms market. Chemical and biological agents can be disseminated by tube and rocket artillery, ground and naval mines, aerial bombs, submunition dispensers for aircraft, and a wide variety of spray devices. An increasing number of countries are also capable of employing unmanned aerial vehicles, cruise missiles, and ballistic missiles for chemical and biological attack. Terrorist use should also be anticipated, primarily in improvised devices, probably in association with an explosive.

(S/NF) Currently, those countries that have a delivery capability for both chemical and biological agents include Russia, Iraq, China, and North Korea. Iran has a chemical weapons capability and probably a limited biological agent delivery means; Libya, Egypt, India, Taiwan, Israel, South Korea, and Syria have chemical weapons capabilities. In addition, Pakistan, Sudan, Serbia, and Croatia are believed to have programs to develop CW capabilities. Moreover, Libya, Syria, and Pakistan probably can produce biological agents on a limited scale and presumably have some means of delivery even if not by military systems.

(U) Chemical and biological agent threats also can derive from sources other than conventional armed forces of hostile states. The nature of agent dissemination devices is such that special operations forces and terrorist groups can use chemical and biological agents

(U) The proliferation of WMD increases the probability that armed conflict or a terrorist attack will have a CW/BW component.

in ways that could have a major impact on national security and warfighting capabilities. The technology required to disseminate agents using aircraft, trucks, small boats, or man-portable devices is readily obtainable in the form of agricultural sprayers and similar forms of equipment. Improvised devices are also likely to be used for agent dissemination.

Nuclear

(S) The proliferation of nuclear weapons and nuclear technology poses a particularly grave threat. A related problem involves unsafe nuclear technology of all types, including that used for peaceful purposes, as well as the improper security and handling of nuclear materials that are dangerous in their natural or processed form. The threat will grow as more nuclear technology is used. Several factors, including international counter-proliferation agreements, general public/political opposition, and the fact that nuclear weapons technology is

expensive and difficult to obtain, will preclude the widespread proliferation of nuclear weapons. Nevertheless, the number of countries acquiring nuclear weapon technology and materials will slowly increase into the next century.

(S) By 2020 Iran, Iraq, and perhaps Libya will have produced or purchased nuclear weapons, assuming their respective leadership maintains the will to do so. Other countries such as Germany and Japan, which have developed their technology base and fissile material production base in support of their civilian nuclear power programs, could develop a nuclear warhead within a year should the political decision be made to pursue such capability.

SECRET/NOFORN

(U) *Indian Shakti-3 nuclear test site.*

Biggest problem: Chemical and biological capabilities used by subnational groups that are not easily deterred or identified.
Growing Threat: Tactical Operations and Terrorism

Selected Worldwide Nuclear Weapons Inventories		
Country	1999	2020
Russia*		
Strategic	8,200-10,600	1,600-2,800
Tactical	8,500-15,900	3,400-6,000
China		
ICBM	40-45	180-220**
SLBM	0-12	28-44
SRBM	100	150-200
India	10-15	50-70
Pakistan	25-35	60-80
Israel	60-80	65-85
North Korea***	1-2	10+
Iran		10-20
Iraq		10-20

* This includes warheads scheduled for dismantling.

** Assumes U.S. NMD & TMD deployment and Chinese build-up in response to U.S. deployment.

*** Assumes noncompliance with international agreements. By 2020, North Korean assets could largely be part of a united Korea.

Russia

(U) Russian troops working for food.

(S) Given the magnitude of the armed forces' problems and the paucity of resources available to deal with them, the condition of Russia's military will not improve substantially over the next decade and in some areas could get worse.

(S) At the extreme, Russia's military could even face institutional collapse, punctuated by military unrest, mutinies, and violent political intervention.

military reform process remains in limbo while the armed forces descend deeper into crisis. Defense-industrial capabilities continue to deteriorate, casting doubt on Russia's ability to produce and deploy future generations of high-tech weapons.

(S) Limited defense funds have forced a Russian emphasis on nuclear weapons, which in turn has accelerated the deterioration in conventional force capabilities. This downward spiral leaves Russia with extremely unattractive options for dealing with the regional conflicts, territorial disputes, peacekeeping operations, and terrorist threats that it will most likely face over the next decade.

UNCLASSIFIED

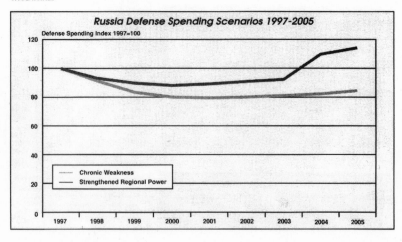

Russia Defense Spending Scenarios 1997-2005

Defense Spending Index 1997=100

Legend:
- Chronic Weakness
- Strengthened Regional Power

Longer-Term Potential

(S) Beyond the next decade, prolonged political and economic difficulty probably will yield a chronically weak military that could do little beyond defend Russia's borders. Such a force would pose less of an external threat than an internal danger due to its instability and questionable reliability, particularly if called on for internal disorders and threats. However, a chronically weak Russia might also have a greater propensity to compensate by resorting to other means, such as covert operations or diplomatic grandstanding.

(S) The possibility also exists that under the right conditions — effective political leadership, sustained economic progress, and successful military reform — Russia could emerge 10 years from now as a strengthened regional power with a significantly reduced but modernized military. A strengthened Russia could play a greater role in international military efforts such as peacekeeping operations. Whether it would employ its new strength in cooperative or less helpful ways, however, would depend on the will of its leaders.

(S) Russia's long-term military direction should become clearer by around 2005, when the lasting impact of leadership transition and the effectiveness of efforts at economic recovery, military reform, and defense industry restructuring, prioritizing and modernizing will be more apparent.

Strategic Forces

(S) As Russian strategic nuclear force levels shrink, the need to maintain a credible missile attack warning system will increase. Russia's priority will be to ensure that a comprehensive detection system is preserved. In the short term, deficiencies in the nuclear warhead security program, coupled with severe economic conditions, increase the risk of nuclear warheads being diverted, especially by insiders. However, in the longer term, U.S. assistance in improving nuclear warhead security is designed to lead to a reduction in the potential for nuclear warhead diversion.

(S) Ratification of START II in its current form probably will not occur. Acceptance with significant modifications and conditions is more likely. These conditions will complicate the implementation of START II and impede progress on a START III treaty. Ultimately, continued economic instability will push START II further down on the Russian government's overall agenda. It will also continue to be held hostage to the machinations of Russo-American relations involving multiple issues such as Iraq and Kosovo.

(S) Problems with START II ratification and, more important, funding shortfalls have delayed the conversion of SS-18 and SS-19 systems to the SS-27. This is a short term problem. Age and life extension operations will force resolution of the issue sometime in the next decade. Deployment of the road-mobile SS-27 is expected between 2002 and 2005 thus supplanting the aging SS-25 systems.

(S) The prospects for Russia's submarine force look bleak for the next decade.

THE AEGEAN

(C) Athens and Ankara will continue to be unable to resolve the practical and political issues in the Aegean that underlie the tensions between the two countries. Both prefer to avoid war. Nonetheless, a crisis involving Aegean sovereignty issues on Cyprus could erupt and escalate into an unwanted conflict because of perceived provocative actions or miscalculations.

(S) In the event of hostilities, Turkey and Greece expect and plan for a short conflict (3-4 days) and assume that the interna-

(U) Turkish Army Aviation Blackhawk.

tional community would intercede by then to stop the fighting. Such a conflict, which probably would start in the Aegean, would be primarily an air and naval fight with a Turkish attack on some of the smaller Greek islands in the Aegean and possibly a limited ground operation in Thrace. A conflict that begins in the Aegean would not necessarily spread to Cyprus, but such expansion should not be ruled out. Turkey is expected to hold a quantitative and qualitative edge on force capabilities, though Greece will make modest improvement to its air and air defense capabilities. Greek military equipment acquisitions in the coming years will lessen the prospects of a catastrophic defeat at the hands of Turkey.

(C/NF) Turkey sees its position as an epicenter of three unstable regions: the Balkans, the Caucasus, and the Middle East. This "tough neighborhood" will continue to be plagued with problems of ethnic strife, regional conflicts, religious fanaticism, international terrorism, and weapons of mass destruction. Turkish relations with Syria will increasingly be strained over distribution of water from the Euphrates River, Syria's support for the PKK, Turkey's military cooperation with Israel, and Syrian claims to Hatay Province. Both Iraq and Iran will complicate Turkish interests in the region. As with Syria, the Kurdish issue further strains relations with Iraq.

(C/NF) These issues are in addition to Turkey's close relations with the United States and budding relations with Israel. Iran has the potential of becoming the more important Turkish adversary in the Middle East. Competing interests in Central Asia and the Caucasus and the fact that Turkey is a secular Muslim state will place Ankara at odds with Iran. Turkey's forceful solutions to regional problems with Iraq and Iran also have the potential for bringing Ankara quickly into conflict with U.S. interests.

(C/NF) Although Turkey appears militarily positioned to survive any of these external challenges and remain a regional power, the Turkish ruling elites will face a fundamental problem that will likely determine if in fact it can do so. It is almost inconceivable that within the next ten years there will not be a point at which the ongoing ideological clash between secularism and an increasingly fervent Islamist political movement will reach a climax. Secular forces, led by the military, are currently in charge and will almost certainly remain so for at least the next five years. It is questionable, however, whether this dominance can last, especially if the religious fervor continues to grow. Just as the military's suppression of the Kurds fed the Kurdish insurgency, continued efforts to quash Islamist political movements in the midst of a religious revival could lead to deeper divisions in society and serious urban violence. The key question, then, would be how long the military — seemingly becoming more and more estranged from civilian society — could maintain control.

BELARUS — UKRAINE — MOLDOVA

(C) These three states will pose opportunities for both cooperation and friction between Europe, Russia, and the United States. Of these, Belarus identifies most closely with Moscow. It already has close military cooperation with Russia, with political integration by 2005 not being ruled out. Though these military ties pose no near-term conventional threat, it is worth noting that the new NATO area of responsibility will be in direct contact with Belarus.

(U) Belarusian President Lukashenko sees the Belarus-Russia Union as a natural merger of two fraternal states.

Given the dismal state of the Belarusian economy, a potentially unstable state already exists on that border. Ukraine will continue a balanced relationship with Russia — if anything as a deterrent, since Russia is considered its only external threat. In addition, Kiev will continue to pursue closer political, economic, and military cooperation with Europe and NATO, eventually establishing both as its primary security relationship. The economic crisis in the Ukraine will limit military capabilities for the next 5 to 10 years. Moldova's problems with its breakaway Transdneister region will continue over the next decade but without significant escalation of the conflict or resolution.

EUROPEAN SECURITY ARCHITECTURE

(C) Europe will have moved closer to building a credible, perhaps much different security structure in NATO, but these efforts face many impediments from the Europeans themselves. Political cohesion of Europe will become equally important to the actual advantages of collective security. The development of ESDI will proceed haltingly for at least the next decade. Its successful implementation will depend on continued support from NATO — but espe-

(U) China is not likely to build the capability to project large conventional forces beyond its immediate borders or nearby seas. China is likely to continue to build a strategic missile/WMD capability.

(U) China's foreign policy will seek to avoid conflict and sustain the trade, investment, and access to technology essential to economic development.

(C) Within this cooperative framework, however, several points of friction will persist. China believes the United States is bent on containing, dividing, and westernizing China, and perceives Japan as its principal rival in the region. Chinese leadership views U.S.-Japanese defense cooperation as increasing the long-term Japanese threat. Taiwan remains the major stumbling block to a coherent and unitary China, and will continue to be a focus for the Beijing government. China believes U.S. policy encourages the independence movement in Taiwan both deliberately and inadvertently. Territorial disputes may flare periodically—though Beijing prefers to defer these disputes until it is strong enough to impose peaceful resolution on its own terms. Furthermore, China remains concerned over ethnic separatism, espe-

(U) Chinese Type 85IIM Tank.

cially in Tibet and the northwest, and the potential threat such movements pose to the country's stability and unity.

Military Trends

(C) The Chinese military will decrease in size during the next two decades to conserve funds for military modernization, although its forces will remain large in comparison with its neighbors. Now numbering about 2.5 million, the People's Liberation Army (PLA) most likely will decline by 10% to 20%.

> The Chinese clock keeps the same time as clocks in the west but the Chinese perception is of decades passing — not hours or days.

SECRET

Expected New Chinese Military Systems	Quantity in 2020
Su-27	320
F-10	320
New Fighter	60
FB-7 Fighter-Bomber	180
New Surface Warships	20
Land-Attack Cruise Missiles	1000
AEW Aircraft	25
New SSBN	1

SECRET

China: Future Military Trends	1999	2020
Tanks	6,960	7,150
Active Divisions	85	70
Rapid Reaction Divisions	11	24
Fighters/Interceptors	3,684	1,550
Ground Attack/Lt Bombers	779	350
Attack Submarines	67	35
Aircraft Carriers	0	1
Other Surface Warships	54	75
Strategic SAMs	512	1,650
Military Satellites	4	15

(U) Absent a major resurgence of Russian power, Beijing sees the air and naval threat from the east as much greater than the ground threat from the north. China's top military priorities will therefore remain its air, air defense, missile, and naval forces, in order to protect Chinese claims in the South China Sea, pose a credible threat to Taiwan, and repel any possible attack from advanced rivals such as the United States or Japan.

(C) With the growth of U.S. long-range strike capabilities, homeland defense requires the PLA Navy to expand its operating area further out to sea. The PLA Navy's main strength is its offensive punch against surface ships, especially its anti-ship cruise missiles launched from ships, submarines, aircraft, and land-based platforms. China's ability to project a naval task force for missions other than coastal defense will remain limited.

(S) China is well aware it would be at a technological disadvantage against any advanced opponent, and would seek to overcome this through force multipliers or unconventional countermeasures and tactics. China believes that information operations will become a major factor in future conflicts and is actively researching offensive information warfare capabilities.

(S) China has recently abandoned all consideration of developing an aircraft carrier and related fighter aircraft for its navy. It is possible that this program will be revived some time in the future, but equally likely that Beijing will decide to rely on anti-ship cruise missiles and fleet air defense, and forego a carrier altogether.

(C) China's nuclear strategy will continue to emphasize a survivable retaliatory capability to deter use of nuclear weapons by the United States, Russia, or India. China feels this deterrent is at risk over the next decade because of U.S. targeting capabilities, missile accuracy, and potential ballistic missile defenses. Beijing is, therefore, modernizing and expanding its missile force to restore its deterrent value. Mobile, solid-fuel missiles and a new ballistic missile submarine will improve the force's ability to survive a first strike, while more launchers, on-board penetration aids, and possibly multiple warheads will improve its ability to penetrate missile defenses. Nothing indicates China will field the much larger number of missiles necessary to shift from a limited, retaliatory strategy to a first-strike, warfighting strategy.

> China's effort to gather technology from open interaction and from industrial and governmental espionage will continue. China's involvement with selected countries in proliferation will also continue.

SECRET

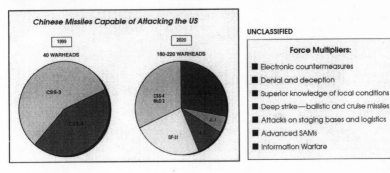

Chinese Missiles Capable of Attacking the US

1999 — 40 WARHEADS
CSS-3
CSS-4

2020 — 180-220 WARHEADS
CSS-4 MoD 2
JL-1
DF-31

UNCLASSIFIED

Force Multipliers:

- Electronic countermeasures
- Denial and deception
- Superior knowledge of local conditions
- Deep strike—ballistic and cruise missiles
- Attacks on staging bases and logistics
- Advanced SAMs
- Information Warfare

Instead, North Korea has prioritized select industrial capabilities, especially a few of its defense industries, relaxed some internal controls to allow its hard-pressed populace more flexibility in acquiring food and other necessities, and boosted the military's internal security role (including enhanced protection for the regime). Ultimately, renewed economic development is likely to hinge on a relaxation of tension and economic accommodation with Seoul.

(C) Lacking economic power and allies upon whom it can depend for military support, North Korea clearly believes it must maintain a credible military capability at all costs. This provides not only deterrence and, if necessary, defense, but Pyongyang also uses it indirectly as leverage in international negotiations and in the policy formulations of concerned governments. In the short term, the North will retain the ability to inflict enormous destruction on South Korea. Its ability to conduct large-scale maneuver warfare against the South is eroding, but it is attempting to balance this erosion with improvements in long-range artillery, ballistic missiles, weapons of mass destruction, and special operations forces and associated delivery platforms. Were conflict to erupt, these elements could wreak heavy damage on the northern part of South Korea.

(S) Social problems, including widespread hunger, increased crime, and corruption among civilian and military officials, have accompanied economic failure. Though the possibility of leadership change cannot be entirely dismissed, the regime, with its enhanced security apparatus, appears firmly in control. The likelihood that North Korea will initiate a war to reunify the peninsula is diminishing, but the possibility of conflict spurred by internal instability, miscalculation, or provocation is increasing.

(C) In the longer term, North Korea is not likely to maintain its capacity for conventional military operations without reversing its economic decline, and it cannot reverse that decline without major reform, without opening itself to the outside world, and

(U) North Korean SANGO-class mini submarine.

without relaxing tensions with the South. If it refuses to follow that path, as is likely, it might be able to muddle through indefinitely, maintaining its missile, nuclear, and special operations capabilities but losing its capacity for conventional maneuver warfare. If it does reconcile or reunify with the South, economic rehabilitation of the North will be an enormous task for many years to come and will influence Seoul's relationships with China, Japan, and the United States.

Military Trends

(S) If North Korea remains hostile, it will maintain its large forward deployed infantry and artillery force, deploying additional long-range systems and emphasizing artillery training. Pyongyang will try to maintain the capabilities of its large special operations forces, including platforms for clandestine insertion of forces into the South. North Korea has thousands of significant underground facilities dispersed widely throughout the country, making precision destruction of warfighting capability very difficult.

(S) North Korean air and air defense capabilities are modest and will remain so in the future. Economic constraints will preclude buying new aircraft to replace its obsolescent inventory, and pilot training will remain inadequate.

(S) Pyongyang will maintain large surface-to-air missile and air defense artillery forces but will have difficulty in investing in newer, more capable systems. The army will continue to harden air and air defense facilities and may upgrade its non-automated air defense command and control system.

Missile and WMD Programs

(S) Pyongyang continues a determined effort to develop and field more capable ballistic missiles, augmenting its existing array of older FROG, SCUD-B, and SCUD-C missiles. The progress of this program, despite the country's severe economic problems, clearly indicates it is a top priority and likely to continue as long as the regime survives. North Korea has deployed medium-range No Dong missiles over the past two years, capable of striking U.S. bases in Japan. The No Dong can deliver a 700 kg payload to a range of 1,300 km.

(S) North Korea recently attempted to launch a satellite using a variant of the Taepo Dong 1 (TD-1) MRBM. This launch may have satisfied Pyongyang's requirement for flight testing of the TD-1. The launch demonstrated critical technologies applicable to MRBMs, IRBMs, and ICBMs, such as stage separation and ignition of the second and third stage at altitude. It also demonstrated the potential to substitute an unguided third stage and a smaller payload for the standard TD-1 warhead and guidance package, extending the missile's range at the expense of greatly reduced payload and accuracy.

(S) North Korea also has a program to develop a larger missile, the Taepo Dong 2 (TD-2) ICBM. Many uncertainties remain, but if this program is successful, Pyongyang could field a TD-2 ICBM within three years that could deliver a 650 kg warhead to Alaska, Hawaii, and the Pacific Northwest, or a much lighter warhead to most of the United States. The system could be capable of delivering a nuclear device.

(S) As a two-stage missile, the TD-1 can deliver a 750 kg warhead, large enough for a first-generation nuclear device, to about 2,500 km, covering all of Japan and Okinawa. A three-stage TD-1 could deliver a 250 kg unguided payload to a range of 5,500 km, reaching Alaska and western Hawaii, or a 75 kg payload to most of the continental United States. Over half the payload would have to be the shielded re-entry vehicle to protect the warhead, leaving a very small explosive device and no room for guidance packages.

(S) In the near term, it is unlikely that the North Korean nuclear weapons program can achieve nuclear yield from a 100 kg device. An early-generation warhead weighing 650-750 kg is the best Pyongyang could achieve. A 100 kg payload is sufficient to deliver chemical, biological, or radiological agents (radioactive contaminants). Of these, only biological agents are lightweight enough to cover a large area with such a small payload. Weight constraints and high re-entry velocity severely limit the effectiveness of any dispersal mechanism, however, so even biological agents are not likely to achieve effective wide-area coverage.

(S) North Korea continues efforts to extend the range of its SCUD missiles. The new 1,000 km extended-range SCUD is currently being fielded at Kumchon-ni, 75km north of the DMZ. With range comparable to the No Dong, but cheaper to construct, the extended-range SCUD (also called SCUD-ER) can deliver a 750 kg warhead to western Japan from Kumchon-ni, or reach all of South Korea even from northern bases near the Chinese border. In addition

> North Korea is not likely to maintain its capacity for conventional military operations without reversing its economic decline, and it cannot reverse that decline without major reform, without opening itself to the outside world, and without relaxing tensions with the South.

(U) SA-2 SAM on parade.

SECRET

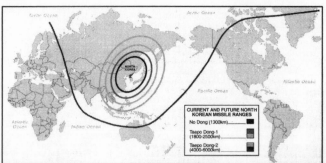

to its increased capability, the SCUD—ER has proven cheaper to produce than the No-Dong.

(S/NF) North Korea is estimated to possess an offensive biological warfare program designed to develop, produce and weaponize agents. Despite limited intelligence on the status of its biological warfare capabilities, North Korea is thought to have developed agents including anthrax, plague, cholera and toxins. The North Korea military will continue to try to increase production rates for traditional biological warfare agents concurrent with Pyongyang's effort to develop its pharmaceutical and biological products industries, but is unlikely to deploy genetically engineered biological warfare agents within the next decade.

(S/NF) North Korea almost certainly is self-sufficient in the production of all necessary precursor chemicals for first-generation chemical agents, including nerve agents. The size of the North Korean chemical agent stockpile is unknown, but is estimated to be between 2,500 and 5,000 metric tons. Many of North Korea's chemical weapons are stored underground, including in railroad tunnels.

SOUTHEAST ASIA

(C) Southeast Asian countries will likely forge greater political and economic cooperation through the next decade, but neither ASEAN nor the larger ASEAN Regional Forum (ARF) will evolve into a cooperative defense alliance similar to Europe's security architecture.

(C) Multilateral mechanisms such as ARF are likely to further enhance ASEAN's regional leadership and promote confidence-building and preventive diplomacy. However, resolution of the area's intractable terri-

(S) Several MENA states could further their economic and political development, becoming more benign. These states might become more responsive to international norms of conduct. Likewise, they could view their strategic military assets as providing stability for their position in the region.

IRAN

Political Outlook

(S) Iran's economic difficulties will influence its domestic and foreign policies through most of the next two decades. Internal demographic-resource tension will drive attempts at internal reform. Iran will evolve into a consensus government with more power-sharing among clerics, technocrats, and secularists. Tehran will reduce emphasis on exporting the revolution, but radical Muslims will probably continue isolated acts of terrorism, some of which will be traceable to Iran. Tehran will continue to seek to undermine regional belief in U.S. security assurances and subvert other regional states that remain pro-Western. Iran will also steadily increase its influence in the Middle East and Central Asia over the next decade as a means of projecting itself as a regional power.

(U) President Khatami

(S) Iran's economy has potential, but economic growth during the rest of the decade is likely to remain sluggish and could suffer significant problems. Oil prices likely will remain weak through 2005, and Iran will have difficulties maintaining the current level of oil exports. Iranian domestic consumption of oil continues to increase, further complicating the economic picture. Natural gas resources will be further exploited, eventually leading to significant amounts of natural gas exports by 2010. Iran is working hard to diversify its economy, develop its industrial base, and increase non-oil exports. Tehran will be moderately successful in these endeavors, particularly in the heavy industrial sectors of mining, metals, and petrochemicals. This should result in a moderate increase in non-oil exports and improvements in the defense industrial sector.

Defense Resources

(S) Declining oil revenues will force Iran to prioritize defense spending and delay or cancel at least some procurement and construction projects. However, Iran will continue to assign priority to resources dedicated to its missile and WMD programs. Temporary delays in these programs are possible if the oil revenue decline lasts beyond 2005. Iran can survive temporary reductions in resources allocated to conventional forces and support entities without having a long-term impact on force structure. Iran is likely to protect personnel, but would cut personnel costs around the edges. Special units, such as the Qods force, could avoid cuts entirely.

Military Outlook

(S) Iran is expected to present a continuing regional threat unless major political change occurs. It will remain suspicious of Iraqi long-term objectives and is increasingly concerned with its eastern border where the extreme orthodoxy of the Sunni Taliban challenges the Shiism of Iran's

Islamic Republic. Iran is developing new military capabilities to deter a post-sanctions Iraq and a hostile Islamic Afghanistan. Enhancements to its conventional forces will be gradual, with a focus on homeland defense. However, underlying difficulties with combat effectiveness and overall readiness will remain in place for at least the next several years. The Islamic Revolutionary Guard Command (IRGC) will continue to compete with the Islamic Republic of Iran Ground Forces (IRIGF) for resources as well as internal responsibilities, adding another challenge to overall Iranian capabilities.

> **Iran seeks to establish political-military hegemony over the Gulf Region.**

(S/NF) Iran should have a greater capability to disrupt the flow of commerce in the Gulf over the next decade, primarily through the use of mine warfare and integrated anti-ship cruise missiles. In fact, absent U.S. intervention, Iran could close the Strait of Hormuz to maritime traffic indefinitely. Even in the face of determined U.S. opposition, Iran could deny or substantially interfere with free passage for several weeks. Tehran's ability to conduct mine warfare will continue to increase both in complexity and tactical proficiency. Any vessel in the Islamic Republic of Iran Navy (IRIN) is

(U) Iranian female troops.

a potential minelayer, and any civil-registered ship also holds the same distinction. Iran does not typically utilize purposeful missions for its naval equipment and allows for a high degree of latitude for mining operations. After 2000, the IRIN should be capable of mine-laying operations with its three KILO-Class submarines. Iran's acquisition of the Chinese C-802 naval cruise missiles and Houdong missile patrol craft gives its navy a credible mobile anti-ship cruise missile capability. With both mine laying and cruise missile operations, however, systemic problems in command and control will inhibit overall combat effectiveness for the foreseeable future.

(S) Advances in WMD programs will remain a priority and extend Tehran's military power projection capability. It will continue to place importance on improved ballistic missile capabilities, in part to acquire a strategic strike capability useful against a variety of regional competitors as well as more distant potential opponents such as Israel. Iran is expected to have an operational Shahab-3 MRBM sometime in 2000 or 2001. The Iranians could readily adapt their existing SCUD production infrastructure — foregoing new production facilities — to manufacture the Shahab-3, with series production beginning about one year after the design is frozen. To adapt existing SCUD facilities, tooling, and equipment to Shahab-3 production is an expedient approach to MRBM production

(U) Iranian soldiers and Cobra helicopter; resourcefulness with aging platforms.

and would allow Iran to employ a readily available workforce rather than train a new cadre of production workers. This option would allow the Iranians to field an MRBM relatively quickly, but at the cost of disrupting the SRBM program.

(S/NF) Iran is already looking ahead to developing a longer range (2,000km) Shahab-4 MRBM, probably with a greater payload. The latter will simplify the implementation of WMD warheads. The greater range will put not only Israel within reach but southeastern Europe as well. With access to Russian technology and expertise, Iran could flight-test such a missile as early as 2001, with operational capabilities as early as 2005. Further missile developments include the Kossar (Shahab-5) IRBM with a potential range between 4,000 and 5,000km. This system could be developed over the next five years and possibly become operational between 2008 and 2010. An operational Kossar system could have the ability to reach all of Europe. Though currently its program goals are ambiguous, Iran could pursue a "Shahab-6" ICBM platform, potentially achieving an initial capability before 2010 with external assistance. This system could have a range of about 10,000km.

(S/NF) Paralleling the expanding missile inventories and capabilities are nuclear, biological, and chemical weapons programs, which by early in the next century are expected to provide Tehran with new warhead types that will make any shortcomings in ballistic missile accuracy and payload size less important to wartime effectiveness. Iran will continue its efforts to acquire a nuclear weapons capability to back its claims to regional dominance. Iran probably will not have the capability to indigenously produce a nuclear weapon before 2009 based on the known state of its R&D efforts. However, Tehran could purchase fissile material before that time. If Iran were to acquire enough suitable fissile material on the black market, it

(U) Iran will continue to place importance on improved ballistic missile capabilities in part to achieve strategic strike capabilities useful within the region. The Shahab-3 pictured above will increase Iran's missile capability to 1300km as early as 2000.

could develop a nuclear weapon capability within the first part of the next decade. Exploitation of both uranium and plutonium weapons technology will aid in this venue once it is advanced beyond the research and development stage. Tehran does not yet have fuel cycle facilities that could serve as critical nodes for the production of nuclear materials for nuclear weapons. Iran is also upgrading its biotechnological infrastructure and is actively seeking foreign scientific cooperation in genetic engineering and other advanced technologies. Advanced biotechnology could be applied to Iran's BW program within 3 to 5 years, resulting in development of enhanced biological agents. Iran is seeking self-sufficiency in dual-use BW agent production equipment, CBW protective clothing, and medical protection against BW agents. An indigenous precursor and CW agent production capability should become a reality for Iran over the next five years. Iran is already self-sufficient in the production of tabun, sarin, and V-series nerve agents, but probably not soman and other so-called fourth generation/novel agents. Unless key foreign suppliers can be dis-

Iran is slowly, but steadily building an offensive capability far in excess of its mere defensive needs.

tate future conflict with Turkey. Demand for water will increase in Iraq's cities and towns over the next two decades as more than 80% of Iraqis are expected to make their homes in urban centers by 2020. Any inhibiting action by the Turks on water flow into Iraq will further stress civil infrastructures as well as the Iraqi leadership.

Military Outlook

(S) Iraq will remain capable of incursions against its Gulf Cooperation Council (GCC) neighbors. Baghdad retains the goal of dominating Kuwait; however, its inability to hold against a determined Western counterattack will limit its options. Relaxed or suspended UN sanctions will allow the Iraqis to modernize their armed forces and will enhance Iraq's ability to pursue this objective. Iraq's conventional priorities will be improved missile, air defense, and ground forces. If sanctions are lifted in the next 10 years, Iraq will focus on acquiring new capabilities specifically intended to provide an asymmetric means to counter U.S. dominance and deter U.S. involvement in the region.

(S/NF) A post-sanctions Iraq will move rapidly and probably clandestinely to rebuild its WMD and ballistic missile production capabilities. Iraq will have the enhanced ability to launch a number of CBW strikes against Israel as well as U.S. deployment areas. For at least the next five to ten years, Iraqi ballistic missile capabilities will probably remain limited to SRBM systems, but purchases of longer range systems or technology as well as earlier deployments cannot be ruled out. Iraq probably has the necessary civil and hidden military assets to resume production of chemical and biological offensive programs within a short time after the removal of sanctions, and has managed to develop a basic indigenous capability for making many BW dual-use products, such as production equipment and media. Iraq has

retained the capability to restart its nuclear weapons program and, from the time sanctions are lifted, Iraq — given intent and foreign assistance — could develop a nuclear device in 5 to 7 years. Such a capability will be alarming to Iran as it will be for Israel, Europe, and the U.S.

(U) Iraqi soldier manning air defense gun.

SAUDI ARABIA
Political — Military Outlook

(S) Crown Prince Abdullah on left, expected successor to King Fahd, is committed to a close US-Saudi bilateral relationship.

(S) Over the next 5 to 10 years, the Kingdom of Saudi Arabia will experience a rapid succession of changes, but U.S.-Saudi relations will remain viable. The Saudi regime will increasingly feel the threat of prolonged economic constraints and internal demographic-resource tensions. Weakened government finances and declining living standards will pose a challenge to the Saudi government. Under opposition pressure, the regime will likely try to distance itself from the United States on a variety of policy and military issues. However, renewed threats from Iraq and Iran counterbalance this circumstance. The Saudi leadership will also try to restrain the growth of government spending while implementing fiscal reforms, but this will be an uphill effort.

Missile Programs

(S) Riyadh will try to reduce military spending by canceling or delaying major arms procurements and reducing the numbers of U.S. combat forces present in the kingdom. Although the Royal Saudi Armed Forces (RSAF) will remain the largest and best equipped of all the militaries, cuts in the military budget will severely degrade capability for the next two to three years if not longer. The RSAF is probably the most affected by these cuts. Without immediate remedial action, foreign military assistance programs will be drastically reduced or canceled. Dependence upon the U.S. and other Western nations in the face of a significant external threat is more critical than ever.

(S/NF) Saudi Arabia maintains a mature CSS-2 MRBM ballistic missile force. No CSS-2 modernization efforts are currently known to be in progress. However, Saudi Arabia will modernize its long-range capability either by refurbishing the CSS-2 or by purchasing new ballistic missile systems or technology within the next ten years. These efforts could be carried out in tandem with

perceived missile threats that arise with the acquisition of advanced ballistic missile systems and capabilities in Iran or Iraq. Once Iran or Iraq appear close to becoming nuclear weapons capable, Saudi Arabia may well try to obtain nuclear weapons for some of its CSS-2 or follow-on MRBM systems.

STRATEGIC IMPLICATIONS

(S/NF) Unless the Arab-Israeli Peace Process succeeds, U.S. influence will be reduced in the Middle East for the next few years because of perceived favoritism toward Israel, policies toward Iraq that seem to hurt the Iraqi people more than Saddam Hussein, and differing perceptions of the Iranian threat. Some states will also distance themselves from U.S. policies and take more independent stands, particularly toward Iraq, because of domestic pressure and challenges. However, Baghdad's recent threats against Saudi Arabia and Kuwait will mitigate criticism of the U.S. over the near term.

(U) The balance of power between GCC states and Iran and Iraq — crucial to the United States — will remain profoundly unfavorable to the GCC states without external influence.

(S) The Arab-Israeli rivalry will persist in some form throughout this period, remaining highly significant to the interests of the United States.

(S) Both Iran and Iraq will continue to pose an enduring unconventional threat to U.S. interests and a conventional threat to our regional allies.

(U) The importance of MENA energy resources to the economies of U.S., Asian, and European allies and partners will guarantee the region's strategic importance to the United States for at least the first part of the new century.

Islam is the only force on the horizon capable of channeling discontent and fear into attempts to change the political status quo in particular states.

(U) Kuwaiti preparations for the possibility of chem/bio attack.

212 RUMSFELD'S WAR

SECRET/NOFORN

Possible Status of MENA WMD Programs in 2020				
Country	**Nuclear** Operational Program/Status	**Biological** Operational Program/Status	**Chemical** Operational Program/Status	**Ballistic Missiles** Operational Program/Status
Egypt	no/possible development	yes/active	yes/active	yes/modernizing SRBM
Iran	yes/modernizing	yes/active	yes/active	yes/active IR/ICBM
Iraq	yes/modernizing	yes/active	yes/active	yes/IR/ICBM development
Israel	yes/modernizing	yes/active	yes/active	yes/active MRBM
Libya	no/possible development	no/development	yes/active	yes/modernizing SRBM — active MRBM
Saudi Arabia	no/possible acquisition	no/possible desire	no/possible development	yes/active MRBM
Syria	no/none	yes/limited	yes/active	yes/modernizing SRBM
UAE	no/none	no/none	no/possible development	yes/possible SRBM
Yemen	no/none	no/none	no/possible development	yes/possible SRBM

*This is an illustrative scenario based on an extension of current and projected MENA NBC/missile capabilities and intentions described in this primer.

(S) The threat posed by weapons of mass destruction (WMD) in the Middle East — already the greatest threat to deployed U.S. forces — will increase. Several rogue states will likely join the nuclear club, chemical and biological weapons will be proliferated, and the numbers of longer-range theater ballistic and cruise missiles will increase significantly in the Middle East. By 2020, the risks will extend beyond the Middle East itself and well into Europe. Several states in the region see WMD as their best chance to preclude U.S. force options and offset our conventional military superiority. Others are motivated more by regional MENA threat perceptions. In either case, the pressure to acquire WMD and missiles is high, and the prospects for limiting them are slim. This dynamic has the potential to fundamentally

(U) Hamas militants torch U.S. flag in Lebanon.

alter theater force balances, the nature of regional war and conflict, and U.S. contingency planning and execution.

SECRET/NOFORN

(U) Gatun Locks, Panama Canal.

Alternative Futures

(C) Though currently unlikely, a prolonged global financial crisis would take its toll on the economies of Brazil and Mexico. An economic collapse would create major instability in these states, compounded by widespread social disorder. This could generate a migration surge and endanger U.S. citizens and interests in the region. In addition, such an environment would disrupt counterdrug efforts in Latin America.

CUBA

(C) Fidel Castro remains in firm control of the Cuban government and is likely to be its chief of state for as long as he desires. His departure from power, however, is virtually certain before 2020, probably from natural death or voluntary resignation. Political calculations will influence heavily any decision by Castro to voluntarily leave office, and he no doubt would name his successor and assume the role of elder statesman with veto power over important policies.

(C) The Cuban Communist Party—even without Castro at the helm—likely will remain in power. However, a post-Castro government—particularly after Castro's death—probably would liberalize the economy more rapidly, and any concomitant relaxation of U.S. foreign policy would

be likely to spark debate over the extent of political liberalization inside and outside the Communist Party. Fundamental political change would probably result.

(C) Cuba's division-riddled and personality-dependent domestic opposition groups are unlikely to gain much future leverage, even in a post-Castro Cuba. The Catholic Church will support democratic reforms, but not regime-destabilizing activities. Cuban exiles lack the military capability or political support in Cuba to destabilize the island, but their activities could provoke a U.S.-Cuban military confrontation.

(C) Maintaining economic stability and growth will be the chief challenge to Castro and the Party over the upcoming 5-10 year period. Poor or declining economic growth would be far more likely than Castro's departure to provoke domestic instability and disagreement over appropriate actions to be taken. State control of the economy and Havana's inability to borrow money from international lenders will continue to hinder economic growth. As a result, Havana will have to choose between continued state control of the economy with accompanying popular frustration, and genuine economic liberalization that may pro-

SECRET

(S) The Cuban MIG-29; an acquisition after its time.

SECRET/NOFORN

(S/NF) Scuttled Cuban Koni Class frigate.

duce autonomous power bases and demands for political reforms.

(C) Continued state control of the economy and/or slow economic recovery will encourage Cuban emigration to the United States. The Cuban government currently seems intent on honoring the migration agreement with the United States, but several hundred thousand Cubans would like to leave the island. A change in Cuba's policy or significant economic or political turmoil on the island could lead to a major outflow of refugees.

(S) The Revolutionary Armed Forces (FAR) will remain loyal to Castro. The high command has demonstrated concern over the speed of economic reforms — they favored more rapid change prior to 1994 — but probably will continue to agree with Castro on the need to maintain the Communist Party's monopoly on political power.

(S) Continuing budgetary constraints will prevent the 50,000-man FAR from deploying substantial numbers of combat troops abroad or substantially improving fighting ability for at least the next decade. A small number deployed in the Congo and Ghana are providing a funded service. However, Cuban security forces are likely to remain fully capable of maintaining internal stability in the face of any spontaneous or organized domestic unrest.

MEXICO

SECRET/NOFORN

(U) Mexican Army on patrol in the troubled southern state of Chiapas.

(S/NF) Mexico will continue its historic democratic transition. Political power will become more diffused as the Institutional Revolutionary Party (PRI) loses its traditional dominance and a multi-party system emerges. Opposition parties will continue to gain a more active role in governing the country, contesting elections at the federal, state, and local levels. The presidential election in July 2000 will shape Mexico's political future, and at this point, any of Mexico's three major parties could win this election.

(S/NF) Mexico's military will become responsive to a more diverse political elite as opposition parties grow more involved in governing the nation. Future civil-military relations may be redefined, and civilian leaders may opt to remove the military from some civil police and control functions.

(C) Narcotics trafficking and its ability to intimidate and corrupt officials at all levels will pose a formidable challenge to Mexico's government and society in general. Mexican criminal groups will become even more involved in both the movement and distribution of cocaine serving the U.S. market. Mexico also will remain a heroin supplier and the main source for most of the foreign-derived methamphetamine and marijuana in the United States through 2020.

(U) Mexico's participation in the North American Free Trade Agreement (NAFTA) will make the transition to a market economy irreversible. Northern Mexican states increasingly will become integrated with the U.S. economy—reflecting new direct foreign investment, substantial infrastructure improvements, and slowly expanding free trade arrangements with the rest of the world—while southern states will continue to lag in job and income growth.

Population Growth In Latin America
(in millions)

	2000	2020
Brazil	169.2	208.5
Mexico	98.9	125.0
Colombia	38.9	50.2
Argentina	37.0	45.3
Peru	25.7	33.8
Venezuela	24.2	32.9
Chile	5.2	18.8
Panama	2.9	3.6

(C) Economic restructuring, underdeveloped safety nets and government services, marginalization of impoverished states, and continued deficiencies in public education will hamper Mexico in resolving pressing social issues, increasing its vulnerability to continued insurgent activity and occasional, localized, violent upheavals.

(S/NF) Long-standing, deeply-rooted Mexican sensitivities over perceived U.S. encroachment on Mexican sovereignty and undue U.S. influence over Mexican affairs will continue to affect and limit the nature of bilateral relations with the United States. Mexico periodically will show its disapproval of perceived U.S. meddling in its internal affairs but will avoid jeopardizing economic ties.

(S/NF) Brazil is attempting to pursue one of the most extensive force modernization programs in Latin America to replace its antiquated military equipment. However, President Cardoso will have to focus on avoiding economic catastrophe, consequently hampering growth in the defense budget and curtailing modernization efforts.

BRAZIL

(C) Brazil should make considerable progress toward asserting itself as the principal political, economic and military power in South America by 2020. Politically, Brazil is solidly democratic. Despite a series of political and public security crises that could have afforded the military the pretext for intervention in politics, the armed forces have shown no interest in involving themselves in the political process except for lobbying on defense matters. The influence of the military service chiefs will diminish even further with the establishment of a unified Defense Ministry within the next year, though the complete subordination of the independent services to the ministry will be gradual.

(C) There are few significant threats that would jeopardize the democratic order in Brazil. Leftist labor parties have won elections at local and state levels as well as in the national legislature, but their agenda has little public support at the national level. Protests and property confiscations by organized landless groups have generated localized conflict and national publicity but have not generated effective political

(U) Future Indian Shishumar Class Submarine (German type 209/1500).

SECRET

SECRET

Selected Future Submarines Operational by 2020	
Type	Country
Dolgorukiy SSBN	Russia
Severodvinsk SSN	Russia
SSBN-P-1	China
SSN-P-1	China
ATV SSN/SSBN	India

Selected Major Countries with Submarine Forces in 2020	
Russia	China
Iran	Korea
UK	Germany
Israel	South Africa
Australia	Sweden
India	Pakistan
Algeria	France
Japan	Egypt
Chile	Brazil
Yugoslavia	Indonesia

CONFIDENTIAL

(S) The Dolgorukiy (Borey) class SSBN, the fate of which hinges on improved funding, will not enter service prior to 2010.

SECRET

SECRET

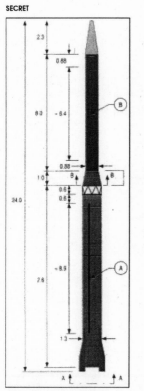

(S) North Korean Taepo Dong 1
(TD-1) MRBM.

BALLISTIC MISSILE SYSTEMS IN DEVELOPMENT		
System	**Country**	**Deployment**
ICBM (> 5,500km)		
SS-27 *	Russia	1998—2001
(standardized system)	Russia	2010—2020
Taepo Dong 2**	North Korea	2002—2005
DF-31	China	2002—2004
DF-31A	China	2006—2009
Shahab 6***	Iran	2010—2015

* Mobile version in development.
** System could have an initial threat capability between 99'—01'
*** System name is speculative

IRBM (3,000—5,500km)		
Agni B	India	2012—2015
Kossar (Shahab 5)	Iran	2008—2010

MRBM (1,000—3,000km)		
CSS-5 Mod 2	China	1999—2002
CSS-5 Mod 2 (conventional)	China	2005—2007
Taepo Dong 1*	North Korea	2000—2001
Agni II	India	2002—2005
Ghauri	Pakistan	1999—2002
Ghauri 2 (Ghaznavi)	Pakistan	2000—2003
Shaheen II	Pakistan	2010—2015
Shahab 3	Iran	2000—2002
Shahab 4	Iran	2005—2007
(solid-fueled system)**	Iran	2008—2010
(solid-fueled system)**	Iraq	2008—2010

* Capability could exist to modify to rudimentary ICBM
** New system in development, name unknown

Missiles with ranges 3,000km and under are also considered Theater
Ballistic Missiles (TBM).

SECRET

SECRET

BALLISTIC MISSILE SYSTEMS IN DEVELOPMENT		
System	Country	Deployment
SRBM (<1,000km)		
Vector	Egypt	2005 — 2007
Al Samoud	Iraq	2000 — 2002
Ababil-100	Iraq	2005 — 2007
Badr 2000	Iraq	2005 — 2010
Iran 170*	Iran	2002 — 2004
Iran 700*	Iran	2005 — 2007
(solid-fueled system)**	Syria	2005 — 2007
Al Fatah	Libya	2009 — 2011
Prithvi II	India	2000 — 2003
Dhanush	India	2002 — 2005
(solid-fueled system)**	India	2010 — 2012
Tarmuk	Pakistan	2005 — 2008
SS-X-26	Russia	1999 — 2000
CSS-X-7 Mod 2	China	2000
CSS-X-9 ***	China	2002-2003
Scud D	North Korea	1999 — 2000

*   U.S. designator, name unknown
** New system in development, name unknown
*** Export model only

SLBM		
JL-1	China	1999 — 2001
JL-2	China	2010 — 2012
Sagarika	India	2010 — 2015
(standardized system)	Russia	2010 — 2020

ICBM — Intercontinental Ballistic Missile
IRBM — Intermediate Range Ballistic Missile
MRBM — Medium Range Ballistic Missile
SLBM — Sea/Submarine Launched Ballistic Missile
TBM — Theater Ballistic Missile
LACM — Land Attack Cruise Missile
ALCM — Air Launched Cruise Missile
SLCM — Sea Launched Cruise Missile

"India has reached a stage where nobody from anywhere would pose a threat."

— George Fernandes
Indian Defense Minister
(After spring 1999 Agni missile tests)

(S) Iraq's Al Samoud SRBM will
have a maximum range of
140km with a projected
payload capability of 300kg.

SECRET   FUTURE THREAT 1999-2020

be national priorities. In particular, North Korea will continue to develop D&D measures in support of its WMD program, and to complicate and degrade U.S. and South Korean indications and warning capabilities. Other countries will increasingly represent D&D challenges over the next 20 years, as will non-state actors, terrorist organizations, organized crime, and narco-traffickers.

Underground Facilities

(S/NF) The proliferation of underground facilities (UGFs) in recent years has emerged as one of the most difficult and significant challenges facing the U.S. Intelligence Community and is projected to become even more of a problem over the next two decades. Increasingly, rogue states and other nations of critical interest to the U.S. are digging deep into mountains and below the surface of the earth to conceal and protect key programs — particularly WMD and missile delivery systems — as well as leadership, command, control, and communications. Many countries also house strategic military production operations in tunneled facilities. In addition, countries such as Russia, China, North Korea and Cuba make extensive use of underground complexes for storage and operational launch sites for ground, naval, and air assets.

(S/NF) Underground facilities are an effective countermeasure to the current U.S. military precision engagement strategy. Facilities at extreme depths, many meters below the surface, may also shield the working area from destruction by nuclear weapons. Underground facilities are often difficult to detect and to characterize (that is, determine or assess facility function, layout, internal and external features, vulnerability, etc.) because of their inherent nature. Emission and activity control are a key feature of the

BAGHDAD BUNKER
Shelters designed by Swiss or German companies reportedly were built under several official buildings in Baghdad. Here is a typical bunker design.

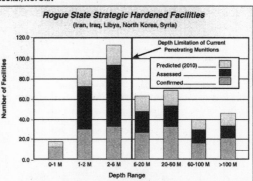

Rogue State Strategic Hardened Facilities
(Iran, Iraq, Libya, North Korea, Syria)

Depth Limitation of Current Penetrating Munitions

Predicted (2010)
Assessed
Confirmed

Number of Facilities: 0.0, 20.0, 40.0, 60.0, 80.0, 100.0, 120.0

Depth Range: 0-1 M, 1-2 M, 2-6 M, 6-20 M, 20-60 M, 60-100 M, >100 M

(S/NF) Although the majority of hardened facilities are relatively shallow and thus vulnerable to our current suite of penetrating munitions, an increasing number of strategic assets are being housed in deeper and harder facilities that are less susceptible to conventional kinetic attack. Greater intelligence granularity is required to identify and exploit alternative methods for holding these facilities at risk.

effectiveness of these facilities. Furthermore, some countries employ very sophisticated active D&D efforts at underground facilities, making analysis even more difficult. This trend is expected to continue and expand.

(S/NF) Russia, China, and North Korea and some other states (Cuba, Libya), already have well-established deep underground infrastructures. Over the next two decades, they will slowly carry out new construction—probably in support of upgrading or replacing current underground facility infrastructure considered vulnerable or outmoded, and also to support new follow-on high-value military programs such as WMD and ballistic missiles.

(S/NF) The continuing growth of deep underground facilities in Iran, Syria, Libya, India and Pakistan and the initiation of deep underground facilities in Iraq—currently only known to possess shallow underground facilities—is expected over the next two decades. All these countries have burgeoning WMD and ballistic missile programs, and they continue to incorporate deep underground facilities into these infrastructures. As more countries commence or expand NBC weapon programs and missile capabilities, the number of underground facilities to conceal and to protect strategic assets is likely to grow.

Nuclear, Biological, and Chemical Warfare

(U) The likelihood of a chemical or biological attack—and to a lesser extent, a nuclear threat—increases with the changing nature of warfare and the recognition

(U) Conflicts in the future are more likely to involve a chemical or biological component.

Iraqi Asymmetric Planning

(S/NF) Iraq has modified its L-29 trainer aircraft into unmanned remotely piloted vehicles (RPV) suitable for "suicide" (one-way) sorties. Some of Iraq's L-29 trainer aircraft have been equipped with spray tanks that could be fitted for biological warfare (BW) delivery. A low-altitude RPV detected at the outer limit of radar could release a BW agent within range of the target before being intercepted. Alternatively, the RPV could lay down an effective BW agent from beyond the radar horizon. Even if an RPV were intercepted and destroyed a few kilometers out, it still could produce a lethal cloud of BW agent that could drift over operational forces.

that asymmetric responses to conventional military dominance can achieve measurable results. Actual or threatened use of NBC warfare places significant stress on both troop morale and national decisionmaking confidence. Protection measures against NBC warfare attacks make it difficult to carry out military missions because they restrict vision, add weight and time, and increase stress. Further logistic burdens are added by the need for decontamination equipment, detection gear, and specialized reconnaissance devices and vehicles. Training is a precursor to effective counter–NBC activity, and few nations have effective training programs.

INFORMATION OPERATIONS

(U) As information technology becomes ubiquitous in military and commercial applications, efforts to attack or manipulate the opponent's information systems, and defend one's own systems against attack, will become an increasingly important part of warfare. Attacks will occur on the information in the systems as well as

Key Challenges to the U.S.

NATIONAL THREATS

(S) **Russia:** Continued political, economic, and social turmoil, as well as lethargic military reform and crisis in defense industries, have forced Russia to rely on strategic forces. Although unlikely to reemerge as a large-scale regional threat over the next two decades, Russia will retain more nuclear weapons and delivery systems than any other state.

(S) **China:** China will continue to prioritize economic reform and development, but military modernization will proceed at a steady but gradual pace, resulting in across the board improvements from a very low baseline. However, China is still 20 years away from developing large-scale regional threat capabilities.

(S) **North Korea:** Worsening economic and internal security situations will steadily erode Pyongyang's conventional military capabilities, but WMD, missiles, artillery, and SOF strike options will remain viable so long as the current political leadership survives. Significant change is likely within the next five years, with the worst case being major theater war.

(S) **Iraq:** Despite being constrained by sanctions and other domestic security issues for the next few years, Iraq will remain militarily capable relative to the GCC. So long as effective sanctions remain in place, Iraq will continue to downsize and consolidate its military, test UN/coalition resolve and capabilities, and have only limited ability to procure WMD. Once sanctions are lifted, nuclear capability could be achieved in less than a decade.

(S) **Iran:** Economic, political, and social-demographic problems will constrain Iran's conventional military development over the next two decades, but expanding WMD, missile, anti-ship and terrorist capabilities will create asymmetric/unconventional threats. Iran is a long-term regional problem.

FUTURE THREAT 1999-2020

SECRET

Alternative Futures 2000-2020

(U) The future security environment described in this Primer encompasses the outcomes that seem most likely, given our current knowledge of economic conditions, technology trends, and the national priorities and threat perceptions of the major and regional powers. Forecasting is a notoriously inaccurate business, however, and some trends could produce significantly different outcomes than those already depicted.

(C/NF) **Chinese economic collapse**: Brought about by a crisis in currency and banking, state-owned enterprises and urban administrations feel the initial impact of an economic collapse. This produces a political crisis resulting in the collapse of the current Communist Party regime. The aftermath sees greater political decentralization, but not fragmentation. The end result is a hostile, xenophobic regime that is still authoritarian.

(U) **Strong, hostile China:** After great economic success and increasing regional influence, China remains disillusioned by perceived U.S. opposition and containment and holds a collective "chip on their

At the U.S. Embassy in Beijing, Chinese protest the accidental bombing of the Chinese embassy in Belgrade.

shoulder" view. However, such economic strength is possible only after a long period of international cooperation and outside investment. Thus a strong, hostile China is only possible in the latter part of the forecast period.

(U) **Russian economic/political collapse:** Russia's failure to cope with the ongoing economic and political crisis results in a steady decrease of central control over the regions, particularly the hinterlands. Most of the regional rulers are authoritarian as well as extremely nationalistic. They are xenophobic and hostile to the West. The remaining vestiges of a central government continue futile efforts to control resources. Most worrisome is the total loss of control of the military/security forces and defense industries, and proliferation of WMD and critical technologies.

(U) **Strong, hostile Russia:** Toward the middle of the forecast period, successful economic reform promotes the resurgence of national power. Russia finances the regeneration of its military capabilities and pushes new R&D. Although it will not return to superpower status in this time frame, Russia is quite capable of regional power projection.

(C/NF) **Confrontation in Northeast Asia**: China and Japan heighten their struggle for regional influence and Korea is the primary point of contention. The U.S. alliance structure in the region is undermined, which subsequently pushes Japan toward development of offensive military capabilities. Japan then becomes a destabilizing factor throughout East Asia.

(C/NF) **Nuclear weapons use:** A conflict either in India-Pakistan; Iran-Iraq; Israel-other; or North-South Korea escalates. One or several of these states — or terrorists — break the nuclear taboo. An interregional nuclear exchange is plausible in light of perceived or actual outside inter-

ference in these conflicts. This fosters a rapid escalation and ends the era when nuclear weapons were regarded as qualitatively different from conventional weapons.

(U) **Strong, coherent Europe:** European economic integration finally succeeds in fostering greater political cohesion. A central European government is able to develop and implement a robust European Security and Defense Identity. Europe is less dependent on U.S. leadership — though not hostile to the U.S. — and is more independent in its actions throughout the world.

(C/NF) **Intra-European conflict:** The 50 to 70 years of peace ends between major European powers. Major disagreements over failed economic integration, the Balkans, the Aegean, or other friction points result in major political/military tensions. There is a breakdown of consensus on security objectives, nationalist agendas surge, and open economic competition among European powers increases accordingly.

(U) **Increased power of hostile non-state actors:** Criminal or terrorist organizations undergo a major increase in size through the acquisition of resources and congruence/merger of political, commercial, and criminal movements. These groups have greater access to high technology and advanced weapons and strategic information technology. They are centrally motivated by hostility to the U.S. or West. It becomes increasingly difficult to trace their connections or distinguish them from legitimate and non-legitimate activities and organizations.

(C/NF) **Collapse of international structures:** The IMF, World Bank, and UN are brought down by a combination of failures and inadequate financial support. Skepticism increases due to their ineptness, and the collective approach to economic/political/social problems falls out of fashion.

(U) **Global recession leading to significant economic transformation:** Several key states fail to implement necessary structural reforms resulting in a chain

(U) Serb policeman aims at Kosovo Liberation Army troops.

reaction of competitive currency devaluations. The G7 is unable to cope, and protectionism rises around the globe. Enthusiasm declines for market reforms and U.S. leadership faces greater pressure. New and shifting alliances develop, and there is a global shift away from the Bretton Woods-era economic and financial arrangements.

(U) **Strategic anti-U.S. alliance:** Two or more major powers (Europe, China, Japan, Russia, India …) join together to oppose, undermine, and counter U.S. leadership, power, and policies around the globe.

(U) **Emergence of anti-U.S. leader or ideology:** The perceived dominance of U.S./Western ideas, institutions, culture, presence, etc. gives rise to an 'anti-American' ideology that eventually enjoys widespread support as an effective counterpoint to U.S. dominance and provides a strategic 'coincidence of interest' among disparate individuals, groups, and states.

(U) **Removal of key U.S. allies:** One or several key pro-U.S. leaders or regimes fail either through natural death, political successions, coups, or economic collapse. U.S. access to resources, markets, bases, and other strategic facilities in the affected region is severely curtailed or eliminated. Diplomatic efforts are hampered — both regionally and globally — in the absence of the compliant partner.

"Gentlemen, I notice that there are always three courses (of action) open to an enemy and that he usually takes the fourth."

— von Molkte the Elder

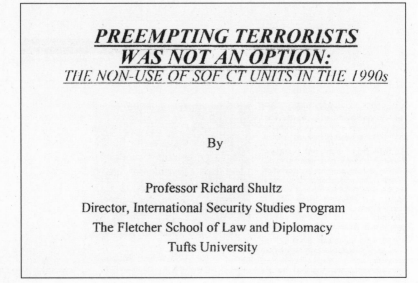

Excerpts from a thirty-seven page secret briefing requested by Rumsfeld's staff to try to understand why President Clinton never used commandos to attack bin Laden and al Qaeda.

TERRORIST TRANSFORMATION

•*Adapting To Globalism*

–In the 1990s al Qaeda passed through an organizational and operational transformation. It adapted to globalization, network-based organization and information age technologies to execute unconventional attacks on the U.S.

–Prior to September 11th the notion that a new kind of war was emerging, and that it would have a dramatic impact on how, when, and where terrorists struck, was considered the unfounded reflections of a handful of strategic iconoclasts.

•*4th Generation Warfare*

–Warfare will be highly irregular, unconventional and decentralized in approach.

–Asymmetrical operations will be employed to bypass the superior military power of nation-states to attack political, economic, population, and symbolic targets. Terrorists will seek to demoralize the psyche of both government and its populace.

–The operations of 4th generation warriors will be masked by deception and related techniques of intelligence tradecraft. They will infiltrate into the populations of the states they seek to attack.

–Terrorist organizations will be profoundly affected by information age technologies. The development of network-based terrorist organizations connected transnationally will provide these non-state actors with global reach.

–Modern technologies will have a profound impact on this new battlefield. There will be no fronts and the distinctions between civilian and military targets will become irrelevant.

–Laws of war will not constrain terrorists and their state sponsors as they seek new and innovative means, to include WMD, to attack civilians and nonmilitary targets to inflict terrible carnage.

–4th generation warriors, frequently in the name of religion, will be remorseless enemies. Their operations will be marked by unlimited violence, unencumbered by compassion.

•*US Government Perspective*

–Far from simpatico with these propositions.

–This was particularly true for the Department of Defense.

SPECIAL OPERATIONS UNITS AND CT POLICY IN THE 1990s

•Escalating Rhetoric

–As terrorist attacks against the US escalated in the 1990s a simultaneous intensification of rhetoric came out of the White House.

–In the forefront of that rhetoric was President Clinton. He asserted he intended to strike offensively at those responsible.

•Tough Policy Initiatives

–In the latter 1990s rhetoric turned into new CT policy initiatives. PDD 62 designated preemption and disruption as one of ten methods for combating those who engage in terrorism.

–A revised CONPLAN 0300 provided the JCS chairman with new CT options including preemptive strikes by SOF units.

–Following the August 1998 bombing of US embassies in Africa President Clinton, according to media reports, signed a finding that authorized killing bin Laden and his senior lieutenants.

•Proposed Operations

–There were several.

•Execution of Proposed Operations

–These examples, and others which could be cited, give the impression of a counterterrorist policy that was increasingly aggressive and offensive.

–But not one of these operations was executed.

–High level discussions, new PDDs, revised CONPLANs, taskers to SOCOM, and dress rehearsals for SOF missions could not penetrate the phalanx of nine constraints described below.

FINDINGS AND RECOMMENDATIONS

•*Nine* self-imposed constraints—showstoppers—throughout the 1990s kept SOF CT units from executing their core mission of combating terrorism through offensive measures.

•These showstoppers may still make it difficult to employ SOF as an offensive/ preemptive CT force.

•Many argue that in the war against terrorism SOF should be the tip of the spear. If the OSD leadership agrees it will have to deconstruct those nine showstoppers that blocked the use of SOF in the 1990s.

•What follows is a series of specific recommendations for that deconstruction.

1. Criminalization of Terrorism

Key Findings

  –During the late 1980s terrorism was defined as a crime. This had a profound impact on DOD.

–The central tool for responding was not the use of military force but extradiction and rendition.

–This reduced DOD to providing transportation for operations carried out by the Department of Justice. There was little opposition in DOD to this marginalization.

Recommendations

  –*Patterns in Global Terrorism—2001* retained the criminal standard. This undermines using SOF to fight al Qaeda and sends the wrong signal. It should be changed.

  –The Justice Department can not have the lead role in fighting errorism. The FBI does not have the capability to go into those lenied areas where al Qaeda has redeployed.

  –Only the military has the SOF capability to do so. OSD should ssert that it has lead agency responsibility for the war on terrorism.

2. Not a Clear and Present Danger and Certainly Not War

Key Findings

–In the Pentagon of the 1990s no senior official deemed terrorism a clear and present danger, let alone a form of war.

–Even after bin Laden declared war on America and bombed US embassies DOD continued to resist regarding terrorism as war.

–As with criminalization, an unwillingness to label terrorism a clear and present danger served as a showstopper for using SOF.

–General Downing explained this reluctance as follows: "people are at war with us and they're using terrorism" but before 9/11 the Pentagon "never wanted to address that as war."

Recommendations

–Since 9/11 Secretary Rumsfeld has often stated the US is engaged in a new kind of war. But resistance to classifying terrorism as war remains a challenge in DOD.

–General Schoomaker observed: "Rumsfeld might think we're at war with terrorism but I'll bet he also thinks he is at war within the Pentagon...The real war's happening right there in his building...It's a war of the culture. He can't go to war because he can't get his team up for it." This must change.

–OSD must carry out its own information and education operations about this new form of war to change the culture.

–This requires officers/warriors who understand it and are committed to fighting it. They must be identified and assigned to the right positions.

3. Somaliized

Key Findings

–The firefight in Mogadishu had a profound impact on the unwillingness of the US to use SOF on offensive CT missions for the rest of the decade. It reinforced an already jaded view.

–For the mainstream military the lesson of Somalia was that here was yet another example of those reckless SOF units attempting operations that end up in disaster.

–Somalia had a profound impact on the Clinton administration. Among the lessons it learned was SOF units can get you into trouble.

Recommendations

–If OSD is to employ SOCOM to conduct a global war on al Qaeda it must learn the right lessons of Mogadishu. Those lessons reveal how good SOF units are, even when policymakers misuse them. Imagine if they were employed properly in the war on terrorism.

–Expect caution from the military leadership for expanding SOF's role in the war. Look at the reaction to preemption. Always in the backdrop will be the refrain remember Mogadishu.

4. DOD Has No Authorities

Key Findings

–As the Clinton administration considered employing SOF's CT units the question arose whether DOD had the legal authority to do so. Similar questions were raised about UW.

–What generated these queries was the fact that CT and UW missions are executed in a clandestine and/or covert manner.

–Pentagon lawyers in the 1990s argued that DOD did not have the legal authority under Title 10. Only the CIA under Title 50 had the license to conduct covert action.

–At the time the assertion that DOD has no authorities stood. It was warmly received at the senior military level in the Pentagon.

Recommendations

–This claim should be rejected. Title 50 does not prevent DOD from conducting covert operations. The president can assign it to DOD under the finding procedures spelled out in Title 50.

–It was DOD's institutional culture and not legal restrictions that stood in the way in the 1990s.

–DOD can avoid the Title 50 canard by employing SOF CT capabilities on a clandestine rather than a covert basis. While both are conducted secretly only the latter requires plausible denial. Using SOF to clandestinely preempt terrorists is within Title 10.

–Supporting resistance movements through SOF's UW mission is likewise authorized under Title 10. It is not a Title 50 issue.

5. Risk Aversion and Failsafe Options

Key Findings

–To employ SOF requires an open-minded political and military leadership, one that considers risks and gains in a context different from the conventional use of force.

–This appreciation in the 1990s was in short supply in DOD. Risk aversion kept SOF on the shelf.

–A lack of understanding of SOF CT options by OSD leaders resulted in the conclusion they were too difficult to execute. That perception was magnified by a propensity to worry about risk

–The military leadership was also risk adverse. It had strong reservations about SOF and insisted on failsafe requirements that ensured it would never be employed.

Recommendations

–OSD policymakers must come to understand the benefits of SOF options, not just the risks. In the 1990s, their mainstream military advisors generally counsel them only on the latter.

–The OSD leadership needs military assistants who provide a balanced assessment of SOF's role in the war on terrorism.

–In the 1990s OSD civilians were cowed every time JCS sought to disabuse them of considering SOF for fighting terrorism. They were unwilling to challenge the chiefs. This should end.

–Appoint an Assistant Secretary of Defense for SOLIC who has the knowledge and confidence to provide policy advice even when it does not coincide with that of the JCS.

6. Interagency Obstructionism and Pariahizing the Aggressive

Key Findings

–The interagency process of the 1990s resulted in bureaucratic infighting over SOF CT options.

–DOD opposed the aggressive CT policy advanced by members the interagency CSG. Such individuals were characterized as proposing ill-conceived ideas that would result in military disasters. They maneuvered to weaken such individuals by pariahizing them.

–To be pariahized means to be characterized as a cowboy, someone who proposes reckless military operations.

–Pariahizing was a way to discredit those advancing aggressive CT options.

Recommendations

–The offensive use of force has caused misgivings in the interagency process. Deterrence and containment are preferred.

–OSD has to challenge this aversion and broaden how the U.S. approaches the functions/purposes of military power.

–Surprisingly, 9/11 did not cause a fundamental change in thinking, as the debate over preemption reveals.

–OSD proponents of preemptive CT options can expect the pariahizing treatment. Indeed, that is already happening.

–While difficult to counter outside the Pentagon there are steps that can be taken to stop such derisive campaigns inside it.

7. The Mantra of Best Military Advice vs. No Military Experience

Key Findings

–During the 1990s professional military status in the form of "best military advice" contested civilian CT proposals.

–This was fostered by senior officers highlighting their own military expertise and the policymakers lack of it. Civilians, insecure in their knowledge of military affairs, were not willing to challenge the "best military advice" of senior officers.

–"Best military advice" trumped civilian officials who advocated aggressive SOF operations. It backed policymakers down and took SOF options off the table. When policymakers kept pushing the Joint Staff employed non-concurrence to dissuade them.

–These subtle and not so subtle challenges became a means for discouraging the use of SOF CT options.

Recommendations

–OSD leaders must respect the "best military advice" of the senior military leadership but also recognize it has limitations has in the past subtly opposed and an activist CT policy. .

–First, remember the mainstream military has little if any experience fighting this new form of warfare.

–Second, be cautious of the advice of the mainstream military when it comes to SOF. They have for a long time disparaged SOF. Distrust of it runs deep. Their advice has to be viewed within this context.

–How can OSD receive the "best military advice" for using SOF in this unconventional global fight? By identifying those SOF colonels and one/two star generals that have the best grasp of the war and assigning them to the right positions.

8. Big Foot Print: Conventionalizing SOF

Key Findings

–The original concept for SOF CT units was unconventional, small, flexible, adaptive, and stealthy. By the 1990s the opposite was the case.

–The footprint for proposed SOF CT missions turned big. This stopped several operations. It scared off policymakers. Small force packages would have had the same result because they would not be failsafe. It was a catch 22.

Recommendations

–Return to the original concept of JSOC. It is a necessary step to fight the global war against al Qaeda.

–Smaller footprints require a new understanding of risk. There is a risk spectrum; it is not just an either/or choice. A prudent and calculated approach to risk is needed.

9. Yes We Have No Actionable Intelligence

Key Findings

–A lack of actionable intelligence was evoked often to stop the employment of SOF CT units. Special operators considered it one of the chief challenges for executing CT operations.

–CT units did not have the necessary operational intelligence/infrastructure support in denied and hostile areas. They lacked Operational Preparation of the Battlefield (OPB).

–A unit was created in the 1980s to establish OPB in areas with the potential for SOF CT missions.

–But it was never permitted to implement the full-range of OPB activities. Therefore, terrorist sanctuaries in the denied areas were off limits.

[ACKNOWLEDGMENTS]

WOULD LIKE TO THANK MY BOSSES—*WASHINGTON TIMES* PRESIDENT
Dr. D. M. Joo, editor in chief Wes Pruden, managing editor Fran
Coombs, and national editor Ken Hanner—for giving me the lati-
tude to write a book and keep my day job.

Two Regnery bestselling authors at the *Times*, my column-mate
Bill Gertz and White House reporter Bill Sammon, gave invaluable
advice. John Sopko in the newsroom library provided critical
research. My editors, Harry Crocker and Paula Decker, worked with
me to make the book better. Publisher Marjory Ross is the one who
got the whole project going. And I especially thank the Pentagon
officials, named and unnamed, who talked to me, some at considerable risk.

[INDEX]

A

Tufts University, 14
Turkey, 45, 146, 152–53, 157

U

United Nations, 46
USA Today, 143
U.S. Central Command (Cent-
   Com), 3, 31, 46

V

Verner, Liipfert, Bernard,
   McPherson, and Hand, 107
Vietnam, 32, 70
Virginia, 23, 141
Voting Rights Act, 70
Vulcans, 38

W

Wall Street Journal, 36
Warner, John, 61, 121, 123
war on terror: Afghanistan and,
   iii, 3, 5, 6, 31–35; al Qaeda
   and, iv, 3–4, 5, 15, 34; bin
   Laden and, 30; bureaucracy
   and, 2, 6–8, 17–19, 21, 56;
   CIA and, 4, 5, 29–30; Defense
   Department and, 14–16;
   duration of, vii; efficiency
   and, 2; enemy and, iii;
   enemy combatants and,
   17–19; Grey Fox and, 22–26;
   high-tech firepower and, 2,

8; intelligence and, 4, 16, 22,
   40–41, 62, 165; Iraq and, 20,
   43–48; Joint Chiefs of Staff
   and, 6; money for hostages
   and, 10–14; Pentagon and, iv,
   4, 6, 14–15, 21, 43; plan for,
   2–5, 29–31; Powell vs. Rumsfeld and, 17–19; Rice vs.
   Rumsfeld and, 6–8; scorecard
   for, 20; September 11 and,
   1–2; Shultz report and, 14–16;
   SOF and, iv, 2, 8, 8–10, 21,
   22–28; Taliban and, 30, 31;
   targets of, 3–4, 31; team for,
   35–43; territorial approach
   to, 4–5; White House and, iv,
   6. *See also* terrorism
Washington Post, 18
Washington Times, i, 17, 18, 34,
   56
Watergate, 72, 74, 82–84
weapons of mass destruction
   (WMDs), 145, 148, 154–55;
   post-Saddam Iraq and, 48,
   55–56
weapons proliferation, 157–59
Weekly Standard, 37, 41
Weinberger, Caspar, 116
"Whip Inflation Now", 76, 82
White, Tom, 121, 126, 127, 130,
   134, 138, 139–40
Winnetka, Ill., 63
Wisconsin, 69
WMDs. *See* weapons of mass
   destruction